DIY CMMC for Small Business

By Richard McInteer

Published by Crossways Concepts, LLC

ISBN: 978-1-7331951-4-0

CMMC, CMMC assessment, technology, and the threat environment continue to evolve. The needs of every organization are different, so any suggestions made may or may not be suitable for any given organization. With variation in assessment philosophy between assessors, the implementation suggestions provided in this book may not always be viewed as conforming to the requirements by any given assessor for any given organization. It remains the responsibility of the organization to implement CMMC in a manner suitable for their organization and their selected C3PAO assessor. Furthermore, after printing, this book remains static so the organization is responsible for considering potential changes to the environment since the book was printed.

Revision 1.02

Publisher:

Crossways Concepts, LLC
2417 Vale Dr
Lexington, KY 40514

A Note From the Author

I thank you for purchasing this book. I hope that this book is a useful tool in obtaining your CMMC, Level 2 certification. Future editions of this book can be improved through your suggestions. Feel free to contact me at richard@cmmc4smb.com with your thoughts. As a community, we can help small businesses achieve CMMC with the least pain.

Richard McInteer

Table of Contents

General CMMC Info

CMMC Cost & Benefit

CMMC presents a tough necessity for many organizations.

CMMC is becoming a challenging reality to those organizations that handle the Government's Controlled Unclassified Information (CUI). This cybersecurity standard is broad-ranging, with 110 specific requirements that address many aspects related to the security of CUI. The DoD seeks to stem the flow of defense-related data to other countries. While there are many controls around classified data, the DoD is now focusing on the data that doesn't quite qualify for being controlled. Much of this Controlled Unclassified Information (CUI) still has significant value to the United States. So, CMMC was created to guide contractors and other non-government organizations so they would handle the Government's CUI with appropriate care.

In early 2025, the DoD is anticipated to begin requiring CMMC for every organization that handles CUI. This will prompt a panic within many organizations as they realize that they must be certified if they want to continue doing any business that involves CUI. They will see that CMMC is not something that can be thrown together in a week or two. The greatest challenge will be with the small companies.

For the small organization, CMMC has 2 major problems: first, it is very expensive and, secondly, the requirements were designed with a large organization in mind.

For many organizations, they will have to choose between CMMC and perishing. This is not a pretty choice, because CMMC is not an easy option. The implementation will be challenging. While most of the steps will feel like they are helping the security of the organization, other steps will seem inappropriate for the organization. Security is always inconvenient and will complicate the lives of users.

But what choice do you have?

The Federal Government and the Department of Defense are making CMMC a requirement for the organizations to do business with them. For Defense contractors, they will begin to see a requirement on their contracts and RFQs that they must be a CMMC organization. In many organizations, CMMC cannot be avoided unless they want to kiss the Federal money goodbye.

For Defense sub-contractors, their primes are likely already applying pressure to ensure that the suppliers are getting certified. In time, that pressure will increase until it finally reaches the point that the prime can't afford to utilize an un-certified supplier. Once again, it becomes a "choice" between losing the business or pursuing a CMMC certification.

If CMMC is a business necessity, then how much is it going to cost? In late 2023, the Government issued a proposed rule covering CMMC. Much of the document was concerning the cost of CMMC. However, seven different times, the document states that the cost estimates do not include the cost of implementation! This ludicrous viewpoint stems from the fact that Defense contracts have contained DFARS clause 252.204-7012. This clause requires contractors to implement the security requirements of NIST SP 800-171. These are the same 110 requirements found in CMMC Level 2.

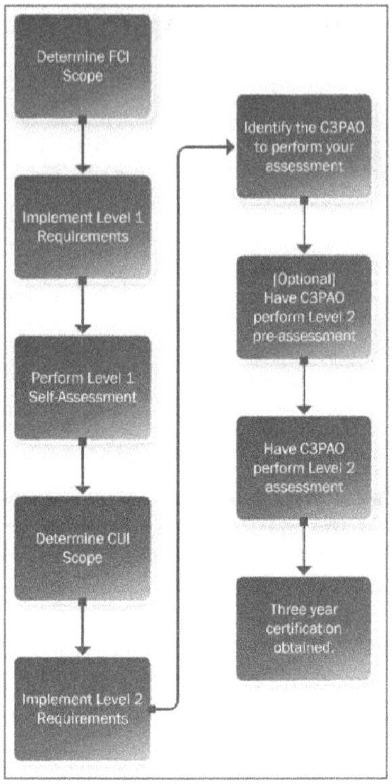

CMMC Certification Process

However, the reality was that many contractors ignored the DFARS clause on their contracts. Other contractors put some effort into implementing the requirements of NIST SP 800-171, but their efforts lacked the rigor necessary to demonstrate to an outside assessor that every CMMC requirement was satisfactorily met.

So, now when CMMC comes around and it requires a third-party assessor to review the implementation of every requirement, suddenly this ups the ante. Hundreds of thousands of companies that are members of the Defense Industrial Base (DIB) will need to perform implementation tasks before certification.

At the time of this writing, having an official assessor (with a C3PAO company) certify a tiny, well-prepared, simple company is estimated to be a minimum of $25,000, although the market is still stabilizing. That cost is just the assessment. The implementation costs include up-front costs and ongoing costs.

What this implementation might cost in your organization depends on:

- Complexity of the Information System
- Availability of Knowledge/Skills to implement controls
- Need to install hardware or software
- Solution selected
- Number of Users
- Types of devices used

This results in huge implementation cost variation from organization to organization.

The folks at Summit 7 have performed an interesting analysis. They looked at the Government's cost estimates for the implementation of 800-53. They pulled out only the items that made their way into NIST SP 800-171 (which was the source for CMMC 2.0, Level 2). Based on that, they derived a small organization cost estimate of $85,000 to $128,000 (for a non-cloud, with some existing system implementation), with an ongoing maintenance cost of $50,000 per year.

For a typical small business, these numbers are reasonably terrifying. However, there is some good news:

- The cost of implementation is likely spent gradually,
- These Government cost numbers are not based on least-cost implementation options,
- Many of the steps taken to implement CMMC will reduce cybersecurity risk,
- This book is full of cost-cutting measures.

The cost of implementing CMMC depends on your starting point and the nature of your organization. For example, there is a requirement for a centralized collection of system event logs. If you already have an SIEM (Security Information & Event Management) system, then you will not need to invest in a system. If your business is geographically spread out, then your event logging system would need to be in the cloud, so it can gather information from your devices wherever they are located. A cloud system will have more ongoing costs than an on-premise system. If you have very few applicable machines, then you might qualify for a free version of event logging software. So, implementation costs can vary widely from organization to organization.

Organizations that have the right resources, can do much of the work themselves at a lower cost than having a consultant perform the same work. Consultants have a huge variety in their level of competence in CMMC. There are a lot of MSP (managed service providers) that had one of their technicians read the CMMC specification or go to a class, so they could be the in-house CMMC expert. CMMC is complex and that does not make an expert! The worst case of having an incompetent implementor is that you might fail your assessment and not get your certification after all the investment! So, ensure that any consultant you hire is CAICO (Cybersecurity Assessor And Instructor Certification Organization) certified.

Within Windows and the domain tools of Active Directory, Group Policy, and PowerShell, you have the means of meeting many of the CMMC requirements. Without putting out a dime to an outside entity, many requirements can be met. However, there are some requirements that likely will require an investment into capabilities not native to Windows and not common within smaller organizations.

Much of what you do to implement CMMC will improve your organization's security. A huge number of small businesses get hit by cyber-attacks. It is reported that about 50% of the small businesses that suffer a major cyber-attack are out of business within a year. Hackers have figured out that small businesses are low-hanging-fruit, and that their low level of defenses make them easy targets. So, an investment into cyber-defenses is potentially good for the company. However, it is hard to quantify the value of the bad things that never happen because of enhanced cybersecurity.

While there is no such thing as a "typical" organization, the following list identifies the requirements that are likely to need extra spending, either as up-front investment or as ongoing expenses.

Requirement(s)	**Cost Considerations**
AU.L2-3.3.1 System Auditing; AU.L2-3.3.2 User Accountability; AU.L2-3.3.3 Event Review; AU.L2-3.3.4 Audit Failure Alerting; AU.L2-3.3.5 Audit Correlation; AU.L2-3.3.6 Reduction & Reporting	Few small organizations have a centralized system of collecting and processing event logs. If you have remote users, this will probably need to be a cloud system. The cost of a system is very dependent upon device count, so limiting the CMMC scope has great value.
CM.L2-3.4.1 System Baselining; CM.L2-3.4.2 Security Configuration Enforcement	Depending upon the number of devices, this could be an expense, or potentially a free product could suffice.
CM.L2-3.4.9 User-Installed Software	Centralized monitoring is not native to Windows and may require an investment.
IA.L2-3.5.3 Multifactor Authentication	This is very likely to require some amount of per-user investment.
PS.L2-3.9.1 Screen Individuals	If you do not have any documented screening tools applied to your personnel, then some expense is possible.
RA.L2-3.11.2 Vulnerability Scan	Many smaller organizations do not have software capable of performing this task so that investment would be required.
SI.L1-3.14.5 System & File Scanning	While most organizations already have some form of antivirus that scans their systems and files, this should be mentioned for any organizations that do not already have that capability.

Even the rest of the 110 CMMC requirements may require significant investments in hours to implement, document, and maintain. If those hours of labor are being performed by an outside person then that will add to the overall cash burden.

It is easy to imagine a small company needing $60,000 to keep doing business with the Federal government. For many small or cash-strapped organizations, this cost might as well be 60 billion dollars, either way, it is an impossibility. The Defense Industrial Base (DIB) will likely shrink as some organizations close their doors or refocus on different sources of revenue instead of getting CMMC.

Given the fact that CMMC is a huge investment, it is vital that it be approached to minimize the cost of each step. Since security is useless if you have to close your doors, this document is created with certification as the primary focus. All through the document, you will find the security advice and implementation suggestions are carefully crafted to achieve certification with minimal expense and with actual security as a real consideration.

For example, for best security the CMMC requirements for Audit & Accountability might suggest a full SIEM system. Aside from the fact that the ongoing maintenance of such a system is beyond the scope of most small organizations, this is a big-dollar investment. Those same requirements can be minimally met by systems with fewer bells-and-whistles. Implementing these systems are still a security improvement for the organization, even if it doesn't have the highest level of cybersecurity technology available.

In a cost-conscious CMMC implementation, most organizations will find that many of the requirements can be implemented by IT staff with a little help, like the guidance provided in this document. Every requirement that can be tackled by internal staff reduces the cost of outside consultants. Even for some requirements that need outside help, when you are knowledgeable about the needs and approaches, you can reduce costs by avoiding unnecessary expenses.

If your IT staff is inexperienced in conformance to standards, documentation, and assessors, you might check with your Quality staff, since those requirements may not be too far from the skills needed for the ISO or similar certification processes. The skill of looking at a requirement and seeing exactly what it says (and what it doesn't say), then looking at a potential solution and making it presentable for an auditor/assessor, is the same whether the standard is AS9100 or CMMC.

In short, CMMC places small government contractors in a bad place. The only choices are to spend a big bunch of money or to sacrifice the government opportunities. If you choose to seek CMMC, then opt for methods that are optimized for small organizations.

CMMC Scope

A valuable tool for reducing CMMC cost and difficulty.

Your CMMC scope defines where your controlled documents can be and how they are limited to that area. If this scope is properly defined and controlled, it may identify portions of your business that are outside of CMMC completely. As a result, if portions of your business are excluded from CMMC, then your CMMC assessor will not be concerned if you have not implemented CMMC controls there. So, the careful use of scope-limiting can potentially reduce all of your CMMC challenges, especially your CMMC cost.

The key to cost reduction is to minimize assets within the CMMC scope. That is fewer computers that need the expensive services and fewer employees that need those per-user licenses. Everything about CMMC implementation and maintenance becomes easier when the scope gets smaller.

The assets (those may be computers or other devices, cloud services, managed service providers, or personnel like employees or consultants) that absolutely cannot be excluded from inclusion are those that process, store, or transmit CUI. These are called, "CUI Assets." For these CUI Assets, all of the CMMC requirements apply. The classification of any assets that touch CUI is non-negotiable.

CMMC provides 2 main ways to exclude those assets that do not see CUI:

> **32 CFR 2002.4 (h)**
>
> **Controlled Unclassified Information (CUI)** is information the Government creates or possesses, or that an entity creates or possesses for or on behalf of the Government, that a law, regulation, or Government-wide policy requires or permits an agency to handle using safeguarding or dissemination controls. However, CUI does not include classified information (see definition above) or information a non-executive branch entity possesses and maintains in its own systems that did not come from, or was not created or possessed by or for, an executive branch agency or an entity acting for an agency.
>
> **IS IT CUI?**
> 1. Is it created or possessed by the Government or by somebody on behalf of the Government,
> 2. Must be a law, regulation, or Government-wide policy that says it must be controlled,
> 3. It is not classified,
> 4. It is not public information,
> 5. It is not information created by your organization (not created from CUI) for your own use and ownership.
>
> Many CUI documents created by the Government are not marked as CUI!

Out-Of-Scope Assets

These assets are invisible to your CMMC assessor. None of the CMMC requirements have to be implemented on these assets. If the assessor walked past one of these devices and it had a big screen demanding a ransom payment, it couldn't affect your assessment (OK, please don't put this extreme example to the test). It is as if these assets are not there.

To define an asset as out-of-scope, it must meet a single rule: It cannot be possible for this asset to connect to any CUI asset. Effectively CUI must be out of reach for any asset to be classified as out-of-scope. You need to be able to show these assets cannot store, process or transmit any CUI.

Each out-of-scope asset must be separated from the CUI assets by one of these methods:

- Physical Separation – This means that there is no wired or wireless connection between this device and the CUI assets. This includes physically non-connected networks or physically locked systems.
- Logical Separation – This is where the asset is wired or wirelessly connected to CUI assets, but software configuration prevents any data flow between the devices. This cannot be user permission restrictions, this restriction must apply box-to-box without regard for the user logging on. This includes firewalls and Virtual Local Area Networks (VLANs).

This level of separation is relatively restrictive. For example, if you have a flat network with a file server that contains CUI, then nothing on that network can be out-of-scope. Even if Windows permissions prohibit anybody but engineering from accessing the CUI share, none of the computers on that network qualify for the "out-of-scope" classification. It would be necessary that some router/firewall or VLAN divide the network, so it is impossible for the out-of-scope machines to connect to any CUI device.

An assessor may seek to investigate or test the separation method to assess risk. Overall, achieving "out-of-scope" classification may present a challenge for small organizations with existing networks.

Contractor Risk Managed Assets

In many small-business implementations of CMMC, Contractor Risk Managed Assets (CRMA) will be the preferred means of exclusion. CRMA has a much lower bar of entry, compared to out-of-scope, yet the added burden associated with these assets is small. These are assets that are capable of, but are not intended to, process, store or transmit CUI because of security policy, procedures, or practices. So, these can be systems that are able to connect to CUI Assets, they do not need to be physically or logically separated. This is much easier to achieve than the separation required for the out-of-scope assets.

For example, you have an accounting computer on the same physical network as machines that handle CUI. CUI has no business on this accounting computer. There is no router or firewall to stop this accounting device from reading CUI (user permissions might prevent access, but that doesn't matter for this determination). So, because the possibility of CUI-access exists for this device, it cannot be considered out-of-scope. It might be feasible to have "security policy, procedures or practices" that prohibit that accounting computer from accessing CUI, so it can be considered a CRMA asset.

The big challenge around CRMA is uncertainty. If the assessor decides that the "security policy, procedures or practices" that restrict the CRMA Assets from CUI are inadequate, then the assessor can check those assets for all 110 CMMC requirements. Since this comes down to a judgment call, it is going to be handled differently from assessor to assessor and cannot be predicted prior to the assessment.

A method to securely establish CUI Assets and CRMA assets on the same network with minimal risk.

1. In Active Directory, establish a security group for CUI_Assets and another for CRMA_Assets.
2. In your DHCP settings, delegate your CUI assets to a specific IP address range, based upon the MAC addresses (or apply static IP addresses if that is better for you).
3. In Group Policy, set Windows Firewall rules that block any inbound or outbound connections to/from the CUI Asset's IP range, apply this rule to all CRMA_Assets members.
4. In Group Policy, create a rule that blocks connection from the CRMA IP range and apply this rule to the CUI_Asset security group.

(This method technically qualifies to make the assets be out-of-scope based on firewall logical separation, but some assessors might balk at that idea. Qualifying the assets as CRMA reduces that risk.)

All of these CRMA assets are supposed to be "Risk Managed," so there needs to be a good effort at controlling the risks. I can well imagine that an assessment would quickly crash and burn if an assessor found any CUI on any CRMA even if there was a policy saying it shouldn't be there.

So, here are CRMA recommendations:

- Layer on as many controls as you reasonably can, so the assessor will believe that there will never be any CUI activities on those assets,
- Implement all CMMC controls on those assets as you can, so you are prepared for an assessor to decide that the assets need to be evaluated,
- Ensure that no CUI is ever stored, processed, or transmitted on those assets

Technically you can control CRMA with an employee policy, but employees don't always comply with policies. A simple way to reduce your dependence on employees obeying a policy is to implement logical protections on top of a policy.

Logical protections can block access to a share of your CUI files. If you create a security group in your Windows domain, for this instruction we will call this CRMA_Assets, Then for every share that is on any CUI machines, you will set the CRMS_Assets group as "No Access." Then, populate the CRMA_Assets group with the computers and users that are classified as CRMA. In this way, you have created a demonstrable barrier between CRMA assets and CUI Assets that should prevent accidents and hopefully satisfy an assessor.

All that your organization is required to do with CRMA is to document the CRMA in the asset inventory. The System Security Plan (SSP) should show each CRMA and identify the security policies, procedures, or practices that keep CUI off these assets. Furthermore, the network diagram in the CMMC Assessment Scope should list each CRMA.

Other CMMS Scope Categories

The CMMC model recognizes that there are some other types of assets that may be found within your systems.

Security Protection Assets – These assets provide CMMC security functions or capabilities to the organization. They may or may not process, store, or transmit CUI. From an implementation/assessment standpoint they are handled much the same way as CUI Assets whether they see CUI or are even located on the same network (for example an external security consultant or cloud-based security consultant). The scoping guide provides this table:

Asset Type	Security Protection Asset Examples
People	• Consultants who provide cybersecurity service • Managed service provider personnel who perform system maintenance • Enterprise network administrators
Technology	• Cloud-based security solutions • Hosted Virtual Private Network (VPN) services • SIEM solutions
Facility	• Co-located data centers • Security Operations Centers (SOCs) • Contractor office buildings

(CMMC Assessment Scope, Level 2, Version 2.0, ©2021 Carnegie Mellon University, The Johns Hopkins University Applied Physics Laboratory LLC, and Futures, Inc.)

Specialized Assets – This is almost like a catch-all for various other less-common categories that are excluded from CMMC. It includes government property, Internet of Things (IoT) devices, Operational Technology (OT), Restricted Information Systems, and Test Equipment. These assets need to be acknowledged in the System Security Plan (SSP), but the other CMMC requirements do not apply. If you potentially have assets that might fall into this category, then you should refer to the scoping guide (see CMMC Assessment Scope, Level 2) for more information.

The CMMC scoping guide provides this helpful reference table:

<table>
<tr><th>Asset Category</th><th>Asset Description</th><th>Contractor Requirements</th><th>CMMC Assessment Requirements</th></tr>
<tr><td colspan="4">Assets that are in the CMMC Assessment Scope</td></tr>
<tr><td>Controlled Unclassified Information (CUI) Assets</td><td>• Assets that process, store, or transmit CUI</td><td rowspan="2">• Document in the asset inventory
• Document in the System Security Plan (SSP)
• Document in the network diagram of the CMMC Assessment Scope
• Prepare to be assessed against CMMC practices</td><td rowspan="2">• Assess against CMMC practices</td></tr>
<tr><td>Security Protection Assets</td><td>• Assets that provide security functions or capabilities to the contractor's CMMC Assessment Scope, irrespective of whether or not these assets process, store, or transmit CUI</td></tr>
<tr><td>Contractor Risk Managed Assets</td><td>• Assets that can, but are not intended to, process, store, or transmit CUI because of security policy, procedures, and practices in place
• Assets are not required to be physically or logically separated from CUI assets</td><td rowspan="2">• Document in the asset inventory
• Document in the SSP
  ○ Show these assets are managed using the contractor's risk-based security policies, procedures, and practices
• Document in the network diagram of the CMMC Assessment Scope</td><td>• Review the SSP in accordance with practice CA.L2-3.12.4
  ○ If appropriately documented, do not assess against other CMMC practices
  ○ If contractor's risk-based security policies, procedures, and practices documentation or other findings raise questions about these assets, the assessor can conduct a limited spot check to identify risks
  ○ The limited spot check(s) shall not materially increase the assessment duration nor the assessment cost
  ○ The limited spot check(s) will be within the defined assessment scope</td></tr>
<tr><td>Specialized Assets</td><td>• Assets that may or may not process, store, or transmit CUI
• Assets include: government property, Internet of Things (IoT) devices, Operational Technology (OT), Restricted Information Systems, and Test Equipment</td><td>• Review the SSP in accordance with practice CA.L2-3.12.4
• Do not assess against other CMMC practices</td></tr>
<tr><td colspan="4">Assets that are not in the CMMC Assessment Scope</td></tr>
<tr><td>Out-of-Scope Assets</td><td>• Assets that cannot process, store, or transmit CUI</td><td>• Assets are required to be physically or logically separated from CUI assets</td><td>• None</td></tr>
</table>

(CMMC Assessment Scope, Level 2, Version 2.0, ©2021 Carnegie Mellon University, The Johns Hopkins University Applied Physics Laboratory LLC, and Futures, Inc.)

Compiling Your Scope

The starting point for compiling your scope is to determine how CUI flows into, within, and out of your organization. Apply that flow to determine the appropriate CMMC status of each device. You may want to critically examine how your CUI flows. Examine that flow to see if there are ways to streamline it and reduce the number of involved assets.

The easy part is to have a listing of all of your devices. Using a scanner can be helpful here to identify all devices. There may be some switches or similar devices that are not visible on an IP scanner because they do not have an IP address. These will need to be added manually. Categorize each asset.

Then, consideration should be given to assets that are not part of your network but might be part of your CUI flow or security controls. These would involve cloud services, like email, storage, or ERP. Also, any outside Managed Service Provider or consultant that controls aspects of your data or network. Then, if you have any cloud-based security services, those would also need to be included.

What to Do With Your Scope

The finished product of your scoping efforts feeds into the SSP. Your Assessor will use the SSP to determine where the CMMC controls apply and where they don't. So, the SSP must contain an organized rendering of how the CMMC scope works in your environment.

Look at section CA.L2-3.12.4 for details concerning your SSP. Your work on scope will feed into several required sections of your SSP:

- Description of the CMMC Assessment Scope
- CMMC Assessment Scope description
- Connections and relationships to other systems and networks

Although it is not listed in the requirements, the documentation has multiple references to a network diagram. This network diagram should show connections and CUI flow.

Scope seems simple enough, however, it can quickly get hairy. Not everybody has assets that fall neatly into the categories. The document linked below goes into many different variations with an educational analysis of each.

HANDY LINK

Multiple scenarios of CMMC scope described and explained:
https://tinyurl.com/CMMC4SMB-627

Introduction to the CMMC Requirements

The following sections list each of the 110 level 2 requirements with suggestions of how a typical small organization might implement them. However, there is no such thing as a "typical" organization. Careful consideration must be given to what will work for the specifics of YOUR organization because every organization is different.

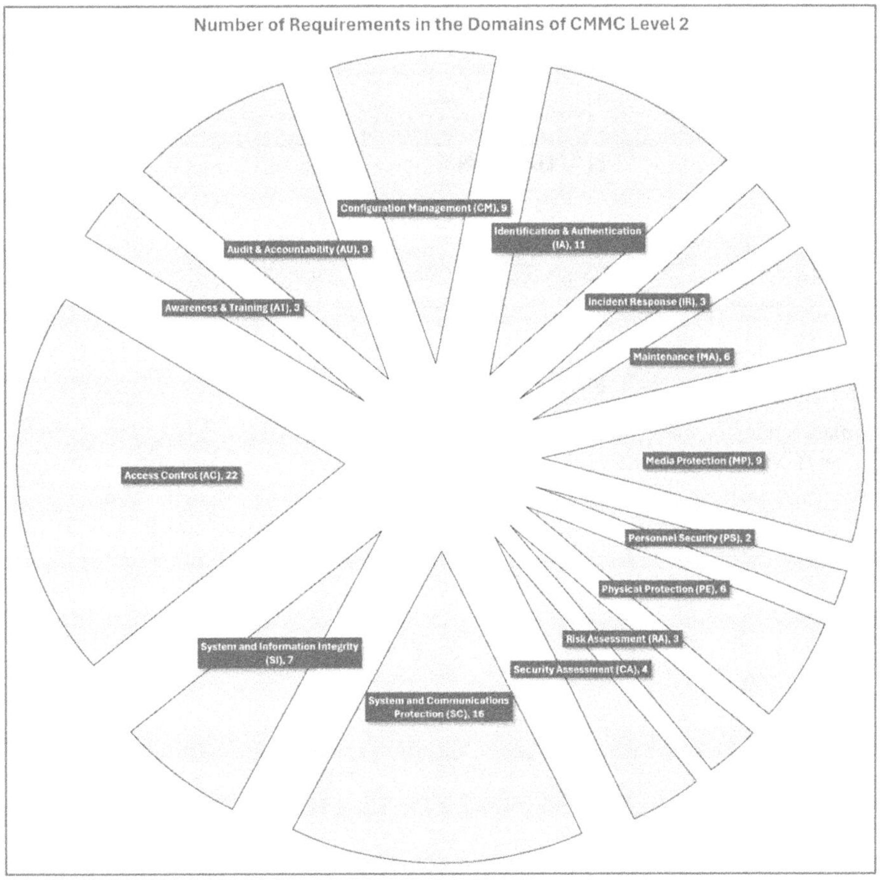

Although this book should be very useful for your implementation of CMMC, the following links go to the base documents for CMMC. These are always the final determiner of what complies with CMMC and what doesn't.

HANDY LINK

The CMMC Model Overview can be downloaded at
https://tinyurl.com/CMMC4SMB-662

HANDY LINK

The CMMC Scoping Guide can be downloaded at
https://tinyurl.com/CMMC4SMB-073

HANDY LINK

The CMMC Assessment Guide can be downloaded at
https://tinyurl.com/CMMC4SMB-273

In addition, these are additional resources that you might find useful in your CMMC journey:

HANDY LINK

SANS Security Policy Templates
https://tinyurl.com/CMMC4SMB-197

HANDY LINK

NIST CSF Templates (pdf)
https://tinyurl.com/CMMC4SMB-081

Access Control

AC.L1-3.1.1

Authorized Access Control

Limit system access to authorized users, processes acting on behalf of authorized users, and devices (including other systems).

Impact

When Tiger Tail Defense was starting, they used a peer-to-peer network for file sharing. One day when schools were closed due to snow, Diane's 12-year-old son was with her in the office. He got on one of the company computers, giving him access to all shared business files. He quickly got bored looking through them. As a prank, he downloaded and saved a file he thought was funny but then worried his mom might get in trouble. When he tried to delete the file, he accidentally deleted all the files in the shared folder instead. Later, when confronted about the missing files, he said (in typical 12-year-old fashion), "Those files couldn't have been that important if I didn't even need a password to access them!"

Official Interpretation

Identify users, processes, and devices that are allowed to use company computers and can log on to the company network. Automated updates and other automatic processes should be associated with the user who initiated (authorized) the process. Limit the devices (e.g., printers) that can be accessed by company computers. Set up your system so that only authorized users, processes, and devices can access the company network.

This requirement, AC.L2-3.1.1, controls system access based on user, process, or device identity. AC.L2-3.1.1 leverages IA.L2-3.5.1 which provides a vetted and trusted identity for access control.

(CMMC Assessment Guide, Level 2, Copyright 2020, 2021 Carnegie Mellon University and The Johns Hopkins University Applied Physics Laboratory LLC and/or CMMC Assessment Guide, Level 2, Version 2.11 - DRAFT, November 2023)

Assessment Focus

Also known as Assessment Objectives, these are the checklist items that an assessor will seek to verify. Each one must be addressed in your implementation and documentation:

1. authorized users are identified;
2. processes acting on behalf of authorized users are identified;

3. devices (and other systems) authorized to connect to the system are identified;
4. system access is limited to authorized users;
5. system access is limited to processes acting on behalf of authorized users; and
6. system access is limited to authorized devices (including other systems).

(CMMC Assessment Guide, Level 2, Copyright 2020, 2021 Carnegie Mellon University and The Johns Hopkins University Applied Physics Laboratory LLC and/or CMMC Assessment Guide, Level 2, Version 2.11 - DRAFT, November 2023)

Implementation

This control is inherent in a Windows domain environment because only authorized personnel and computers can log onto the network. The controls in Active Directory restrict access to the processes and devices. Assure that resources are only accessible to authenticated domain members (look at the security tab on the resource's properties).

Consider any non-Windows devices that might seek participation in the data environment. Typical examples are cell phones and printers. Because Windows may not control access on these devices through Windows's Active Directory, special care must be taken to limit the devices to appropriate data.

An assessor will want to look at lists of authorized users and devices. Active Directory is the first resource to obtain this information. If your network has devices or users that Active Directory does not control, then it will be essential that they are presented as well.

One of the sub-requirements says that there must be device control. A Windows device is easy because it has to be joined to the domain, but non-Windows devices do not have a record in AD. The easy way to accomplish this device control is to have MAC address filtering on your DHCP. With this in place, a device plugged into an Ethernet port isn't automatically connected. The device's MAC address must be added to the DHCP filters before it can get an IP address. While MAC address filtering does not provide a very high level of security, it can be pointed out as a form of control, and the filter exception list can be provided as a listing of your authorized devices.

Windows is very good at assuring that any process a user initiates is specifically associated with that user.

Your documentation should include a description of the authorized users, their processes, and the devices they use. Then it should describe how system access is controlled for those users, processes, and devices.

Assessment Stats

- Assessment Points: 5
- Assessment POAM Eligible: No

Keys

- Be prepared to demonstrate that your users and computers authenticate to the domain controller.
- Compile a list of all authorized users and devices.
- Establish authorization processes (potentially MAC address filtering) for your assets not under Active Directory.

Access Control

AC.L1-3.1.2

Transaction & Function Control

Limit system access to the types of transactions and functions that authorized users are permitted to execute.

Impact

Kelsey knows she isn't very good with computers, but her new boyfriend is full of computer advice. Not wanting to appear dumb, she tells him about her computer issues at work, he gives her ideas of what she can try, and she does her best to do what he says the next day. Her current problem is getting the shared server files to display in the order she wants. She thinks this is one of those times to use the right-mouse click he had told her about. She doesn't see a "re-arrange" option, but there is one called "format." That should be the answer because she wants the file list to be formatted differently. It just took a few more mouse clicks until something went wrong with the file server. She would have to get somebody to fix that problem.

Official Interpretation*

Limit users to only the information systems, roles, or applications they are permitted to use and are needed for their roles and responsibilities. Limit access to applications and data based on the authorized users' roles and responsibilities. Common types of functions a user can be assigned are create, read, update, and delete.

(CMMC Assessment Guide, Level 2, Copyright 2020, 2021 Carnegie Mellon University and The Johns Hopkins University Applied Physics Laboratory LLC and/or CMMC Assessment Guide, Level 2, Version 2.11 - DRAFT, November 2023)

Assessment Focus

Also known as Assessment Objectives, these are the checklist items that an assessor will seek to verify. Each one must be addressed in your implementation and documentation:

1. the types of transactions and functions that authorized users are permitted to execute are defined; and
2. system access is limited to the defined types of transactions and functions for authorized users.

(CMMC Assessment Guide, Level 2, Copyright 2020, 2021 Carnegie Mellon University and The Johns Hopkins University Applied Physics Laboratory LLC and/or CMMC Assessment Guide, Level 2, Version 2.11 - DRAFT, November 2023)

Implementation

Careful consideration must be given to the digital "transactions and functions" that a given user should be permitted to perform. If the capability is not needed, it only serves as an opportunity for problems.

This is primarily controlled through the setting of permissions within the domain control. This way, an individual's permissions are tied directly to their login. Within the domain access, permissions can be controlled to a very granular level or with as broad of strokes as necessary. Permissions to perform specific functions can be granted or denied to groups or individual users.

For example, you might have a "Finance" folder, which needs access limitations. Within the authorized users, you can create a security group you might call "Finance Team." Then, the security properties of the Finance folder can be set so only the Finance Team members can access the folder.

Beyond the Windows functions and transactions, there are also controls over other applications. For example, your organization may have Office 365 permissions, ERP access, or other applications that can be controlled.

When compiling your documentation of authorized transactions and functions, focus on the following:

- The systems they can access,
- Roles they are given, and
- Applications they can access.

The authorizations to perform actions and functions should be appropriate to the user's role. The accounting data-entry clerk would not be permitted to perform the same range of activities as the IT technician.

Assessment Stats

- Assessment Points: 5
- Assessment POAM Eligible: No

Keys

- 🔧 Documentation – Create a document that shows which users (or groups) are granted which permissions
- 🔧 System Change – Divide your users into security groups based on the appropriate capabilities for their role.
- 🔧 System Change -- Use those capability-based security groups to assign Group Policies that permit or deny various capabilities.

Access Control

AC.L2-3.1.3

Control CUI Flow

Control the flow of CUI in accordance with approved authorizations.

Impact

Damon is a summer intern who is responsible for documenting some processes. While doing this work, he realized that his employer had no idea where their CUI was located. He had stumbled upon large amounts of CUI residing on the shared drive that all employees had access to. Being a poor college student, he always looked for ways to make a buck. He wasn't sure if these documents had any market value, but he loaded them onto his personal thumb drive, just in case. He didn't figure that anybody would be hurt if he managed to sell some of this data.

Official Interpretation*

Typically, companies will have a firewall between the internal network and the internet. Often multiple firewalls or routing switches are used inside a network to create zones to separate sensitive data, business units, or user groups. Proxy servers can be used to break the connection between multiple networks. All traffic entering or leaving a network is intercepted by the proxy, preventing direct access between networks. Companies should also ensure by policy and enforcement mechanisms that all CUI allowed to flow across the internet is encrypted.

(CMMC Assessment Guide, Level 2, Copyright 2020, 2021 Carnegie Mellon University and The Johns Hopkins University Applied Physics Laboratory LLC and/or CMMC Assessment Guide, Level 2, Version 2.11 - DRAFT, November 2023)

Assessment Focus

Also known as Assessment Objectives, these are the checklist items that an assessor will seek to verify. Each one must be addressed in your implementation and documentation:

1. information flow control policies are defined;
2. methods and enforcement mechanisms for controlling the flow of CUI are defined;
3. designated sources and destinations (e.g., networks, individuals, and devices) for CUI within the system and between interconnected systems are identified;
4. authorizations for controlling the flow of CUI are defined; and

5. approved authorizations for controlling the flow of CUI are enforced.

(CMMC Assessment Guide, Level 2, Copyright 2020, 2021 Carnegie Mellon University and The Johns Hopkins University Applied Physics Laboratory LLC and/or CMMC Assessment Guide, Level 2, Version 2.11 - DRAFT, November 2023)

Implementation

To meet the requirements of this item, you must provide controls over the movement and locations of CUI. It is focused on the "where" instead of the "who" of data. Determine where CUI can exist within your organization, who can send CUI to outside entities, and what restrictions are there on methods, destinations, and documentation. Implementing a Data Loss Prevention (DLP) system would be excellent for monitoring users' actions and ensuring they conform to specific rules. Still, implementing and maintaining a DLP system is typically beyond consideration for the SMB.

The more realistic solution for the smaller organization is a published policy so all users can conform to prescribed rules for handling CUI. Each CUI-handling employee should be able to look at the policy and clearly understand how CUI should flow as they transmit, process, or store CUI in their jobs. If the employee is authorized to send or receive CUI with outside entities, then the policy should communicate the process and restrictions of their flow. The policy should also address obtaining special authorization if circumstances require activities outside the authorizations outlined in the policy.

If you have physical or logical controls that limit the flow of CUI, this is an opportunity to take credit for those controls. For example, if your CUI is limited to a specific VLAN and the is a router that controls what kinds of communication can occur between the CUI VLAN and the rest of the network, then that applies to this requirement.

Assessment Stats

- Assessment Points: 1
- Assessment POAM Eligible: Yes

Keys

- Documentation – Define the movement of CUI within your organization. Identify how the CUI arrives, where it is stored, used, or processed, and where it might be sent outside your organization. In mapping out this movement, note any firewalls or routers restricting data flow. Document precisely who is authorized to change the restriction on the movement of CUI.
- Policy Change – Establish a policy that designates the only places where electronic CUI may reside, the acceptable locations for paper CUI, and under what circumstances. Define how the policy will be enforced.

AC.L2-3.1.4

Separation of Duties

Separate the duties of individuals to reduce the risk of malevolent activity without collusion.

Impact

A familiar movie character is the bank official who "goes rogue" and seeks to extract large sums of money from the bank. Perhaps they are the victim of blackmail, their loved ones are being threatened, the mob wants to recover their loans, or the individual has just gotten greedy, but the result is the same. Within most real-world organizations, some individuals have great power over those assets that the company considers greatly valuable. Those assets may be intellectual property (like the "secret recipe," product designs, customer information, etc.) or of more direct monetary value (like bank accounts, investments, etc.). The idea of this requirement is to prevent any single individual from being able to cause too much damage to the company if something were to cause them to "go rogue."

Official Interpretation*

No one person should be in charge of an entire critical task from beginning to end. Documenting and dividing elements of important duties and tasks between employees reduces intentional or unintentional execution of malicious activities.

(CMMC Assessment Guide, Level 2, Copyright 2020, 2021 Carnegie Mellon University and The Johns Hopkins University Applied Physics Laboratory LLC and/or CMMC Assessment Guide, Level 2, Version 2.11 - DRAFT, November 2023)

Assessment Focus

Also known as Assessment Objectives, these are the checklist items that an assessor will seek to verify. Each one must be addressed in your implementation and documentation:

1. the duties of individuals requiring separation are defined;
2. responsibilities for duties that require separation are assigned to separate individuals
3. access privileges that enable individuals to exercise the duties that require separation are granted to separate individuals.

(CMMC Assessment Guide, Level 2, Copyright 2020, 2021 Carnegie Mellon University and The Johns Hopkins University Applied Physics Laboratory LLC and/or CMMC Assessment Guide, Level 2, Version 2.11 - DRAFT, November 2023)

Implementation

The intent of this is to keep any single individual from having too much power. In a small organization, this can be very challenging. There are a lot of 2 or 3 person Defense contractors. In these organizations, there has to be a lot of trust in each other. The value of the Separation of Duties increases as the number of employees increases, so it borders on stupid in a tiny organization, while it is of great value in a larger organization.

The designers of CMMC would probably like to see a separation of duties applied specifically to handling CUI, but that isn't what they asked for. In a small organization, where the IT department is very small, perhaps only one person, this can be challenging because that single person is likely all-powerful (admin). In a larger organization, this discussion would start with "What duties carry the greatest risk to the organization?" Within the smaller organizations, the question will likely be, "What duties can we conceivably apply this to?" The good news is that the organization can choose where and how to apply separation of duties. The only guidance provided about where separation of duties should be applied is that it should serve to "reduce the risk of malevolent activity."

To comply, it is necessary to construct a list of tasks controlled by a separation of duties. This list should have at least two items to look like a list (just a suggestion). The requirement does not specify that this needs to be cybersecurity. Because of a tradition of controls around money, the most likely area where separation of duties can be easily applied, or might even already exist, is in accounting (for example, one person issues checks, then somebody else signs them). If the company has any particular trade secrets (secret sauce recipe), then the risk to the organization might help guide implementation.

Avoid setting Separation of Duties on tasks that are performed frequently. The restrictions could quickly become a stress point if this cooperative work were required multiple times a week. Also, consider vacations and illnesses that require people to be away from the office. "I'm sorry, we can't run payroll because Tom has gone on a cruise" will not be popular.

For a small organization, creativity will often have to be required to develop some duty that can be split between 2 individuals without impeding the organization's essential functioning. Remember that an assessor may ask how a selected task carries risk if somebody abuses it. So, for an extreme example, making it so one person unlocks the dumpster and somebody has to throw in the trash bags would be tough to justify as an operation that could be abused if only one person were involved.

Also, unlike the trash example, the assumption is made that the individuals will be prohibited (by mechanism) from performing the part of the task assigned to the other individual. Thus, a policy that specifies that two people are required to be present for a specified activity may not be considered conforming to the requirement.

In virtually any environment where separation of duties is implemented, someone who sets this up could perform the restricted task themselves. So, if a task were set up to require the participation of 2 technicians, but the admin could do the task anytime she wants, do not let this reality affect your implementation of this requirement. You are setting up the separation for those employees assigned to conduct the task.

There are many methods to create a Separation of Duties situation. For example, you might create a locked box/cabinet/room with 2 locks. If 2 people can unlock 1 of the locks, both are required to open the secure container. Alternately, SoD can be set for a computer task.

This is an example of how a Separation of Duties scenario might be configured in Active Directory:

Use Case: Apply Separation of Duties to the ability to create, modify, and assign membership to groups. This is to be applied to 2 IT technicians.

1. In AD, create a security group in your domain called "Limited Permission."
2. Assign the users that you want as members of this security group
3. Right-click on the OU where your users reside, this is typically the "users" folder, and select Delegate Control
4. After the introductory page comes a page to select users (not a best practice) or groups. Add the "Limited Permission" group to the Delegation of Control Wizard.

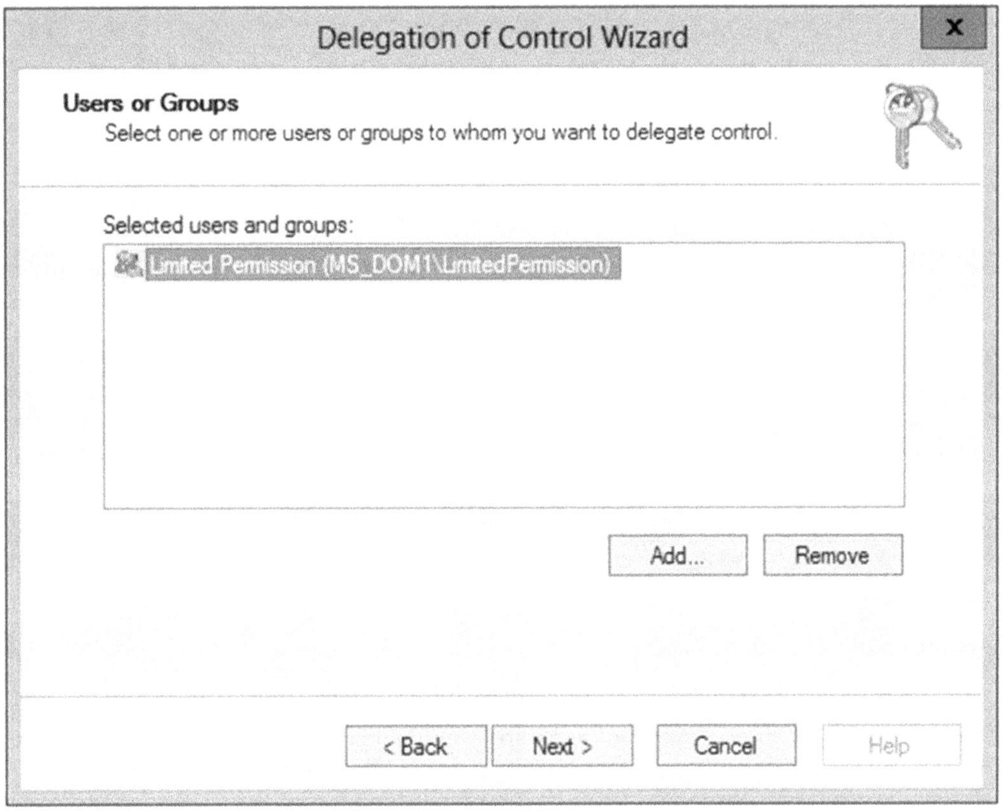

5. On the "Tasks to Delegate" page, you can check the tasks that you want the individuals to be able to do independently. Leave unchecked the tasks where you want separation of duties.

6. Click Finish on the next page
7. Create a new user with the username "GroupSOD" and assign a long passphrase
8. Create a new security group called "Group Admin"
9. Assign user "GroupSOD" to the "Group Admin" security group.
10. Use the Delegation of Control Wizard to assign minimal permissions, plus the permissions where you want to apply Separation of Duties.
11. Give each of the users one-half of the passphrase for the GroupSOD
12. Now, neither of the users can assign or modify group assignments, but working together, they can log in as "GroupSOD" to perform these tasks.

If your organization finds the Separation of Duties helpful, you might consider a third-party application.

Assessment Stats

- Assessment Points: 1
- Assessment POAM Eligible: Yes

Keys

- System Configuration – identify and implement two or more high-risk permissions which can be set to require more than one person to proceed with the process
- Documentation – Provide assessors with a list of the Separation of Duties tasks, who are the individuals that share these responsibilities, and what controls prevent them from operating independently.

Access Control

AC.L2-3.1.5

Least Privilege

Employ the principle of least privilege, including for specific security functions and privileged accounts.

Impact

If an employee's job is to watch the door at the daycare and make sure that no children wander out, then a machine gun is not a necessary tool for the successful execution of their responsibilities. In the world of computers, it is easy to fall into the trap of doing the equivalent of issuing guns to wranglers of toddlers. In a secure computer environment, users would only have the tools to do their job and nothing more. This restriction keeps people from accidentally causing damage as much as it might stop a malicious individual. It can be challenging to restrict users from absolutely everything that is not needed to do their job, so some level of common sense needs to be applied, restricting the most dangerous things that are the furthest from the responsibilities of the user.

Official Interpretation*

The principle of least privilege applies to all users and processes on all systems, but it is critical to systems containing or accessing CUI. Least privilege:

- restricts user access to only the machines and information needed to fulfill job responsibilities; and
- limits what system configuration settings users can change, only allowing individuals with a business need to change them.

(CMMC Assessment Guide, Level 2, Copyright 2020, 2021 Carnegie Mellon University and The Johns Hopkins University Applied Physics Laboratory LLC and/or CMMC Assessment Guide, Level 2, Version 2.11 - DRAFT, November 2023)

Assessment Focus

Also known as Assessment Objectives, these are the checklist items that an assessor will seek to verify. Each one must be addressed in your implementation and documentation:

1. privileged accounts are identified;

2. access to privileged accounts is authorized in accordance with the principle of least privilege;
3. security functions are identified; and
4. access to security functions is authorized in accordance with the principle of least privilege.

(CMMC Assessment Guide, Level 2, Copyright 2020, 2021 Carnegie Mellon University and The Johns Hopkins University Applied Physics Laboratory LLC and/or CMMC Assessment Guide, Level 2, Version 2.11 - DRAFT, November 2023)

Implementation

The idea behind this is the old "need to know" concept. Unless an individual needs to use privileges, those privileges should be inaccessible to that individual. Especially in the case of the "specific security functions and privileged accounts," those should be inaccessible as the default and only be made accessible where there is a need.

The two areas of concern here are the privileged accounts and the security functions. You will need to develop a list for both areas. For the benefit of implementation, these are what you say they are. Thus, if a specific permission is particularly problematic to control in your organization, then it might not make it onto your list (as long as it isn't too obvious as a problem).

The items you define as privileged accounts might include anything from an administrator on the workstation to a domain administrator. This would be any user with an account having permissions above the practical minimum of power. Then, the goal would be to ensure that the users possessing these accounts have justified reasons for this greater power.

The listing of security functions would include capabilities that have greater security implications. These might include adding users, changing security settings, and accessing security monitoring software. There might be additional security functions specific to ERP, email, or other software.

You can use the Delegation of Control Wizard to create roles with very granular permissions, as described in AC.L2-3.1.4.

Assessment Stats

- Assessment Points: 3
- Assessment POAM Eligible: No

Keys

- Documentation – Create a list of the privileged accounts in your system
- Documentation – Create a list of the controlled Security Functions in your operations.
- System Change – Control access to the Privileged Accounts to only those individuals who need those accounts.
- System Change – Control the users' access to the identified security functions so they are only accessible to users as they need them.

Access Control

AC.L2-3.1.6

Non-Privileged Account Use

Use non-privileged accounts or roles when accessing nonsecurity functions.

Impact

Abby didn't think she was doing anything risky on that fateful Tuesday. All she was doing was checking her email. The message about the past-due invoice concerned her, so she clicked on the attachment. The attachment was malware. However, the malware would not have been able to do much except that Abby was working as a local administrator on her computer. Since the malware was able to operate with Abby's permissions, it was able to install itself and make registry changes. What might have been a non-issue was rapidly turning into a disaster.

Official Interpretation*

A user with a privileged account can perform more tasks and access more information than a person with a non-privileged account. Tasks (including unauthorized tasks orchestrated by attackers) performed when using the privileged account can have a greater impact on the system. System administrators and users with privileged accounts must be trained not to use their privileged accounts for everyday tasks, such as browsing the internet or connecting unnecessarily to other systems or services.

(CMMC Assessment Guide, Level 2, Copyright 2020, 2021 Carnegie Mellon University and The Johns Hopkins University Applied Physics Laboratory LLC and/or CMMC Assessment Guide, Level 2, Version 2.11 - DRAFT, November 2023)

Assessment Focus

Also known as Assessment Objectives, these are the checklist items that an assessor will seek to verify. Each one must be addressed in your implementation and documentation:

1. nonsecurity functions are identified; and
2. users are required to use non-privileged accounts or roles when accessing nonsecurity functions.

(CMMC Assessment Guide, Level 2, Copyright 2020, 2021 Carnegie Mellon University and The Johns Hopkins University Applied Physics Laboratory LLC and/or CMMC Assessment Guide, Level 2, Version 2.11 - DRAFT, November 2023)

Implementation

Start by generating a list of activities that should never be performed with higher privileges. This list is likely to include checking email and browsing the Internet. This might require separate accounts or even separate devices for administrators to use to avoid having higher privileges when performing higher-risk activities.

In some implementations, the IT administrators use a tablet for their email and Internet research, so their computers can be used for system administration activities. This provides an efficient way to isolate high-risk activities from the high-permission persona.

Regular users should never be the local administrator on their computers. They might rarely run into a situation where they need administrator credentials. This does create a bit of inconvenience for the user. There are two reasonable options for handling this need. In the first case, the user can simply request help from the IT staff (this gives the IT personnel a chance to evaluate exactly what the user is attempting to do). The next option is to create a local administrator account where the user is not permitted to change passwords, and the password is crazy. This long and complex password is provided to the user, but the complexity discourages the user from using this account for day-to-day activities.

That second assessment focus item says that "users are required to use non-privileged accounts or roles when accessing nonsecurity functions." This does not necessarily mean that the users are technologically blocked from ever using the higher-privilege accounts for dangerous activities, so a policy and training will suffice. However, the users need the means to accomplish their jobs without excessive difficulty (like logging out and back in every few minutes). If security restrictions make it too hard on the users, then they WILL find a way around the limits. Furthermore, when the assessors interview your users, they may discover that this requirement has not been successfully implemented.

Sometimes, management personnel will insist that they must always have administrator privileges. This requires significant tact and persuasion. Remind them of the financial risk to the company if ransomware were to rampage through the network.

IT staff are sometimes a challenge. They often feel that their greater computer knowledge makes them immune from risk. In actuality, their position makes them an appealing target. No IT admin should not be using their privileged account for day-to-day activities; that account should only be used as needed. The admin personnel should have an unprivileged account or separate device for all other activities. Whenever possible, the power should be concentrated in accounts different than those used for day-to-day activities. The more an account is utilized, the higher the probability that the account might be compromised. It would be best if you did not carry the keys to the (proverbial) royal treasury on your person at all times.

Assessment Stats

- Assessment Points: 1
- Assessment POAM Eligible: Yes

Keys

- Create a list of those activities which should never be performed under a privileged account.
- Assure that all users normally use a logon that is not a local administrator and does not have special powers.
- Users who need higher-level capabilities should perform the security tasks under a unique logon. This logon should never be used for normal day-to-day activities.

Access Control

AC.L2-3.1.7

Privileged Functions

Prevent non-privileged users from executing privileged functions and capture the execution of such functions in audit logs.

Impact

There are always a few drivers on the road who should never have been trusted with something as dangerous as a car. Similarly, in an organization, there are always a few people with no business having access to the powerful functions that might cause damage to the company. Many times, those people also have no business justification for having access to those. In a perfect world, nobody would have access to any functions except for what they require for their specific role. If a person's job can be performed entirely using Microsoft Office, why would they have access to PowerShell? The second part of this requirement says that the use of the various identified "privileged functions" should be logged so it can be seen who is using them.

Official Interpretation*

Non-privileged users should receive only those permissions required to perform their basic job functions. Privileged users are granted additional permissions because their jobs require them. Privileged functions typically involve the control, monitoring, or administration of the system and its security measures. When these special privileged functions are performed, the activity must be captured in an audit log, which can be used to identify abuse. Non-privileged employees must not be granted permission to perform any of the functions of a privileged user.

This requirement, AC.L2-3.1.7, manages non-privileged users by logging any attempts to execute privileged functions. AC.L2-3.1.7 leverages AU.L2-3.3.2, which ensures logging and traceability of user actions. AC.L2-3.1.7 also extends AC.L2-3.1.2, which defines a requirement to limit types of transactions and functions to those that authorized users are permitted to execute.

(CMMC Assessment Guide, Level 2, Copyright 2020, 2021 Carnegie Mellon University and The Johns Hopkins University Applied Physics Laboratory LLC and/or CMMC Assessment Guide, Level 2, Version 2.11 - DRAFT, November 2023)

Assessment Focus

Also known as Assessment Objectives, these are the checklist items that an assessor will seek to verify. Each one must be addressed in your implementation and documentation:

1. privileged functions are defined;
2. non-privileged users are defined;
3. non-privileged users are prevented from executing privileged functions; and
4. the execution of privileged functions is captured in audit logs.

(CMMC Assessment Guide, Level 2, Copyright 2020, 2021 Carnegie Mellon University and The Johns Hopkins University Applied Physics Laboratory LLC and/or CMMC Assessment Guide, Level 2, Version 2.11 - DRAFT, November 2023)

Implementation

Create a list of the "privileged functions" within your organization. This might include command line, PowerShell access, establishing system accounts, modifying system logging, or administering cryptographic key management activities.

Also, it is essential to identify the users that have no business need for those "privileged functions." Avoid creating a list of individuals that needs frequent updates. The list might be by exclusion, for example, "all users outside of IT." Use titles instead of names so the list requires less maintenance. It may be easiest if this list resides as an active directory security group.

You can use group policy to block the identified privileged functions. As you address each of these activities, you should turn on logging so the use of any of these functions will generate visibility.

Assessment Stats

- Assessment Points: 1
- Assessment POAM Eligible: Yes

Keys

- Documentation – Create a list of the privileged functions you will control.
- Documentation – Identify the users that have no reason to be using those privileged functions
- System Configuration – Restrict the use of privileged functions among non-privileged users.
- System Configuration – Activate logging for those restricted privileged functions.

AC.L2-3.1.8

Unsuccessful Logon Attempts

Limit unsuccessful logon attempts.

Impact

When all a person talks about is their dog, then it isn't too hard of a stretch to guess that a person's password might be their dog's name or some variation of the name. So, a malicious person might try breaking into their computer by trying different variations on the dog's name. Beyond that, there are many programs out on the Internet that hackers can use, by lightning-fast trial and error, to guess passwords. If the computers have a control that locks out the computer after some number of failed logon attempts, then this guessing game suddenly gets much more challenging.

Official Interpretation*

Consecutive unsuccessful logon attempts may indicate malicious activity. OSAs can mitigate these attacks by limiting the number of unsuccessful logon attempts, typically by locking the account. A defined number of consecutive unsuccessful logon attempts is a common configuration setting. OSAs are expected to set this number at a level that fits their risk profile with the knowledge that fewer unsuccessful attempts provide higher security.

After an unsuccessful login attempt threshold is exceeded and the system locks an account, the account may either remain locked until an administrator takes action to unlock it, or it may be locked for a predefined time after which it unlocks automatically.

(CMMC Assessment Guide, Level 2, Copyright 2020, 2021 Carnegie Mellon University and The Johns Hopkins University Applied Physics Laboratory LLC and/or CMMC Assessment Guide, Level 2, Version 2.11 - DRAFT, November 2023)

Assessment Focus

Also known as Assessment Objectives, these are the checklist items that an assessor will seek to verify. Each one must be addressed in your implementation and documentation:

1. the means of limiting unsuccessful logon attempts is defined; and
2. the defined means of limiting unsuccessful logon attempts is implemented.

(CMMC Assessment Guide, Level 2, Copyright 2020, 2021 Carnegie Mellon University and The Johns Hopkins University Applied Physics Laboratory LLC and/or CMMC Assessment Guide, Level 2, Version 2.11 - DRAFT, November 2023)

Implementation

This is a straightforward control in Group Policy. (Computer Configuration→ Windows Settings→ Security Settings→ Account Policies→ Account Lockout Policy) Use caution with account lockout, or this can be used to induce denial of service.

When a person is distracted, it isn't too odd for them to take 3 attempts at getting their password correctly typed. If they have recently had to change a long-standing password, then this might also contribute to a valid user taking multiple attempts to type the correct password. If somebody is already having a bad day, you don't want to add to that by locking them out of their computer. You might also consider that 10 attempts do not go very far at brute-forcing a password.

While choosing a small number of unsuccessful logon attempts before account lockout, might feel like greater security, it might be bringing on more stress without any appreciable improvement in security. You are allowed to set this value wherever you decide it is appropriate, so consider carefully what is the best choice for your organization.

It is typically considered best practice to log both successful and failed logon attempts.

Assessment Stats

- Assessment Points: 1
- Assessment POAM Eligible: Yes

Keys

- Documentation – Be prepared to present the settings for unsuccessful password attempts
- System - Configure the Group Policy for Account Lockout Policy and apply it to all users.

Access Control

AC.L2-3.1.9

Privacy & Security Notices

Provide privacy and security notices consistent with applicable CUI rules.

Impact

In our world, a "No Trespassing" sign prevents visitors from being able to say, "I didn't know I wasn't supposed to be here!" From an Information Technology standpoint, we use an informational posting to ensure people recognize their rights, responsibilities, and possible repercussions of using or accessing controlled resources. These notices may be physical signs or login notifications, but the purpose is always to ensure people understand what they need to do.

Official Interpretation*

Every system containing or providing access to CUI has legal requirements concerning user privacy and security notices. One method of addressing this requirement is the use of a system-use notification banner that displays the legal requirements of using the system. Users may be required to click to agree to the displayed requirements of using the system each time they log on to the machine. This agreement can be used in the civil and/or criminal prosecution of an attacker that violates the terms.

The legal notification should meet all applicable requirements. At a minimum, the notice should inform the user that:

- information system usage may be monitored or recorded, and is subject to audit;
- unauthorized use of the information systems is prohibited;
- unauthorized use is subject to criminal and civil penalties;
- use of the information system affirms consent to monitoring and recording;
- the information system contains CUI with specific requirements imposed by the Department of Defense; and

- use of the information system may be subject to other specified requirements associated with certain types of CUI such as Export Controlled information.

(CMMC Assessment Guide, Level 2, Copyright 2020, 2021 Carnegie Mellon University and The Johns Hopkins University Applied Physics Laboratory LLC and/or CMMC Assessment Guide, Level 2, Version 2.11 - DRAFT, November 2023)

Assessment Focus

Also known as Assessment Objectives, these are the checklist items that an assessor will seek to verify. Each one must be addressed in your implementation and documentation:

1. privacy and security notices required by CUI-specified rules are identified, consistent, and associated with the specific CUI category; and
2. privacy and security notices are displayed.

(CMMC Assessment Guide, Level 2, Copyright 2020, 2021 Carnegie Mellon University and The Johns Hopkins University Applied Physics Laboratory LLC and/or CMMC Assessment Guide, Level 2, Version 2.11 - DRAFT, November 2023)

Implementation

The prudent thing is to seek legal counsel for the exact language you use. If your legal counsel agrees, your statement might be something like this:

> *This system may contain Controlled Unclassified Information (CUI) from the United States Government. All unauthorized use of the information system is prohibited. Unauthorized access may be subject to criminal and civil penalties. By proceeding, you acknowledge that you are authorized to access this information system and accept that there will be monitoring and recording of your activities within this system.*

HANDY LINK

Access this suggested text at https://tinyurl.com/cmmc4smb-706

In the government implementation of their corresponding requirement, they present warning information that must be acknowledged before logging into their system. A message can be set up in Group Policy (Computer Configuration→ Windows Settings→ Security Settings→ Local Policies→ Security Options→ Interactive Logon: Message text for users attempting to log on)

Assessment Stats

- Assessment Points: 1
- Assessment POAM Eligible: Yes

Keys

- Documentation – Be prepared to present your configuration setting concerning the logon notifications.
- System Change – Establish a Logon message within Group Policy

Access Control

AC.L2-3.1.10

Session Lock

Use session lock with pattern-hiding displays to prevent access and viewing of data after a period of inactivity.

Impact

Troy wanted his systems to be as secure as possible, so he required the users to use an extremely long and complex password. He got into a discussion about security with the summer intern. She bet him that before the morning was up, she could bypass the password security and send him a message from somebody else's email. Troy was sure she could not do that.

A few minutes later, when Ron, the engineer, had left for lunch, she sat down at Ron's unlocked workstation and sent Troy the "I told you so!" email. In her email, she bragged about how she could view, copy, delete, or change any files Ron could access.

Official Interpretation*

Session locks can be initiated by the user or, more fundamentally, enabled automatically when the system has been idle for a period of time, for example, five minutes. Session locks are a quick way to prevent unauthorized use of the systems without having a user log off. Minimum configuration requirements are left up to the organization to define.

A locked session shows pattern-hiding information on the screen to mask the data on the display.

(CMMC Assessment Guide, Level 2, Copyright 2020, 2021 Carnegie Mellon University and The Johns Hopkins University Applied Physics Laboratory LLC and/or CMMC Assessment Guide, Level 2, Version 2.11 - DRAFT, November 2023)

Assessment Focus

Also known as Assessment Objectives, these are the checklist items that an assessor will seek to verify. Each one must be addressed in your implementation and documentation:

1. the period of inactivity after which the system initiates a session lock is defined;
2. access to the system and viewing of data is prevented by initiating a session lock after the defined period of inactivity; and

3. previously visible information is concealed via a pattern-hiding display after the defined period of inactivity.

(CMMC Assessment Guide, Level 2, Copyright 2020, 2021 Carnegie Mellon University and The Johns Hopkins University Applied Physics Laboratory LLC and/or CMMC Assessment Guide, Level 2, Version 2.11 - DRAFT, November 2023)

Implementation

This can be accomplished by establishing a mandatory screen-saver function in Group Policy. A short period before the screen saver activates is best for security but most inconvenient for the users. So, this period of inactivity should be as short as your user population will tolerate.

In Group Policy, the setting can be found at User Configuration → Administrative Templates → Control Panel → Personalization. You will want to set Screen Saver Timeout, Enable Screen Saver and Password Protect the Screen Saver.

If the screensaver kicks in too quickly, then you will get user resistance. If it is too long, then computers will be sitting logged in and unattended, creating a security vulnerability.

It is also good if you teach your users to use ⊞-L to lock their screens immediately. This is especially useful when the users have sensitive materials on their screen but need to get up from their computer. This tool has value with all computers, all the time.

Assessment Stats

- Assessment Points: 1
- Assessment POAM Eligible: Yes

Keys

- Documentation – Be prepared to show your Screen Saver settings to an assessor.
- System Change – Set the group policy setting for a mandatory, password-protected screen saver.

AC.L2-3.1.11

Session Termination

Terminate (automatically) a user session after a defined condition.

Impact

Imagine a highly secure bank vault where the bank employees decide it is simply too much trouble to go through all the hassle of locking and unlocking the vault, so they always leave it open. This step will save them lots of time but has obvious security implications. Similarly, with our computer networks, we have employees who would be happy if they only had to log in once; then, the network access is always available when they step up to their computer. Like the bank vault, this leaves the "valuables" available to anybody who wants them.

Official Interpretation*

Configure the system to terminate user sessions based on the organization's policy. Session termination policies can be simple or sophisticated. Examples are inactivity (end the session after a specified duration (e.g., one hour) of inactivity), day/time (all sessions are terminated at the end of the established workday), misbehavior (end the session due to an attempted policy violation), and maintenance (terminate sessions to prevent issues with an upgrade or service outage). If there is no automatic control of user sessions, an attacker can take advantage of an unattended session.

(CMMC Assessment Guide, Level 2, Copyright 2020, 2021 Carnegie Mellon University and The Johns Hopkins University Applied Physics Laboratory LLC and/or CMMC Assessment Guide, Level 2, Version 2.11 - DRAFT, November 2023)

Assessment Focus

Also known as Assessment Objectives, these are the checklist items that an assessor will seek to verify. Each one must be addressed in your implementation and documentation:

1. conditions requiring a user session to terminate are defined; and
2. a user session is automatically terminated after any of the defined conditions occur.

(CMMC Assessment Guide, Level 2, Copyright 2020, 2021 Carnegie Mellon University and The Johns Hopkins University Applied Physics Laboratory LLC and/or CMMC Assessment Guide, Level 2, Version 2.11 - DRAFT, November 2023)

Implementation

When it comes to the actual termination of a network user session, Windows is weak. They have a setting for termination of Remote Desktop or SMB sessions, but not Active Directory network sessions. Microsoft has built-in ways to block or hide the session but not actually to terminate it.

Because Windows does not make this easy, I suggest setting any logged-in workstations to reboot in the middle of the night. This way, any active session is firmly terminated.

Some users will have difficulty with this because they are in the habit of leaving unsaved work open on their computers until they return the next day. So, to help prevent grumbling or screaming, it is essential to thoroughly publicize this change in advance. There will still be a bit of data loss because people are slow to change their habits, but they will blame themselves instead of you if they were well warned.

The method used here is to create a Group Policy to place a Scheduled Task on each user's computer to reboot at a specified hour. In the following example, computers are to reboot at 3:00 a.m. Tuesday through Saturday morning. The Group Policy is created at Computer Configuration -> Preferences -> Control Panel Settings -> Scheduled Tasks.

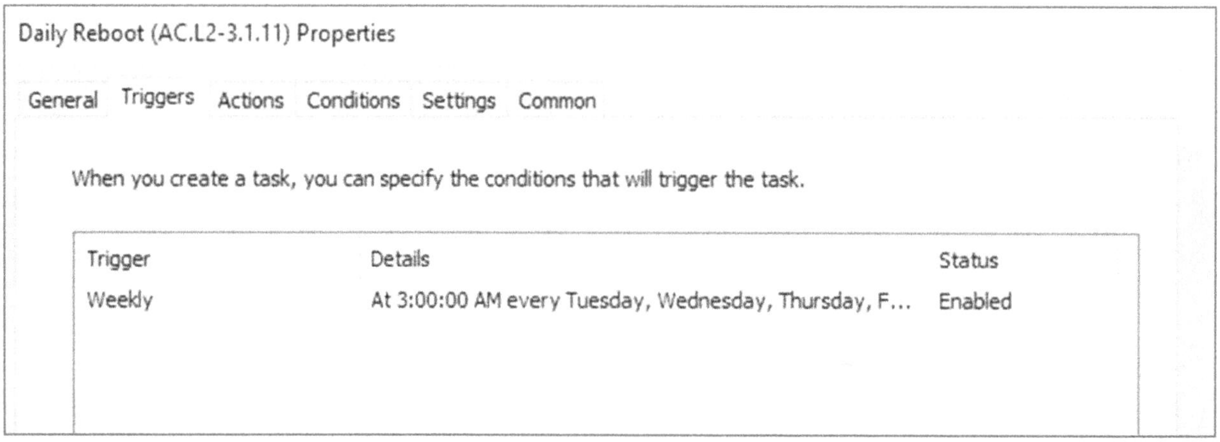

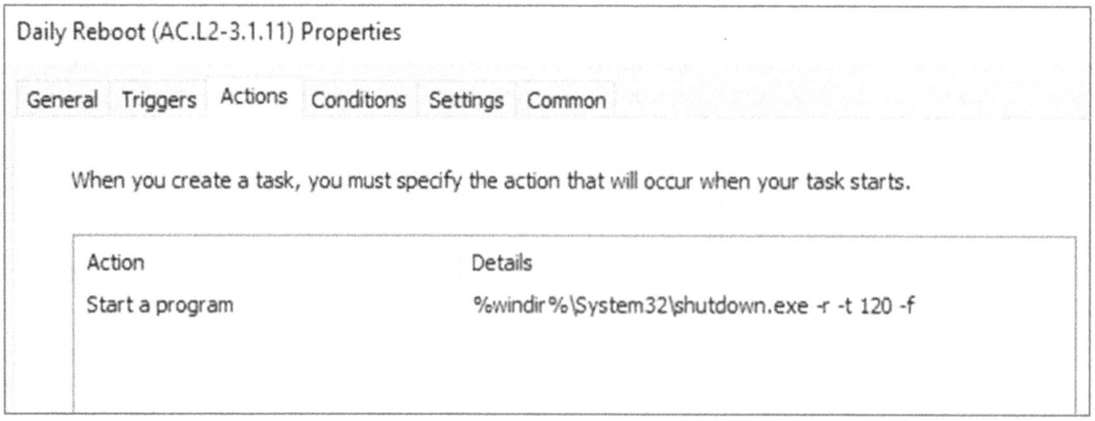

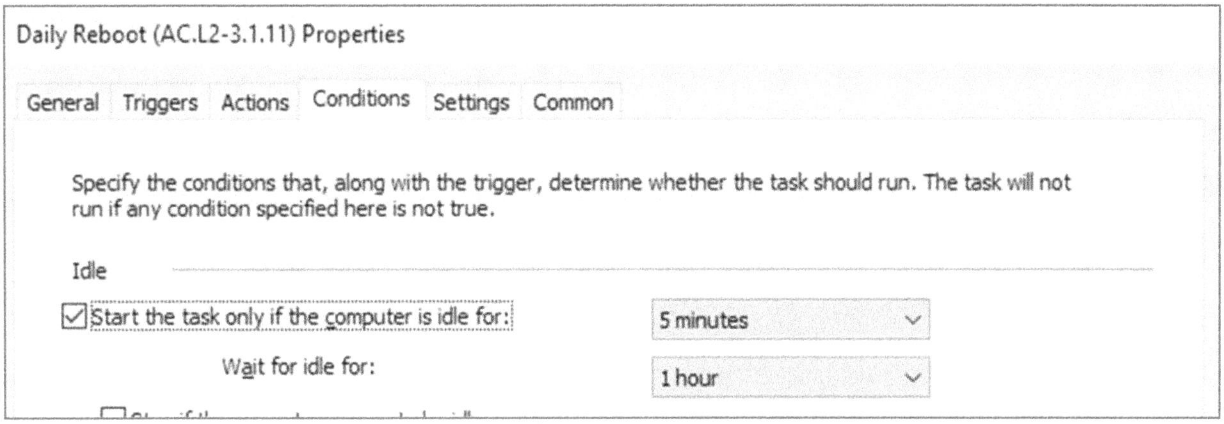

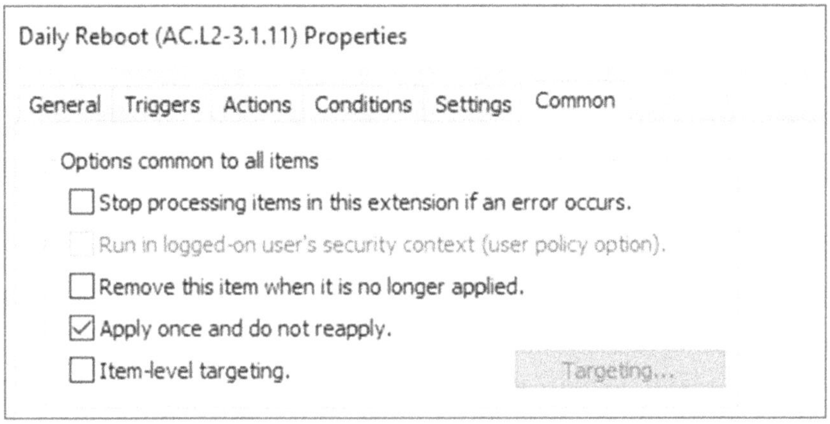

This sort of implementation meets the letter of the law. While it might be argued that the writers of the standard had a different expectation, this implementation does perform what the words of the standard require.

Assessment Stats

- Assessment Points: 1
- Assessment POAM Eligible: Yes

Keys

- Policy – Define the condition(s) for forced session termination.
- Documentation – Be prepared to provide the assessor with a copy of your session-termination settings.
- System Configuration – Use Group Policy to push out session termination settings in accordance with your policy.

Access Control

AC.L2-3.1.12

Control Remote Access

Monitor and control remote access sessions.

Impact

In 2014, Home Depot had to endure announcing that 56 million of their customer's credit and debit cards had been hacked. The hackers took advantage of the company's remote access capabilities to perform this crime. If you have employees who access your network from remote locations, you must have controls limiting what they are allowed to do. Furthermore, you must monitor what they are doing within the network while they are connected.

Official Interpretation*

Remote access connections pass through untrusted networks and therefore require proper security controls such as encryption to ensure data confidentiality. Initialization of all remote sessions should ensure that only authorized users and devices are connecting. After the remote session is established, the connection is monitored to track who is accessing the network remotely and what files are being accessed during the session.

Remote access sessions can encompass more than just remote connections back to a headquarters network. Access to cloud-based email providers or server infrastructures also are relevant to this requirement if those environments contain CUI.

This requirement, AC.L2-3.1.12, requires the control of remote access sessions and complements five other requirements dealing with remote access (AC.L2-3.1.14, AC.L2-3.1.13, AC.L2-3.1.15, IA.L2-3.5.3, and MA.L2-3.7.5):

- AC.L2-3.1.14 limits remote access to specific access control points.
- AC.L2-3.1.13 requires the use of cryptographic mechanisms when enabling remote sessions.
- AC.L2-3.1.15 requires authorization for privileged commands executed during a remote session.
- IA.L2-3.5.3 requires multifactor authentication for network access to non-privileged accounts.
- MA.L2-3.7.5 requires the addition of multifactor authentication for remote maintenance sessions.

Assessment Focus

Also known as Assessment Objectives, these are the checklist items that an assessor will seek to verify. Each one must be addressed in your implementation and documentation:

1. remote access sessions are permitted;
2. the types of permitted remote access are identified;
3. remote access sessions are controlled; and
4. remote access sessions are monitored.

(CMMC Assessment Guide, Level 2, Copyright 2020, 2021 Carnegie Mellon University and The Johns Hopkins University Applied Physics Laboratory LLC and/or CMMC Assessment Guide, Level 2, Version 2.11 - DRAFT, November 2023)

Implementation

Note: This requirement is one of 6 regarding remote access. These requirements should all be considered together when designing controls. The remote-access-related controls are:

AC.L2-3.1.12	control of remote access	AC.L2-3.1.15	privileged commands on remote sessions
AC.L2-3.1.14	remote access control points	IA.L2-3.5.3	multifactor authentication
AC.L2-3.1.13	cryptography for remote sessions	MA.L2-3.7.5	MFA for remote maintenance sessions

Remote access inherently carries a higher risk than the days when all of your users were plugging into an Ethernet cable within your building. A remote access session could originate from next door or across the globe. While a stranger wanting to plug his laptop into your network would be suspicious, that same stranger could seek to connect remotely without generating any suspicion. In today's business environment, remote access has, for many organizations, become a necessary evil.

There should be a process for granting the right to access your networking resources remotely. The users that are authorized for remote access must be clearly identified. Even if you have a 100% virtual organization, a policy statement should indicate that all users will operate by using remote access. The majority of organizations have only certain users that are granted remote access. Those users should be distinctly selected, whether this means that they are members of a security group or licensed to use the remote access software. However this list might manifest itself, a distinct list must define who is in this club.

In most remote access configurations, the user still has to log onto Active Directory and operate according to the permissions granted to that user in AD. The users should only access materials and operate by assigned privileges. It would be foolish from a security standpoint if all remote users operated as Domain Administrators (plus, that would not comply with this requirement).

You should be prepared to show your assessor a listing of all the controls applied to your remote access. This would include things like:

- Who gets remote access?
- How are remote access permissions granted?
- Who can allow remote access?
- Are there any geographic restrictions on remote access?
- What authentication processes do the users have to go through (like MFA) to connect?
- What steps are taken to ensure users connect from clean devices?

The final element of this requirement is that activities performed remotely are monitored. You will need to be able to provide the assessor with configuration data concerning the logging of authentications and access to CUI or other controlled materials. These logs may or may not be separate from logs of normal on-premise activities. This requirement is a good candidate for the assessor to ask for a demonstration to see if it works.

Beyond users that remote into your organization, you will also want to consider any CUI-containing external systems that users might access. So, if you have users accessing a cloud service or email provider's system and CUI is involved, those "remote access sessions" should be addressed for this requirement, just like the inbound remote sessions.

Assessment Stats

- Assessment Points: 5
- Assessment POAM Eligible: No

Keys

- System Change – Establish remote access processes with adequate security controls and control of who can gain access and what access privileges they have when using the remote access.
- System Change – Establish monitoring of who is accessing your systems remotely and what activities they are performing through that access.
- Evidence of Conformance – You should be able to provide a remote access security plan, information about the process of granting remote access, and be able to show how remote access activities are limited based on the users' needs. Be prepared to show remote access and activity logs.

Access Control

AC.L2-3.1.13

Remote Access Confidentiality

Employ cryptographic mechanisms to protect the confidentiality of remote access sessions.

Impact

A remote session is a little bit like having a confidential conversation across a crowded restaurant. Unless steps are taken to protect confidentiality, just like in the restaurant analogy, it is unclear who might be paying attention. So, when the remote session is encrypted, that significantly increases the difficulty for anybody to "listen in" to the content of the communication. When a remote access session is conducted, the communication packets may pass through many locations, networking equipment, and, potentially, different countries on the way from one machine to another. Although the user experience might make it feel like the two computers are directly communicating, that data passes through many "hands" getting from place to place.

Official Interpretation*

A remote access session involves logging into the organization's systems such as its internal network or a cloud service provider from a remote location such as home or an alternate work site. Because the use of cryptography in this requirement is to protect the confidentiality of CUI, the cryptography used must meet the criteria specified in requirement SC.L2-3.13.11. Although not explicitly required to meet AC.L2-3.1.13 requirements, this remote access session must be secured using FIPS-validated cryptography to provide confidentiality and prevent anyone from deciphering session information exchanges.

This requirement, AC.L2-3.1.13, requires the use of cryptographic mechanisms when enabling remote sessions and complements five other requirements dealing with remote access (AC.L2-3.1.12, AC.L2-3.1.14, AC.L2-3.1.15, IA.L2-3.5.3, and MA.L2-3.7.5):

- AC.L2-3.1.12 requires the control of remote access sessions.
- AC.L2-3.1.14 limits remote access to specific access control points.
- AC.L2-3.1.15 requires authorization for privileged commands executed during a remote session.

- IA.L2-3.5.3 requires multifactor authentication for network access to non-privileged accounts.
- MA.L2-3.7.5 requires the addition of multifactor authentication for remote maintenance sessions.

(CMMC Assessment Guide, Level 2, Copyright 2020, 2021 Carnegie Mellon University and The Johns Hopkins University Applied Physics Laboratory LLC and/or CMMC Assessment Guide, Level 2, Version 2.11 - DRAFT, November 2023)

Assessment Focus

Also known as Assessment Objectives, these are the checklist items that an assessor will seek to verify. Each one must be addressed in your implementation and documentation:

1. cryptographic mechanisms to protect the confidentiality of remote access sessions are identified; and
2. cryptographic mechanisms to protect the confidentiality of remote access sessions are implemented.

(CMMC Assessment Guide, Level 2, Copyright 2020, 2021 Carnegie Mellon University and The Johns Hopkins University Applied Physics Laboratory LLC and/or CMMC Assessment Guide, Level 2, Version 2.11 - DRAFT, November 2023)

Implementation

Note: This requirement is one of 6 regarding remote access. These requirements should all be considered together when designing controls. The remote-access-related controls are:

AC.L2-3.1.12	control of remote access	AC.L2-3.1.15	privileged commands on remote sessions
AC.L2-3.1.14	remote access control points	IA.L2-3.5.3	multifactor authentication
AC.L2-3.1.13	cryptography for remote sessions	MA.L2-3.7.5	MFA for remote maintenance sessions

There are many different options for remote access solutions. To comply with CMMC Level 2, the solution must utilize FIPS-validated cryptography to encrypt the sessions. Many available packages boast that they utilize DoD-grade encryption, but this is inadequate. To achieve FIPS compliance, the provider must prove the validity of their specific cryptography implementation and appear on the CMVP list (see SC.L2-3.13.11 for a full explanation). This FIPS validation must be a minimum criterion for selecting a remote access solution.

Assessment Stats

- Assessment Points: 5
- Assessment POAM Eligible: No

Keys

- System Change – Assure that any remote access solution utilized to gain access to your networks only communicates through FIPS-validated encryption for session data.
- Documentation – Be prepared to show your assessor how your remote access method utilizes FIPS-validated encryption.

Access Control

AC.L2-3.1.14

Remote Access Routing

Route remote access via managed access control points.

Impact

Imagine a building with an electric fence and guard dogs all around it, but there is also an unprotected tunnel passing under all that security. Remote access can be that tunnel.

Remote access to your network typically bypasses all of your regular boundary security, so it is essential that it has adequate security controls. If an employee installs unauthorized consumer-grade remote access software on their work computer, that route into the company network has no company-administered controls. Even if the employee is basically honest, they might be using a compromised home computer. This sort of uncontrolled access is a dream come true for a hacker. So, the only remote access to the network must be through controlled entry points.

Official Interpretation*

The OSA can route all remote access through a limited number of remote access control points to reduce the attack surface and simplify network management. This allows for better monitoring and control of the remote connections.

This requirement, AC.L2-3.1.14, limits remote access to specific access control points and complements five other requirements dealing with remote access (AC.L2-3.1.12, AC.L2-3.1.13, AC.L2-3.1.15, IA.L2-3.5.3, and MA.L2-3.7.5):

- AC.L2-3.1.12 requires the control of remote access sessions.
- AC.L2-3.1.13 requires the use of cryptographic mechanisms when enabling remote sessions.
- AC.L2-3.1.15 requires authorization for privileged commands executed during a remote session.
- IA.L2-3.5.3 requires multifactor authentication for network access to non-privileged accounts.
- MA.L2-3.7.5 requires the addition of multifactor authentication for remote maintenance sessions.

(CMMC Assessment Guide, Level 2, Copyright 2020, 2021 Carnegie Mellon University and The Johns Hopkins University Applied Physics Laboratory LLC and/or CMMC Assessment Guide, Level 2, Version 2.11 - DRAFT, November 2023)

Assessment Focus

Also known as Assessment Objectives, these are the checklist items that an assessor will seek to verify. Each one must be addressed in your implementation and documentation:

1. managed access control points are identified and implemented; and
2. remote access is routed through managed network access control points.

(CMMC Assessment Guide, Level 2, Copyright 2020, 2021 Carnegie Mellon University and The Johns Hopkins University Applied Physics Laboratory LLC and/or CMMC Assessment Guide, Level 2, Version 2.11 - DRAFT, November 2023)

Implementation

Note: This requirement is one of 6 regarding remote access. These requirements should all be considered together when designing controls. The remote-access-related controls are:

AC.L2-3.1.12	control of remote access	AC.L2-3.1.15	privileged commands on remote sessions
AC.L2-3.1.14	remote access control points	IA.L2-3.5.3	multifactor authentication
AC.L2-3.1.13	cryptography for remote sessions	MA.L2-3.7.5	MFA for remote maintenance sessions

Remote access systems fall into two different categories. Some, like Microsoft VPN, pass through a company-owned, access-controlling server. Alternatively, there are systems that connect computer-to-cloud-to-computer.

This requirement says remote access should enter the network through specific managed access points. At first glance, the systems that connect through computer-to-cloud-to-computer would seem to fail to meet this requirement. However, to comply with the letter of the requirement, the cloud service, with its settings, restrictions, and logging, meets the requirement of being a managed point of control. Since these computer-to-cloud-to-computer remote access systems are often better suited to a small organization, it is good that the cloud systems can be considered to be the "managed access control points" for the purposes of this requirement.

You will need to be able to demonstrate your "managed access control points" and how all remote access passes through these points. These must be points where some level of management is applied to remote access.

If you use a managed service provider that remotes into organization systems, ensure their access is addressed alongside employees' remote access. It is important to note that this requirement does not specify that there has to be a single remote access method, so an MSP may use one managed access point while employees might use another.

Assessment Stats

- Assessment Points: 1
- Assessment POAM Eligible: Yes

Keys

- System Configuration – Assure that any remote access into your systems passes through a specified management point. This might be an on-premise server or a cloud controller.
- Evidence of Conformance – Be prepared to demonstrate which systems are the management control points for all remote access and how they manage the access.

AC.L2-3.1.15

Privileged Remote Access

Authorize remote execution of privileged commands and remote access to security-relevant information.

Impact

When Todd was at the office performing his IT job, he was always very aware that his boss watched what he did. He made a point of always operating "by the book." He was recently granted remote access to address problems that might crop up outside of his regular shift. From his apartment's privacy, he felt free to do a lot more exploring, probing, and testing. As he poked around, he found some really intriguing things. In time, he began thinking he could make some extra money from what he was finding.

Official Interpretation*

Privileged users are not necessarily allowed to perform their job functions from a remote location. Likewise, not all privileged commands may be executed remotely. Allowing remote execution of privileged commands or remote access to security-relevant information should be avoided if possible. If absolutely necessary, the privileged commands authorized for remote execution should be identified and documented. Document which user roles have permissions to remotely execute privileged commands to make changes and to access security relevant information. Documentation must be used to establish security mechanisms that enforce the policy.

This requirement, AC.L2-3.1.15, requires authorization for privileged commands executed during a remote session and complements five other requirements dealing with remote access (AC.L2-3.1.12, AC.L2-3.1.14, AC.L2-3.1.13, IA.L2-3.5.3, and MA.L2-3.7.5):

- AC.L2-3.1.12 requires the control of remote access sessions.
- AC.L2-3.1.14 limits remote access to specific access control points.
- AC.L2-3.1.13 requires the use of cryptographic mechanisms when enabling remote sessions.
- IA.L2-3.5.3 requires multifactor authentication for network access to non-privileged accounts.
- MA.L2-3.7.5 requires the addition of multifactor authentication for remote maintenance sessions.

This requirement, AC.L2-3.1.15, also extends AC.L2-3.1.2, which limits the types of transactions and functions that authorized users are permitted to execute.

(CMMC Assessment Guide, Level 2, Copyright 2020, 2021 Carnegie Mellon University and The Johns Hopkins University Applied Physics Laboratory LLC and/or CMMC Assessment Guide, Level 2, Version 2.11 - DRAFT, November 2023)

Assessment Focus

Also known as Assessment Objectives, these are the checklist items that an assessor will seek to verify. Each one must be addressed in your implementation and documentation:

1. privileged commands authorized for remote execution are identified;
2. security-relevant information authorized to be accessed remotely is identified;
3. the execution of the identified privileged commands via remote access is authorized; and
4. access to the identified security-relevant information via remote access is authorized.

(CMMC Assessment Guide, Level 2, Copyright 2020, 2021 Carnegie Mellon University and The Johns Hopkins University Applied Physics Laboratory LLC and/or CMMC Assessment Guide, Level 2, Version 2.11 - DRAFT, November 2023)

Implementation

Note: This requirement is one of 6 regarding remote access. These requirements should all be considered together when designing controls. The remote-access-related controls are:

AC.L2-3.1.12	control of remote access	AC.L2-3.1.15	privileged commands on remote sessions
AC.L2-3.1.14	remote access control points	IA.L2-3.5.3	multifactor authentication
AC.L2-3.1.13	cryptography for remote sessions	MA.L2-3.7.5	MFA for remote maintenance sessions

In a typical small organization, there are only a few individuals who are allowed to exercise the power of a privileged user remotely. This requirement is all about those individuals and the elevated privileges they can utilize remotely.

This requirement becomes significantly more complex in a larger organization where administrators have various tiers of permissions. In a smaller organization, it is possible to take a significant shortcut, which makes compliance simple.

For a minimum complexity implementation:

1. Develop your list of privileged commands that administrators use. This may include generalizations like "all PowerShell, all Windows command line, and all Cisco CLI commands" for an easier listing process.
2. Make a list of your security-relevant controls that administrators can access. These might include Active Directory, Firewall, MFA controls, Networking Device controls, and Cloud Service settings.
3. Authorize all your administrators to utilize <u>all</u> of the commands and security controls from your lists remotely.

Alternately, when you have remote access restrictions, you must implement controls to enforce those restrictions. When you go with "All," then there are no restrictions and no need to enforce them.

If you choose to make a different set of privileges for remote users than for local users, then you need to document these things:

- For each privileged remote user, you need a listing of the security-relevant information that they have access to. This may include Active Directory, logging, log management, settings for security devices, etc. It is also possible to describe the settings by category or say "all" or "all except…"
- For each privileged remote user, you should list the select commands they are allowed to use. Rather than listing them individually, it might make sense to describe them by category or say "all" or "all except…"
- A description of how these restrictions (if any) are enforced

The documentation of user permissions may look something like this (the enforcement details would be a separate document):

Privileged Remote Access

Users	Security Relevant Information	Privileged Commands
IT Manager	Active Directory Logging System System Firewall Settings	All Powershell Commands All Command-Shell Commands
IT Technician	Active Directory Logging System	All Powershell Commands All Command-Shell Commands

Assessment Stats

- Assessment Points: 1
- Assessment POAM Eligible: Yes

Keys

- Documentation – You should have a document that identifies the privileged commands and security information that will be accessible remotely, along with identifying the users that will have that access.
- System – Implement and verify the permissions and enforced restrictions, as defined in your document.

Access Control

AC.L2-3.1.16

Wireless Access Authorization

Authorize wireless access prior to allowing such connections.

Impact

Your local burger joint might have WiFi that anybody can log onto. However, if you have a company network with sensitive materials, you need better control over who is gaining access. Although you could set up a wireless connection with a shared password required for access, that does not give visibility of exactly who is connecting. Imagine the ugly firing of an employee; what would keep that angry person from connecting to the network and causing havoc? So, from a practical standpoint, this authorization of wireless access needs to be user-by-user.

Official Interpretation*

Guidelines from management form the basis for the requirements that must be met prior to authorizing a wireless connection. These guidelines may include the following:

- types of devices, such as corporate or privately owned equipment;
- configuration requirements of the devices; and
- authorization requirements before granting such connections.

AC.L2-3.1.16, AC.L2-3.1.17, and AC.L2-3.1.18 are complementary requirements in that they all establish control for the connection of mobile devices and wireless devices through the use of authentication, authorization, and encryption mechanisms.

Assessment Focus

Also known as Assessment Objectives, these are the checklist items that an assessor will seek to verify. Each one must be addressed in your implementation and documentation:

1. wireless access points are identified; and
2. wireless access is authorized prior to allowing such connections.

(CMMC Assessment Guide, Level 2, Copyright 2020, 2021 Carnegie Mellon University and The Johns Hopkins University Applied Physics Laboratory LLC and/or CMMC Assessment Guide, Level 2, Version 2.11 - DRAFT, November 2023)

Implementation

Implementing this depends significantly on what the wireless access is giving the users access to. If the WiFi is Internet-only and isolated from the company network, then the wireless network is outside the scope of your CMMC assessment. However, to be accepted as out of scope, the wireless system must have absolute data separation from any system containing CUI. WPA-2 with a pre-shared key is adequate if the WiFi is Internet-only.

If the WiFi is attached to your CUI-containing network, it is considered in-scope, and all other network controls must apply. The best way to authorize wireless connections to your network would be through a RADIUS server, where each user has unique credentials. This would also need to have multi-factor authentication applied.

This gets complicated pretty fast, but you must consider that a hacker can sit in your parking lot and work at their leisure trying to hack your system. So, if you can avoid in-scope network access through WiFi, then that is best.

If you have an in-scope wireless system, you must do two things to comply with this requirement. You must document all of your access points and have an authorization process before allowing any connection. This connection must meet all the same requirements of authentication that would apply if the user plugged a network Ethernet cable into their laptop.

If you have no wireless network connecting to your CUI-containing systems, this requirement is "not applicable."

Assessment Stats

- Assessment Points: 5
- Assessment POAM Eligible: No

Keys

- Documentation – a listing of all of your access points must be available for any in-scope wireless system
- System – Any in-scope wireless system must have an authorization process before making a connection.

AC.L2-3.1.17

Wireless Access Protection

Protect wireless access using authentication and encryption.

Impact

Wireless access is highly convenient. However, it is also extremely convenient for hackers. A hacker can sit in their car outside your business and work at their leisure to get into your network. When wireless access to a network requires authentication, that should limit who can access the network. If authentication occurs without encryption, it is easy for a hacker to "listen" to the packets on the wireless network until they eavesdrop on what is needed to authenticate. When both authentication and encryption are used hand-in-hand, wireless access security increases.

Official Interpretation*

Use a combination of authentication and encryption methods to protect the access to wireless networks. Authenticating users to a wireless access point can be achieved in multiple ways. The most common authentication and encryption methods used include:

- WPA2-PSK (WiFi Protected Access-Pre-shared Key) – This method uses a password or passphrase known by the wireless access point and the client (user device). It is common in small companies that have little turnover because the key must be changed each time an employee leaves in order to prevent the terminated employee from connecting to the network without authorization. WPA2 is typically configured to use Advanced Encryption Standard (AES) encryption.
- WPA2 Enterprise – This method may be better for larger companies and enterprise networks because authentication is based on the identity of the individual user or device rather than a shared password or passphrase. It typically requires a Remote Authentication Dial-in User Service (RADIUS) server for authentication and can provide higher security than WPA2-PSK.

Open authentication must not be used because it authenticates any user and lacks security capabilities.

Because the use of cryptography in this requirement is to protect the confidentiality of CUI, the cryptography used must meet the criteria specified in requirement SC.L2-3.13.11.

AC.L2-3.1.16, AC.L2-3.1.17, and AC.L2-3.1.18 are complementary requirements in that they all establish control for the connection of mobile devices and wireless devices through the use of authentication, authorization, and encryption mechanisms.

(CMMC Assessment Guide, Level 2, Copyright 2020, 2021 Carnegie Mellon University and The Johns Hopkins University Applied Physics Laboratory LLC and/or CMMC Assessment Guide, Level 2, Version 2.11 - DRAFT, November 2023)

Assessment Focus

Also known as Assessment Objectives, these are the checklist items that an assessor will seek to verify. Each one must be addressed in your implementation and documentation:

1. wireless access to the system is protected using authentication; and
2. wireless access to the system is protected using encryption.

(CMMC Assessment Guide, Level 2, Copyright 2020, 2021 Carnegie Mellon University and The Johns Hopkins University Applied Physics Laboratory LLC and/or CMMC Assessment Guide, Level 2, Version 2.11 - DRAFT, November 2023)

Implementation

If your wireless network is out of scope (does not connect to your CUI-containing network, like Internet-only WiFi), then this requirement can be considered "not applicable."

This requirement covers the minimum requirement for wireless networking. Unless your wireless networking is wholly isolated from anything containing CUI (and therefore out-of-scope), plenty of other CMMC requirements will apply.

Both the WPA2-Enterprise and the WPA2-PSK wireless modes meet this requirement because they both use authentication and encryption for the connections. If used on Windows 10, the encryption also meets the FIPS requirements. So, this requirement appears easy to comply with.

However, if you are using a Pre-Shared Key on an in-scope network, it becomes more difficult to show compliance with PS-L2-3.9.2 (Personnel Actions), since you cannot turn off a single user's access when it is no longer applicable. While it is possible to change the PSK each time an employee leaves the company, the process will create some chaos (which increases as the number of authorized employees increase).

Your documentation will only need to show how your wireless connection uses a WPA2 connection.

Assessment Stats

- Assessment Points: 5
- Assessment POAM Eligible: No

Keys

- 🔧 System Change – Use WPA2 for wireless connections. If the connection provides access to a network containing CUI data, use Enterprise mode with a Radius Server. If the connection is Internet only, then a Pre-Shared Key is adequate.

Access Control

AC.L2-3.1.18

Mobile Device Connection

Control connection of mobile devices.

Impact

Having devices networked without wires or in a fixed location has revolutionized our world. The effects have been both very good and very bad. The idea that a person with a diabetic child could go through their typical day while their phone continuously reports their child's blood sugar levels, could never have happened without networked devices that no longer need wires. However, with that mobile capability has come significant risk. The fact that somebody might hack into your wireless network from their car parked in the street in front of your building is terrifying. The very thought that somebody might connect to your secure network using the same device used to surf some of the less savory areas of the Internet is enough to cause nightmares. In this requirement, there is a need to place controls on factors like:

- Who can connect?
- What devices are they allowed to use to connect?
- When and under what circumstances are they allowed to connect?
- When are these connections allowed?
- What aspects of the network can be accessed from a mobile device?

Official Interpretation*

Establish guidelines and acceptable requirements for proper configuration, use, and management of mobile devices. Devices that process, store, or transmit CUI must be identified with a device-specific identifier. There are many different types of identifiers, and it is important to select one that can accommodate all devices and be used in a consistent manner. These identifiers are important for facilitating the required monitoring and logging function.

In addition to smartphones, consider the security of other portable devices such as e-readers and tablets.

AC.L2-3.1.16, AC.L2-3.1.17, and AC.L2-3.1.18 are complementary requirements in that they all establish control for the connection of mobile devices and wireless devices through the use of authentication, authorization, and encryption mechanisms.

(CMMC Assessment Guide, Level 2, Copyright 2020, 2021 Carnegie Mellon University and The Johns Hopkins University Applied Physics Laboratory LLC and/or CMMC Assessment Guide, Level 2, Version 2.11 - DRAFT, November 2023)

Assessment Focus

Also known as Assessment Objectives, these are the checklist items that an assessor will seek to verify. Each one must be addressed in your implementation and documentation:

1. mobile devices that process, store, or transmit CUI are identified;
2. mobile device connections are authorized; and
3. mobile device connections are monitored and logged.

(CMMC Assessment Guide, Level 2, Copyright 2020, 2021 Carnegie Mellon University and The Johns Hopkins University Applied Physics Laboratory LLC and/or CMMC Assessment Guide, Level 2, Version 2.11 - DRAFT, November 2023)

Implementation

If your wireless network does not connect to your CUI-containing network, then this requirement is "not applicable." This is undoubtedly a simple way to check off this requirement.

People carry so much technology and often desire to hook their personal devices to the business network. However, since you have no idea how these devices have been used or protected, you have no idea whether they might contain malware. The most secure response to the demand to use personal devices is to deny using all devices not under the specific control and protection of the company IT staff to connect to the company network.

However, "just say 'No'" is not always an option. If it is necessary to allow network access through personal devices, setting specific standards is perfectly reasonable to protect the network and sensitive data.

However, demonstratable control must be exerted before mobile devices can connect to any network containing CUI, whether company-owned or personal.

If you have any mobile devices connecting to your CUI-containing network, you must know exactly what devices are connecting. Each device that connects must be authorized to connect. A list of all the authorized devices is part of the documentation needed to demonstrate conformance to this requirement. User authentication (username/password/MFA) does not verify the device, only the user, so it is a separate issue.

So, there must be a mechanism that only allows the authorized devices to connect. The simplest control for this is establishing MAC address filtering on your WiFi. While this is simple to set up, it does have some problems. The most important of these problems is that it isn't very secure. Acquiring and spoofing an authorized MAC address is simple for somebody who knows what they are doing. Secondly, depending on your WiFi hardware, you may not have a function that will pass for having those connections "monitored and logged."

Another option to address many of the needs associated with this requirement is to use a variety of Mobile Device Management (MDM) systems on the devices that are allowed to connect. These systems enable the devices to be monitored for conformance to security standards and remotely managed as necessary. Many people resent that this manner of software might be installed on their personal devices, but this should be considered a prerequisite for connecting to the organization's secure networks. It does not make sense that we would install antivirus, monitoring, and control on all the company computers before they are allowed to be used on the networks and that similar controls would not be applied before any mobile device could be connected. While there might be a perception that a phone is much safer than a computer, reality shows there is no difference.

NOTE: If an MDM system is part of your remote device controls, you may want to consider using the capabilities of this system to aid in the satisfaction of CM.L2-3.4.1 for system baselining. This would require obtaining licensing for all computers in your network, not just mobile devices.

The next key part of the requirement is that the mobile device connections to any CUI-containing network are monitored and logged. If your authorization system records what devices are connected and when, your network logging systems established to meet the CMMC Audit and Accountability requirements will provide data about what activities are being performed while the devices are connected. Combining both systems provides a complete picture of what these mobile devices are doing. To comply with the "monitoring" aspect of the requirement, you will want to set up a documented periodic review of the device authorization logs.

Assessment Stats

- Assessment Points: 5
- Assessment POAM Eligible: No

Keys

- Identification – You will want to have a list of the mobile devices that are authorized to connect
- System – You must have a system allowing only authorized mobile devices to connect.
- System – You need to demonstrate that you are logging and monitoring the mobile devices that connect. Monitoring implies that either there is an automated or manual process of periodically examining the logs for unacceptable activity.

Access Control

AC.L2-3.1.19

Encrypt CUI on Mobile

Encrypt CUI on mobile devices and mobile computing platforms.

Impact

Bernie was frustrated about his flight delays. Although this should be an excellent opportunity to get some work done, his aggravation made him unable to concentrate. So, he sets his laptop aside. While he is stressing over whether he will be stuck in this airport until the next day, the airline personnel call him up to the counter. In his haste to gather his stuff and go up to the counter, he leaves his laptop. When he finishes at the counter, somebody else sits in his seat. It takes him a few minutes to realize his laptop is not with him. It also isn't where he was previously sitting.

Now Bernie has a new stress. Laptops aren't cheap, but more than that, he thinks of all the confidential data on the computer. He may be in serious trouble with his employer for his momentary lapse of focus.

Many companies have had leaks of sensitive materials from a lost or stolen mobile device. The laptop's new owner may find that the data on the laptop is far more valuable than the laptop itself. People will always lose mobile devices; the trick is to either have no sensitive data on the mobile device or encrypt it so it cannot be easily accessed. You cannot assume for a minute that the login password provides any security when a hacker has physical access to the device. Unless the device has good encryption, accept that the new owner has access to every file on the device.

Official Interpretation*

Ensure CUI is encrypted on all mobile devices and mobile computing platforms that process, store, or transmit CUI including smartphones, tablets, and e-readers.

Because the use of cryptography in this requirement is to protect the confidentiality of CUI, the cryptography used must meet the criteria specified in requirement SC.L2-3.13.11.

This requirement, AC.L2-3.1.19, specifies that CUI be encrypted on mobile devices and extends three other CUI protection requirements (MP.L2-3.8.1, MP.L2-3.8.2, and SC.L2-3.13.16):

- MP.L2-3.8.1 requires that media containing CUI be protected.
- MP.L2-3.8.2 limits access to CUI to authorized users.

- Finally, SC.L2-3.13.16 requires confidentiality of CUI at rest.

This requirement, AC.L2-3.1.19, also leverages SC.L2-3.13.11, which specifies that the algorithms used must be FIPS-validated cryptography, and SC.L2-3.13.10, which specifies that any cryptographic keys in use must be protected.

(CMMC Assessment Guide, Level 2, Copyright 2020, 2021 Carnegie Mellon University and The Johns Hopkins University Applied Physics Laboratory LLC and/or CMMC Assessment Guide, Level 2, Version 2.11 - DRAFT, November 2023)

Assessment Focus

Also known as Assessment Objectives, these are the checklist items that an assessor will seek to verify. Each one must be addressed in your implementation and documentation:

1. mobile devices and mobile computing platforms that process, store, or transmit CUI are identified; and
2. encryption is employed to protect CUI on identified mobile devices and mobile computing platforms.

(CMMC Assessment Guide, Level 2, Copyright 2020, 2021 Carnegie Mellon University and The Johns Hopkins University Applied Physics Laboratory LLC and/or CMMC Assessment Guide, Level 2, Version 2.11 - DRAFT, November 2023)

Implementation

There are several ways to accomplish this. The simplest method is to prohibit CUI on mobile devices, but that may not be an option in your organization. If the CUI can be accessed on a platform that does not create local copies, then this may be a path to allow the user to access CUI without CUI being on the device.

The second option is to require all in-scope mobile devices to employ encryption* to protect the CUI. This may be in full disk encryption (FDE), where everything stored on the device is encrypted. In a Windows device, Full Disk Encryption can be achieved through the use of BitLocker, which is part of Windows. The next encryption option is to establish an encrypted partition or encrypted mountable file. This last option is the hardest to enforce because it requires that the user only places the files where they are supposed to be, even though that requires an additional step in accessing them. If your mobile device encryption depends on the user, then it should be specifically addressed in your policy.

For some companies, BYOD is the norm. If you need to gain control over a mass of mobile phones, tablets, and other devices, a tool like Microsoft Intune may be required. While a tool like this will add implementation costs, it may be required for certain organizations.

Remember that those laptops used like a desktop and never moved are still "mobile devices and platforms." Even if the devices do not move, they are a mobile platform and should receive the same protections as a device carried around all the time.

*When encryption protects CUI, then SC.L2-3.13.11 applies, so the encryption implementation must be FIPS-validated.

Assessment Stats

- Assessment Points: 3
- Assessment POAM Eligible: No

Keys

- System Change – Set up full disk encryption or an encrypted container on any laptops that handle CUI. Any encryption used here must have received the FIPS validation.
- System Change – Address the requirement for encryption on any tablets, phones, or other mobile devices that might store CUI.
- Policy Change – Ensure all users understand that CUI must always be encrypted in any mobile device.
- Documentation – Be prepared to identify those mobile devices that contain CUI and what protections are applied to each.

Access Control

AC.L1-3.1.20

External Connections

Verify and control/limit connections to and use of external systems.

Impact

The term "External Information Systems" from this requirement refers to networks and data systems outside your IT management's control. The biggest and most obvious example of this is the Internet, which contains many things that are not appropriate for access for business purposes. So, access to the Internet needs to be controlled or limited. But then, if an employee sets up an unauthorized (rogue) wireless access point to access blocked websites, this is another example of an "External Information System." Other examples include connecting to personal devices or using public networks to connect to your controlled network. Anytime that your network hooks up to an external information system, it needs to be done in a manner that is carefully controlled.

Official Interpretation*

Control and manage connections between your company network and outside networks. Outside networks could include the public internet, one of your own company's networks that falls outside of your CMMC Assessment Scope (e.g., an isolated lab), or a network that does not belong to your company. Tools to accomplish include firewalls and connection allow/deny lists. External systems not controlled by your company could be running applications that are prohibited or blocked. Control and limit access to corporate networks from personally owned devices such as laptops, tablets, and phones. You may choose to limit how and when your network is connected to outside systems or only allow certain employees to connect to outside systems from network resources.

(CMMC Assessment Guide, Level 2, Copyright 2020, 2021 Carnegie Mellon University and The Johns Hopkins University Applied Physics Laboratory LLC and/or CMMC Assessment Guide, Level 2, Version 2.11 - DRAFT, November 2023)

Assessment Focus

Also known as Assessment Objectives, these are the checklist items that an assessor will seek to verify. Each one must be addressed in your implementation and documentation:

1. connections to external systems are identified;
2. the use of external systems is identified;
3. connections to external systems are verified;

4. the use of external systems is verified;
5. connections to external systems are controlled/limited; and
6. the use of external systems is controlled/limited.

(CMMC Assessment Guide, Level 2, Copyright 2020, 2021 Carnegie Mellon University and The Johns Hopkins University Applied Physics Laboratory LLC and/or CMMC Assessment Guide, Level 2, Version 2.11 - DRAFT, November 2023)

Implementation

The "External Information Systems" the standard refers to are those networks and data systems outside your IT management's control.

Of all the systems that your employees connect to, the most prominent of those is the Internet. In general, that system would be considered out-of-scope for the purposes of CMMC. However, this requirement demands careful documentation of the limiting controls that exist between the Internet and your organization's systems.

There might be some corners of the Internet that are part of your scope. For example, you might use a cloud service to store some CUI. Now, even though this service is part of the Internet it will need to be separately addressed as an External System. However, a cloud service that is used by your quality department for calibrations, which never sees CUI or FCI, can be lumped into the broader Internet.

You likely have controls between your users and the Internet, like firewalls or DNS filtering. However, there is always the possibility of Internet access that bypasses your controls or other external information systems. You will need policies or other controls that prevent employees from using hotspots or other systems that bypass the protections between your systems and the Internet.

Controlling access to the Internet can best be achieved by limiting what Internet traffic enters your facility. Your basic Internet firewall is a key element of this control. Products such as web filtering devices and software go a long way toward providing the required restrictions. High-quality filtering can be obtained for free through the NSA for DoD contractors. If you have remote users, they will need an app allowing them to have their DNS filtered wherever they access the Internet.

HANDY LINK

Link to NSA PDNS: https://tinyurl.com/*CMMC4SMB*-867

In addition to the broader, out-of-scope Internet, other connections must be addressed. Other examples of External Information Systems might include:

- Cloud Systems that are in scope due to CUI: like email, cloud storage, ERP, or security services
- Personal devices
- Partner networks (customers or suppliers)

It must be understood that if unfiltered access is made between a system with CUI and an External Information System, then that External System is technically in scope for your CMMC certification. This is unlikely to be your intent. It is, therefore, necessary to provide tools to isolate or control these connections.

Each identified External Information System (Internet through your ISP may be the only one) must have documented verification with controls or limits. So your documentation may be a table like:

External Information Systems (Example)

System	Verification	Controls/Limits
Internet through Company ISP	Annually, logs of the MX64W will be examined to verify that it is working correctly. The PDNS is set to provide daily log emails sent to the IT Manager to verify that filtering is occurring.	The Meraki MX64W provides users with firewall and web filtering for users accessing the Internet within the building. In addition, the NSA PDNS provides DNS filtering.
Remote users' Internet Access	PDNS logs will be examined annually to verify that DNS filtering works correctly for remote users.	Remote users use company laptops with the PDNS remote application installed, so DNS is filtered regardless of Internet source.

If your CMMC assessor interviews users and discovers any external systems that should be covered by this requirement but aren't covered, that could cause a NOT MET. So, careful brainstorming should be applied to think of all possible External Systems that should be addressed.

Assessment Stats

- Assessment Points: 1
- Assessment POAM Eligible: No

Keys

- Documentation – Construct a listing of the External Information Systems that your systems connect to and the applicable controls.
- System Change – Provide filtering to the Internet access provided to your users.
- Policy Change – Publish a policy that states that users must refrain from setting up any unauthorized means of accessing outside digital resources, like the Internet, on company systems.
- Records of conformance – There should be logs of the verification processes of the external system controls and limitations.

Asset Management

AC.L2-3.1.21

Portable Storage Use

Limit use of portable storage devices on external systems.

Impact

One thing feared by cybersecurity practitioners is called "exfiltration of data." This is where company secrets or other valuable data are removed from the systems in an unauthorized manner. Exfiltrated data might include customer credentials, credit card numbers, employee personal information, or trade secrets. Being entrusted with CUI from the government, it is essential that nobody can simply plug in and download vast amounts of CUI, easily carrying it out in their pocket. This requirement addresses those tools that can attach to a computer and carry the data away.

Official Interpretation*

A portable storage device is a system component that can be inserted or attached and easily removed from a system. It is used to store data or information. Examples of portable storage devices include:

- compact/digital video disks (CDs/DVDs);
- Universal Serial Bus (USB) drives;
- external hard disk drives;
- flash memory cards/drives; and
- floppy disks.

This requirement can be implemented in two ways:

- identifying the portable storage device usage restrictions, identifying portable storage devices that may be used on external systems, identifying associated external systems on which a portable storage device may be used, and administratively (through the use of a written policy) limiting the usage of the devices to those systems; or
- configuring devices to work only when connected to a system to which the portable storage device can authenticate, limiting the devices' use on external systems to those that the OSA has the ability to manage.

(CMMC Assessment Guide, Level 2, Copyright 2020, 2021 Carnegie Mellon University and The Johns Hopkins University Applied Physics Laboratory LLC and/or CMMC Assessment Guide, Level 2, Version 2.11 - DRAFT, November 2023)

Assessment Focus

Also known as Assessment Objectives, these are the checklist items that an assessor will seek to verify. Each one must be addressed in your implementation and documentation:

1. the use of portable storage devices containing CUI on external systems is identified and documented;
2. limits on the use of portable storage devices containing CUI on external systems are defined; and
3. the use of portable storage devices containing CUI on external systems is limited as defined.

Implementation

This requirement concerns any portable data storage devices with CUI and how they can connect to "external systems." If you never have CUI on any portable storage devices, then this requirement is not applicable.

So, unless you can completely avoid ever having CUI on portable devices, steps must be taken to control those devices from ever getting on an external system. For this requirement, an "external system" is any system outside of your CUI scope. Under this requirement, it is just as "external" to plug a CUI-containing thumb drive into the accountant's Contractor Risk Managed Asset (CRMA) computer as it is to plug it into somebody's home computer. Either way, the organization is not controlling the asset for CUI.

It is possible to configure BitLocker through Group Policy in such a way that it encrypts all portable storage devices in a way that cannot be read away from the domain. Approach these controls with caution to ensure that they won't cause any problems in your normal operations.

HANDY LINK

More information about using BitLocker to control storage devices can be found at: https://tinyurl.com/CMMC4SMB-823

Because the organization does not control the external system, there are challenges for the organization to establish technical controls on that system to block the portable storage device. As a result, this is typically controlled through policy.

You know your organization. You will have to ask yourself if a written policy will be effective. Certainly, an assessor will want to determine if it provides effective control. If there is doubt about whether a policy will be complied with, then other controls would be mandated.

The policy is the cleanest if it is possible to simply ban the use of any CUI-containing portable storage device on any system except those in the organization's CUI scope. With secure cloud storage and file-sharing, this is not onerous in most organizations. If there is a special circumstance where using a portable storage device with CUI on a system outside the CUI scope cannot be avoided, you will want to thoroughly document what is allowed and what is not. Then, you will need to create and enforce a policy that clarifies those limits.

HANDY LINK

The author's preferred tool for secure and compliant cloud storage of CUI for the small organization can be found here https://tinyurl.com/CMMC4SMB-938

It is helpful if you have some controls that limit the use of unauthorized portable storage devices on any of your CUI systems. In addition to several 3rd party solutions, you can control the use of USB devices with group policy. The controls available within Group Policy allow the application of very granular restrictions on the use of USB and other portable storage devices. (Computer Configuration→ Administrative Templates→ System→ Removable Storage Access) It is possible to place a ban on portable storage devices and then apply exceptions for specific devices.

Assessment Stats

- Assessment Points: 1
- Assessment POAM Eligible: Yes

Keys

- Policy – Create a policy that limits the use of any CUI-containing portable storage device on any computer that is not within the organization's CUI scope. The policy must clearly communicate under what circumstances this is allowed and prohibit all other uses. The policy needs to be communicated and enforced.

AC.L1-3.1.22

Control Public Information

Control CUI posted or processed on publicly accessible systems.

Impact

Tad is working hard to get noticed in his first marketing job. He has devised a plan to try to grab new customers. He feels that the potential customers need to see the great things his employer, a defense contractor, is making. He is slightly annoyed by the hoops he has to jump through to get product drawings, but he promptly starts posting these on social media and the company website. He is sure that if potential customers get greater visibility into the cool stuff they are making, they will be lining up to place orders, and he will be the hero.

It didn't take long before the stuff hit the fan. Since he had received training in CUI but did this anyway, Tad was being fired. His manager said Tad, as a company representative, had violated the trust that the government had placed in their company by giving them CUI and that his actions threatened the company's existence.

Official Interpretation*

Only government officials can be authorized to release CUI to the public. Do not allow CUI to become public – always safeguard the confidentiality of CUI by controlling the posting of CUI on company-controlled websites or public forums, and the exposure of CUI in public presentations or on public displays. It is important to know which users are allowed to publish information on publicly accessible systems, like your company website, and implement a review process before posting such information. If CUI is discovered on a publicly accessible system, procedures should be in place to remove that information and alert the appropriate parties.

(CMMC Assessment Guide, Level 2, Copyright 2020, 2021 Carnegie Mellon University and The Johns Hopkins University Applied Physics Laboratory LLC and/or CMMC Assessment Guide, Level 2, Version 2.11 - DRAFT, November 2023)

Assessment Focus

Also known as Assessment Objectives, these are the checklist items that an assessor will seek to verify. Each one must be addressed in your implementation and documentation:

1. individuals authorized to post or process information on publicly accessible systems are identified;
2. procedures to ensure CUI is not posted or processed on publicly accessible systems are identified;

3. a review process is in place prior to posting of any content to publicly accessible systems;
4. content on publicly accessible systems is reviewed to ensure that it does not include CUI; and
5. mechanisms are in place to remove and address improper posting of CUI.

(CMMC Assessment Guide, Level 2, Copyright 2020, 2021 Carnegie Mellon University and The Johns Hopkins University Applied Physics Laboratory LLC and/or CMMC Assessment Guide, Level 2, Version 2.11 - DRAFT, November 2023)

Implementation

It is not uncommon that individuals will make materials Internet-accessible for a reason that seems reasonable at the time but does not make any sense from the company's big-picture standpoint. This is one area where the SMB may have an advantage over the large company with its sprawling web presence.

This requirement is limited to the potential exposure of CUI and FCI, so the simplest answer is to have the people who handle social media and websites be out-of-scope so they can't get their hands on CUI or FCI. Often, in a small organization, folks wear many hats, so that level of separation just isn't possible. When the person who handles the external marketing has legitimate access to FCI or CUI, it might be possible to provide the person with alternate logons for the different roles. In many cases, this control will just come down to policy and training.

In a small organization, posting FCI or CUI is often the fault of some manager who tells a assistant to post it. This is where training comes in. It also justifies why the training needs to have a broad scope.

An assessor will expect to see a list of the individuals authorized to post information on behalf of the organization publicly, a procedure that shows how FCI and CUI will be kept off the Internet. They will be looking for a procedure for reviewing postings before going live. Finally, there needs to be a periodic review of posted materials with a corresponding procedure of how any FCI/CUI accidentally posted shall be removed.

Assessment Stats

- Assessment Points: 1
- Assessment POAM Eligible: No

Keys

- Documentation – Compile a list of individuals authorized to post materials online.
- Procedure Development -- Create a public information policy that includes what information may be posted on the Internet and what is prohibited, how postings will be reviewed before going live, how the organization's posting will be periodically scanned for FCI and CUI, and the process for removing any materials that shouldn't be posted.
- Documentation - Materials being posted should receive a documented review (even if the review is performed by the same person who is doing the posting, it checks the box.) Document the periodic review of all publically accessible materials for any FCI or CUI and the removal of any controlled information accidentally posted.

AT.L2-3.2.1

Role-Based Risk Awareness

Ensure that managers, systems administrators, and users of organizational systems are made aware of the security risks associated with their activities and of the applicable policies, standards, and procedures related to the security of those systems.

Impact

Anthony was working to repair the office copier. He made sure to unplug the device before beginning the repairs. Around the corner, Tom spotted the unplugged cord that he knew belonged to the copier, so he tried to be helpful by plugging it in. This resulted in a big surprise for Anthony.

"I didn't know" is a common refrain when things go wrong. In the world of data security, many people don't understand much about the issues involved. More importantly, they often don't understand how their actions support or negate efforts to assure good security. In many areas of hacking, the human is the clear "path of least resistance" to gain unauthorized access. The uninformed human can be tricked into doing various activities to help the hacker. The best defense against this is to educate your people about what they should be doing and the risks associated with their job.

Official Interpretation*

Awareness training focuses user attention on security. Several techniques can be used, such as:

- synchronous or asynchronous training;
- simulations (e.g., simulated phishing emails);
- security awareness campaigns (posters, reminders, group discussions); and
- communicating regular email advisories and notices to employees.

Awareness training and role-based training are different. This requirement, AT.L2-3.2.1, covers awareness training, which provides general security training to influence user behavior. This training can apply broadly or be tailored to a specific role. Role-based training focuses on the knowledge, skills, and abilities needed to complete a specific job and is covered by AT.L2-3.2.2.

(CMMC Assessment Guide, Level 2, Copyright 2020, 2021 Carnegie Mellon University and The Johns Hopkins University Applied Physics Laboratory LLC and/or CMMC Assessment Guide, Level 2, Version 2.11 - DRAFT, November 2023)

Assessment Focus

Also known as Assessment Objectives, these are the checklist items that an assessor will seek to verify. Each one must be addressed in your implementation and documentation:

1. security risks associated with organizational activities involving CUI are identified;
2. policies, standards, and procedures related to the security of the system are identified;
3. managers, systems administrators, and users of the system are made aware of the security risks associated with their activities; and
4. managers, systems administrators, and users of the system are made aware of the applicable policies, standards, and procedures related to the security of the system.

(CMMC Assessment Guide, Level 2, Copyright 2020, 2021 Carnegie Mellon University and The Johns Hopkins University Applied Physics Laboratory LLC and/or CMMC Assessment Guide, Level 2, Version 2.11 - DRAFT, November 2023)

Implementation

This awareness program can be conducted in a manner that is appropriate to your organization. However, the required content of the training is clearly defined. It will be necessary that all the boxes get checked and that the delivered content is well documented.

Because the requirement says that it is necessary to "ensure" that the individuals are aware, that implies some evaluation that the messages have been effectively communicated. So, the records of this training should consist of some "test" completed by each applicable employee.

The training content must include the applicable policies, standards, and procedures. There have been many cases where such directive documents had been published, but interviews revealed that the employees were unaware of their existence.

The security-awareness box cannot be checked by just training the users. The individuals that need to receive the training are the managers, system administrators, and system users. The range of individuals receiving the training should extend beyond the boundary of CUI-accessing users for maximum benefit.

Security and the threat environment continually evolve. Training will need to be refreshed periodically to ensure that it remains applicable. Also, you must ensure that new employees, promotions, and transferred employees receive the awareness training.

You will need to compile a list of risks involving CUI. These can be organized around the cybersecurity triad of accessibility, confidentiality, and integrity. The list could be never-ending if the identified risks are too specific, but if they are too broad then the whole training process becomes useless. This list will be the basis of the awareness training.

You will also need to include information about the system security policies, standards, and procedures in the user training. Your CMMC assessor will likely want to see your listing of these documents and how they are communicated in the user training.

This requirement might seem like a pain and a "soft" requirement, but it can provide a tangible security benefit.

Assessment Stats

- Assessment Points: 5
- Assessment POAM Eligible: No

Keys

- Documentation – Develop a list of CUI-related risks and the policies and procedures that apply to the employees. Create documented training materials to include security policies, procedures, and CUI-associated risks. Have records of the training of individuals. Have documented assessment of their absorption of the content.
- Procedure Change – Establish a procedure that outlines how security principles and risks will be communicated with employees, including existing employees, employees transferring to new roles, and new hires.

Awareness & Training

AT.L2-3.2.2

Role-Based Training

Ensure that personnel are trained to carry out their assigned information security-related duties and responsibilities.

Impact

Perhaps the most common issue in information technology is the "PEBCAK" family of problems. PEBCAK stands for "Problem Exists Between Chair And Keyboard." It is in this user zone that many issues occur. We expect our users to know what to do and what not to do, but they frequently astonish us with the multitude of ways that they find to perform tasks in manners that are contrary to the correct procedure. Within information security, the stakes are much higher than for the user with an app that won't work as expected. A security PEBCAK issue can cause damage to the organization and incur a significant cost. The best defense against PEBCAK issues is training.

Official Interpretation*

Training imparts skills and knowledge to enable staff to perform a specific job function. Training should be available to all employees for all organizational roles to accommodate role changes without being constrained by the training schedule. Awareness training and role-based training are different. Awareness training provides general security training to influence user behavior and is covered by AT.L2-3.2.1. This requirement, AT.L2-3.2.2, covers role-based training that focuses on the knowledge, skills, and abilities needed to complete a specific job. Role-based training may include awareness topics specific to individual roles such as ensuring systems administrators understand the risk associated with using an administrative account.

(CMMC Assessment Guide, Level 2, Copyright 2020, 2021 Carnegie Mellon University and The Johns Hopkins University Applied Physics Laboratory LLC and/or CMMC Assessment Guide, Level 2, Version 2.11 - DRAFT, November 2023)

Assessment Focus

Also known as Assessment Objectives, these are the checklist items that an assessor will seek to verify. Each one must be addressed in your implementation and documentation:

1. information security-related duties, roles, and responsibilities are defined;
2. information security-related duties, roles, and responsibilities are assigned to designated personnel; and

3. personnel are adequately trained to carry out their assigned information security-related duties, roles, and responsibilities.

(CMMC Assessment Guide, Level 2, Copyright 2020, 2021 Carnegie Mellon University and The Johns Hopkins University Applied Physics Laboratory LLC and/or CMMC Assessment Guide, Level 2, Version 2.11 - DRAFT, November 2023)

Implementation

Although AT.L2-3.2.1 may sound similar, that requirement concerns general awareness and security principles. This requirement is the specific training an individual should receive of how to perform the employee's security-related responsibilities. Any individual with no security responsibility beyond what is covered by the awareness training does not need training under this requirement. The primary recipients of this specialized training will be IT staff. Occasionally, some managers have privileged accounts or access to security resources, so they will also need this training.

Like AT.L2-3.2.1, this requirement says you should "ensure" the training occurs. Based on this need to ensure the training, the users should be tested to show their comprehension.

This training might be simpler and more effective if it is broken up into modules instead of trying to do everything in a one-size-fits-all barrage. For example, there might be training about the risks associated with using administrator credentials, which may have different participants than training about Active Directory. This training might be focused on a specific task common to a group of users. For example, the employees who use a sensitive cloud application might be given training on how to perform this task safely (even though the individuals might be performing diverse activities on this application).

Your HR folks likely have job descriptions that describe the duties, roles, and responsibilities of various positions in the company. For this requirement, it will be necessary to accumulate the duties, roles, and responsibilities, assigned to those same positions, specific to information security. Then the training, to meet this requirement, will provide the individuals with the necessary information to carry out those security duties, roles, and responsibilities.

Beware of those situations where people are performing security tasks that are not really part of their job. If an assessor found out about those and determined that those people had not received training for what they do, then that might result in this requirement being found non-compliant.

If you have individuals who have completed external security-related classes or achieved security-related certifications, this is where you can take credit for those activities.

Security and the tools we use continually evolve. Training will need to be refreshed periodically to ensure that it remains applicable. Your training system should also ensure that new employees and those transferred or promoted receive applicable training.

The training can take any form. Classroom, videos, online, or written training is acceptable. Assure that there is some assessment of comprehension after the employee has completed the training.

Assessment Stats

- Assessment Points: 5
- Assessment POAM Eligible: No

Keys

- Data Gathering – A listing of the security-related tasks and who is assigned those tasks must be compiled.
- Procedure Change – Establish a procedure that outlines how employees will be trained to perform their security responsibilities in their job (those that go beyond what was covered in the awareness training).
- Evidence of Conformance – Be able to produce records indicating that the security training has been effectively communicated to all applicable employees.

Awareness & Training

AT.L2-3.2.3

Insider Threat Awareness

Provide security awareness training on recognizing and reporting potential indicators of insider threat.

Impact

Often, people will surprise you. You think you know somebody and know what they are capable of doing, only to find out that they have done something that completely shocks you. While we don't expect our coworkers ever to do anything to harm the organization intentionally, we also know how often an "insider" has been responsible for something awful. In the smaller organization, we would like to believe that this risk is lower, but while the risk might be lower, it still isn't zero. Therefore, we need to recognize the real risk of the insider threat and help our people to detect the threat and identify it before it becomes an "I should have recognized the signs" regret.

Official Interpretation*

An insider threat is the threat that an insider will use their authorized access, wittingly or unwittingly, to do harm. Insider threat security awareness training focuses on recognizing employee behaviors and characteristics that might be indicators of an insider threat and the guidelines and procedures to handle and report it. Training for managers will provide guidance on observing team members to identify all potential threat indicators, while training for general employees will provide guidance for focusing on a smaller number of indicators. Employee behaviors will vary depending on roles, team membership, and associated information needs. The person responsible for specifying insider threat indicators must be cognizant of these factors. Because of this, organizations may choose to tailor the training for specific roles. This requirement does not require separate training regarding insider threat. Organizations may choose to integrate these topics into their standard security awareness training programs.

(CMMC Assessment Guide, Level 2, Copyright 2020, 2021 Carnegie Mellon University and The Johns Hopkins University Applied Physics Laboratory LLC and/or CMMC Assessment Guide, Level 2, Version 2.11 - DRAFT, November 2023)

Assessment Focus

Also known as Assessment Objectives, these are the checklist items that an assessor will seek to verify. Each one must be addressed in your implementation and documentation:

1. potential indicators associated with insider threats are identified; and
2. security awareness training on recognizing and reporting potential indicators of insider threat is provided to managers and employees.

(CMMC Assessment Guide, Level 2, Copyright 2020, 2021 Carnegie Mellon University and The Johns Hopkins University Applied Physics Laboratory LLC and/or CMMC Assessment Guide, Level 2, Version 2.11 - DRAFT, November 2023)

Implementation

In the SMB, where people tend to know other employees, the insider threat is likely a less significant risk than within a large organization. The NIST SP 800-53 (R4) lists out a series of "indicators and precursors" of insider threat, saying that it can include behaviors such as:

- Inordinate, long-term job dissatisfaction,
- attempts to gain access to information not required for job performance,
- unexplained access to financial resources,
- bullying or sexual harassment of fellow employees,
- workplace violence and other serious violations of organizational policies, procedures, directives, rules, or practices.

Provide your employees with documented training about the signs of insider threat and what they should do if these signs are observed. This training can be lumped in with the security awareness training developed to meet AT.L2-3.2.1.

Assessment Stats

- Assessment Points: 1
- Assessment POAM Eligible: Yes

Keys

- Documentation – Construct a list of potential indicators of insider threat.
- Procedure Change – Establish a procedure where employees are provided documented training in detecting possible insider threats and the actions that should be taken based on suspicion.
- Evidence of Conformance – Be able to produce records indicating that insider threat training has been effectively communicated to all applicable employees.

Audit & Accountability

AU.L2-3.3.1

System Auditing

Create and retain system audit logs and records to the extent needed to enable the monitoring, analysis, investigation, and reporting of unlawful or unauthorized system activity.

Impact

Parents must keep a close eye on their young kids to prevent problems. They can't watch them 24/7, but they need to understand their kids enough to know the most critical times and circumstances when they should monitor them especially closely. Similarly, we need to carefully consider how we collect data on the activities of our network users. This requires the application of wisdom to maximize the meaningful data while minimizing the useless data. This needs to be done without knowing the nature of the unauthorized activities that might be occurring in the future of your network.

Official Interpretation*

OSAs must ensure that all applicable systems create and retain audit logs that contain enough information to identify and investigate potentially unlawful or unauthorized system activity. OSAs must define the audit logs it needs to collect as well as the specific events to capture within the selected logs. Captured audit records are checked to verify that they contain the required events.

In defining the audit log retention period, OSAs must ensure that logs are retained for a sufficiently long period to allow for the investigation of a security event. The retention period must take into account the delay of weeks or months that can occur between an initial compromise and the discovery of attacker activity.

(CMMC Assessment Guide, Level 2, Copyright 2020, 2021 Carnegie Mellon University and The Johns Hopkins University Applied Physics Laboratory LLC and/or CMMC Assessment Guide, Level 2, Version 2.11 - DRAFT, November 2023)

Assessment Focus

Also known as Assessment Objectives, these are the checklist items that an assessor will seek to verify. Each one must be addressed in your implementation and documentation:

1. audit logs needed (i.e., event types to be logged) to enable the monitoring, analysis, investigation, and reporting of unlawful or unauthorized system activity are specified;
2. the content of audit records needed to support monitoring, analysis, investigation, and reporting of unlawful or unauthorized system activity is defined;
3. audit records are created (generated);
4. audit records, once created, contain the defined content;
5. retention requirements for audit records are defined; and
6. audit records are retained as defined.

(CMMC Assessment Guide, Level 2, Copyright 2020, 2021 Carnegie Mellon University and The Johns Hopkins University Applied Physics Laboratory LLC and/or CMMC Assessment Guide, Level 2, Version 2.11 - DRAFT, November 2023)

Implementation

Windows networks are capable of collecting extremely granular audit records. Audit records can explode into a mountain of data that becomes useless just because of its volume. Compliance with the standard does not require specific activities to be audited. While Microsoft does set some actions to log by default, there are some deficiencies in the defaults. For example, Windows will log a failed logon attempt by default but not a successful one. So, in the logs, you might see a series of suspicious failed attempts, but you can't tell if the attempts were finally successful.

Across different organizations, there are different opinions on what exact auditing provides the greatest benefits while minimizing useless information. In general, you will want to establish a group policy object that enables advanced auditing (Computer Configuration => Policies => Windows Settings => Security Settings => Local Policies => Security Options, set Audit: Force audit policy subcategory settings to enabled). Then, create an audit policy in Computer Configuration => Policies => Windows Settings => Security Settings => Advanced Audit Policy Configuration => Audit Policies. There, you will find several categories of events where logging can be turned on.

Here are some suggested settings for a typical environment.

	Subcategory	Audit Events
Account Logon	Audit Credential Validation	Success and Failure
	Audit Kerberos Authentication Service	Not Configured
	Audit Kerberos Service Ticket Operations	Not Configured
	Audit Other Account Logon Events	Success and Failure

	Subcategory	Audit Events
Account Management	Audit Application Group Management	Success and Failure
	Audit Computer Account Management	Success and Failure
	Audit Distribution Group Management	Success and Failure
	Audit Other Account Management Events	Success and Failure
	Audit Security Group Management	Success and Failure
	Audit User Account Management	Success and Failure

Category	Subcategory	Audit Events
Detailed Tracking	Audit DPAPI Activity	Not Configured
	Audit PNP Activity	Success
	Audit Process Creation	Success and Failure
	Audit Process Termination	Not Configured
	Audit RPC Events	Success and Failure
	Audit Token Right Adjusted	Success
DS Access	Audit Detailed Directory Service Replication	Not Configured
	Audit Directory Service Access	Not Configured
	Audit Directory Service Changes	Success and Failure
	Audit Directory Service Replication	Not Configured
Logon/Logoff	Audit Account Lockout	Success
	Audit User / Device Claims	Not Configured
	Audit Group Membership	Success
	Audit IPsec Extended Mode	Not Configured
	Audit IPsec Main Mode	Not Configured
	Audit IPsec Quick Mode	Not Configured
	Audit Logoff	Success
	Audit Logon	Success and Failure
	Audit Network Policy Server	Success and Failure
	Audit Other Logon/Logoff Events	Success and Failure
	Audit Special Logon	Success and Failure
Object Access	Audit Application Generated	Success and Failure
	Audit Certification Services	Success and Failure
	Audit Detailed File Share	Success
	Audit File Share	Success and Failure
	Audit File System	Success
	Audit Filtering Platform Connection	Success
	Audit Filtering Platform Packet Drop	Not Configured
	Audit Handle Manipulation	Not Configured
	Audit Kernel Object	Not Configured
	Audit Other Object Access Events	Not Configured
	Audit Registry	Success
	Audit Removable Storage	Success and Failure
	Audit SAM	Success
	Audit Central Access Policy Staging	Not Configured

Category	Subcategory	Audit Events
Policy Change	Subcategory	Audit Events
	Audit Audit Policy Change	Success and Failure
	Audit Authentication Policy Change	Success and Failure
	Audit Authorization Policy Change	Success and Failure
	Audit Filtering Platform Policy Change	Success
	Audit MPSSVC Rule-Level Policy Change	Not Configured
	Audit Other Policy Change Events	Not Configured
Privilege Use	Subcategory	Audit Events
	Audit Non Sensitive Privilege Use	Not Configured
	Audit Other Privilege Use Events	Not Configured
	Audit Sensitive Privilege Use	Success and Failure
System	Subcategory	Audit Events
	Audit IPsec Driver	Success
	Audit Other System Events	Failure
	Audit Security State Change	Success and Failure
	Audit Security System Extension	Success and Failure
	Audit System Integrity	Success and Failure
Global Object Access Auditing	Resource Manager	Audit Events
	File system	Not configured
	Registry	Not configured

Assessors will be looking for specific items of evidence that you have complied with this requirement. The assessors will be looking for evidence that your implementation was planned out. They will want to see a document listing audit logs you will use to accomplish your goals.

Instead of just being a list of logs, they want to know what content is recorded in each log. Consider this description from the Assessment Guide:

> *Audit record content that may be necessary to satisfy this requirement includes time stamps, source and destination addresses, user or process identifiers, event descriptions, success or failure indications, filenames involved, and access control or flow control rules invoked. Event outcomes can include indicators of event success or failure and event-specific results (e.g., the security state of the system after the event occurred).* (CMMC Assessment Guide, Level 2, Copyright 2020, 2021 Carnegie Mellon University and The Johns Hopkins University Applied Physics Laboratory LLC and/or CMMC Assessment Guide, Level 2, Version 2.11 - DRAFT, November 2023)

You must turn on the planned auditing and verify that it works as expected. This included assuring that the content of the logs complies with the plan. This verification process should be documented.

Determine and document the planned retention period for your logs. Then, there should be a documented verification that data is actually being retained according to the plan. Because of the massive size of Windows logs, a longer retention period has costs associated with it. However, in a security incident, a shorter retention period might find critical data already deleted. Your retention period can theoretically be anything you choose, but many assessors would expect it to be 90 days or more.

Consider that your retention time might be limited by storage space, so adding more users or more logging might reduce your effective retention time. Therefore, future actions might have the effect of causing nonconformance to your documented retention time. Based on this, you might define your retention period very conservatively and define it as a minimum value. For example, if your logging server looks like it can hold 120 days of data, then you might want to define your retention time as, "a minimum of 90 days," to provide a margin of error.

Assessors will want to see that the records you audit help with your security goals. They will want to see that you have verified that the actual audit records produce the anticipated content. Finally, they will want you to be able to show your audit data retention plans and your confirmation that your system is accurately conforming to those retention plans.

Assessment Stats

- Assessment Points: 5
- Assessment POAM Eligible: No

Keys

- Documentation – Be prepared to show how your audit items are planned with an effort to assure that your selected items meet your goals. List out the data to be saved for each event. Produce evidence that the auditing is being performed in accordance with the plans.
- Documentation – Define a log retention period and verify that your logging system retains the records per that plan.
- System Configuration – Use Group Policy to establish logging requirements for your member systems.

Audit & Accountability

AU.L2-3.3.2

User Accountability

Ensure that the actions of individual system users can be uniquely traced to those users so they can be held accountable for their actions.

Impact

It was the Tuesday after Memorial Day. Larry started getting complaints as he was en route to the office. The basic complaint was the same, the shared directory was empty. While he was a little annoyed, he wasn't terribly concerned. Chances are that a quick reboot of the server would fix everything.

Shortly after getting to the office, his concern grew. He found that the non-technical folks had hit the nail on the head, the directory for the shared drive was completely empty. The directory should have had 10 years of files, but now there was nothing. To abate the screaming, he began a restore from backup and his mind turned to understand what happened to all those files.

He opened his logs and groaned out loud. A few months earlier, they had created a single logon to be shared by a group of interns from the local technical school. The file deletions were all performed by that username. He had no idea which of them might have caused this disaster.

Official Interpretation*

Capturing the necessary information in audit logs ensures that you can trace actions to a specific user. This may include capturing user IDs, source and destination addresses, and time stamps. Logging from networks, servers, clients, and applications should be considered in ensuring accountability.

This requirement, AU.L2-3.3.2, which ensures logging and traceability of user actions, supports the control of non-privileged users required by AC.L2-3.1.7 as well as many other auditing, configuration management, incident response, and situation awareness requirements.

(CMMC Assessment Guide, Level 2, Copyright 2020, 2021 Carnegie Mellon University and The Johns Hopkins University Applied Physics Laboratory LLC and/or CMMC Assessment Guide, Level 2, Version 2.11 - DRAFT, November 2023)

Assessment Focus

Also known as Assessment Objectives, these are the checklist items that an assessor will seek to verify. Each one must be addressed in your implementation and documentation:

1. the content of the audit records needed to support the ability to uniquely trace users to their actions is defined; and
2. audit records, once created, contain the defined content.

(CMMC Assessment Guide, Level 2, Copyright 2020, 2021 Carnegie Mellon University and The Johns Hopkins University Applied Physics Laboratory LLC and/or CMMC Assessment Guide, Level 2, Version 2.11 - DRAFT, November 2023)

Implementation

Within a Windows domain, network resources are accessed based on an individual login for each user. This capability comes without much effort. Many logged actions by a signed-in domain user will be automatically recorded as attributed to that user.

It should be pointed out that each person should have their own login credentials and they are the only person who knows their password. If you have even one shared account or one password known by multiple people, then the ability of your system to identify users is suspect.

As audit logs are designed, ensure that the necessary information is included to connect logged events to users.

Assessment Stats

- Assessment Points: 3
- Assessment POAM Eligible: No

Keys

- Evidence of Conformance – On a domain controller, open the event viewer and look in the Windows Logs -> Security events. Within that list, you can look for Logon events to show how they are specifically attributed to a user.
- Evidence of Conformance – If audit records are processed or stored on any device for analysis, correlation, or archiving, then the ability to attribute records of actions to specific users should be documented.
- Network Configuration – Ensure your network is free of shared accounts and credentials.

Audit & Accountability

AU.L2-3.3.3

Event Review

Review and update logged events.

Impact

Everything changes over time. Our networks change. Our organization changes. The threat landscape changes. Technology changes. So, what we monitor in our networks needs to be adjusted accordingly. The best way for these changes to occur is to stop and review the current monitoring and how it fits into the current environment. Then, to plan and implement the appropriate changes.

Official Interpretation*

This requirement is focused on the configuration of the auditing system, not the review of the audit records produced by the selected events. The review of the audit logs is covered under AU.L2-3.3.5 and AU.L2-3.3.6.

(CMMC Assessment Guide, Level 2, Copyright 2020, 2021 Carnegie Mellon University and The Johns Hopkins University Applied Physics Laboratory LLC and/or CMMC Assessment Guide, Level 2, Version 2.11 - DRAFT, November 2023)

Assessment Focus

Also known as Assessment Objectives, these are the checklist items that an assessor will seek to verify. Each one must be addressed in your implementation and documentation:

1. a process for determining when to review logged events is defined;
2. event types being logged are reviewed in accordance with the defined review process; and
3. event types being logged are updated based on the review.

(CMMC Assessment Guide, Level 2, Copyright 2020, 2021 Carnegie Mellon University and The Johns Hopkins University Applied Physics Laboratory LLC and/or CMMC Assessment Guide, Level 2, Version 2.11 - DRAFT, November 2023)

Implementation

What you will audit should continue to be tweaked as the organization evolves and threats evolve. Establishing a schedule by which the audit events are reviewed and then making a record of those reviews and the changes suggested by those reviews will serve to show conformance to this requirement.

You will need to define a process for making this review. A checklist like this may be adapted to the needs of your organization to serve as a process and record:

AU.L2-3.3.3 Events Logged Review

Date of Review	
Review Leader	
Review Participants	

Were inadequacies seen since the last review?	□ Yes □No
Do organization changes suggest any changes to event logging?	□ Yes □No
Do changes to the threat landscape suggest any changes to event logging?	□ Yes □No
Do changes to our implemented technology suggest changes to event logging?	□ Yes □No
Are there changes to event logging that can make us more effective?	□ Yes □No

Changes that need to be made

I acknowledge that the changes have been implemented by my signature below:

____

Date _____________________________

If the proposed changes are logged in the POAM system, their progress can be documented there.

There might be some changes proposed in this review, that the organization decides not to implement for any reason. That determination and the reasons for it should be documented. You do not want it to look, to a CMMC assessor, like the proposals were ignored.

Assessment Stats

- Assessment Points: 1
- Assessment POAM Eligible: Yes

Keys

- Procedure Development – Create a schedule and process to perform a periodic review of the events that are being logged.
- Evidence of Conformance – Have a document showing that the reviews were performed and any identified changes were implemented. Any proposed changes that are declined should also be documented.

Audit & Accountability

AU.L2-3.3.4

Audit Failure Alerting

Alert in the event of an audit logging process failure.

Impact

Surrounding the high-speed industrial robot is a light curtain. Because this robot would pose a significant risk to anyone who gets too close, the light curtain stops the robot immediately if anybody crosses the danger line. What happens if the light curtain stops working one day? The robot becomes an accident looking for a victim. It is essential to monitor your monitoring systems. While monitoring your network for any actions that might be useful in identifying or understanding any unwanted activities is critical, it is also important to be alerted if your monitoring system stops working.

Official Interpretation*

Audit logging keeps track of activities occurring on the network, servers, user workstations, and other components of the overall system. These logs must always be available and functional. The company's designated security personnel (e.g., system administrator and security officer) need to be aware when the audit log process fails or becomes unavailable [a]. Notifications (e.g., email, Short Message Service (SMS)) should to be sent to the company's designated security personnel to immediately take appropriate action. If security personnel are unaware of the audit logging process failure, then they will be unaware of any suspicious activity occurring at that time. Response to an audit logging process failure should account for the extent of the failure (e.g., a single component's audit logging versus failure of the centralized logging solution), the risks involved in this loss of audit logging, and other factors (e.g., the possibility that an adversary could have caused the audit logging process failure).

Assessment Focus

Also known as Assessment Objectives, these are the checklist items that an assessor will seek to verify. Each one must be addressed in your implementation and documentation:

1. personnel or roles to be alerted in the event of an audit logging process failure are identified;
2. types of audit logging process failures for which alert will be generated are defined; and

3. identified personnel or roles are alerted in the event of an audit logging process failure.

(CMMC Assessment Guide, Level 2, Copyright 2020, 2021 Carnegie Mellon University and The Johns Hopkins University Applied Physics Laboratory LLC and/or CMMC Assessment Guide, Level 2, Version 2.11 - DRAFT, November 2023)

Implementation

This requirement requires the organization to establish a system that notifies if the audit system itself fails to function. This could be a hardware/software failure, encountering a storage space limit, a communication issue, or a failure in the system that captures the audit data.

For the CMMC assessor, you need to prepare a document that describes how you are defining an auditing process failure, that is, what will trigger an alert. Then, you should also specify who is to be alerted in the event of a failure. Then, of course, the implementation of the alerting system should be tested to perform in accordance with the planning documents.

This logging system failure alerting cannot be done natively within Windows. Details of how this might be accomplished are specific to the logging system implemented in your organization. More information concerning a system that will address several auditing requirements that cannot be addressed within Windows can be found in section AU.L2-3.3.5.

Assessment Stats

- Assessment Points: 1
- Assessment POAM Eligible: Yes

Keys

- Documentation – Document what events will trigger alerts and who will receive the alerts
- Implement & Test – Confirm that your alerting system works as defined in your documentation.
- See section AU.L2-3.3.5 for information about creating a log handling system that will address a range of these requirements.

AU.L2-3.3.5

Audit Correlation

Correlate audit record review, analysis, and reporting processes for investigation and response to indications of unlawful, unauthorized, suspicious, or unusual activity.

Impact

After the September 11, 2001 attacks on the World Trade Center in New York City and elsewhere, many of the investigators looked at the available data and saw many pieces of evidence concerning the attacks. However, the disparate systems could not "connect the dots" to see the attack coming.

Similarly, computing systems across our organizations collect large amounts of data about activity across the network. We must create the capacity to "connect the dots" about those activities.

Official Interpretation*

Companies must review, analyze, and report audit records to help detect and respond to security incidents in a timely manner for the purpose of investigation and corrective actions. Collection of audit logs into one or more central repositories may facilitate correlated review. Small companies may be able to accomplish this manually with well defined and managed procedures. Larger companies will use an automated system for analysis that correlates log data from across the entire enterprise. Some companies may want to orchestrate the analysis process to include the use of Application Programming Interfaces (APIs) for collection, correlation, and the automation of responses based on programmed rulesets.

(CMMC Assessment Guide, Level 2, Copyright 2020, 2021 Carnegie Mellon University and The Johns Hopkins University Applied Physics Laboratory LLC and/or CMMC Assessment Guide, Level 2, Version 2.11 - DRAFT, November 2023)

Assessment Focus

Also known as Assessment Objectives, these are the checklist items that an assessor will seek to verify. Each one must be addressed in your implementation and documentation:

1. audit record review, analysis, and reporting processes for investigation and response to indications of unlawful, unauthorized, suspicious, or unusual activity are defined; and
2. defined audit record review, analysis, and reporting processes are correlated.

(CMMC Assessment Guide, Level 2, Copyright 2020, 2021 Carnegie Mellon University and The Johns Hopkins University Applied Physics Laboratory LLC and/or CMMC Assessment Guide, Level 2, Version 2.11 - DRAFT, November 2023)

Implementation

The logging mechanisms in many different computers generate large amounts of data. Until this data is pulled together and viewed as a whole, it is like identifying the image on a jigsaw puzzle based on a single piece. For example, if you saw a few failed login attempts in a computer's event log, that would not be very suspicious. If you saw those same login attempts on a dozen computers within seconds of each other, that would be highly suspicious. This sort of analysis is not feasible by moving from computer to computer.

When each computer dumps its log data into a central dataset, then the data of the individual systems can be examined as a single system. In addition to bringing the data together, this requirement wants you to monitor the data for "indications of unlawful, unauthorized, suspicious, or unusual activity." This could be a manual process for minimalist requirement-box-checking. However, to gain any benefit from your investment in logging software, you would want this to be an automated process. There is no suggestion that you will monitor for all possible "indications of unlawful, unauthorized, suspicious, or unusual activity," so you can likely meet the letter of the requirement by simply monitoring for just a few risky behaviors. Those things you choose to monitor should be documented.

When these "indications of unlawful, unauthorized, suspicious, or unusual activity" are found, then there needs to be "review, analysis, and reporting" that goes on. These responses can be manual, automatic functions performed by your log analysis software, or a combination of manual and automatic functions. Whether automatic or manual, there should be documentation that these functions were performed. Most logging systems have some built-in functions that could satisfy this need. You might choose to start with what is easy to implement and then build from there.

You will need to document the processes:

1. The review function will consist of gathering all pertinent data. The data should provide information identifying the scope (computers/users involved, the software/modules involved), the timing (sequence and progression), and all other data about the incident.
2. The analysis function seeks to build a picture of what transpired. This is putting flesh onto the skeleton of the data. The analysis will want to determine the fix for this specific incident and also find the root failure that allowed the incident to occur. At the same time, the analysis should determine any other system areas that might have been affected or are vulnerable to the same issue.
3. The reporting phase involves determining who needs to hear about this incident. This may include company management, law enforcement, or some Federal authorities. This reporting would be in accordance with written incident reporting plans.

The log data correlation demanded by this requirement cannot be met by Windows OS software, so it will be necessary to use third-party software to meet this need. Many solutions will satisfy this need, solutions that vary widely in cost and capabilities. This acquired capability should also satisfy the needs of these requirements:

- AU.L2-3.3.3 -- Review and update logged events.

- AU.L2-3.3.4 -- Alert in the event of an audit logging process failure.
- AU.L2-3.3.1 - System Auditing -- Create and retain system audit logs and records to the extent needed to enable the monitoring, analysis, investigation, and reporting of unlawful or unauthorized system activity.
- AU.L2-3.3.5 -- Correlate audit record review, analysis, and reporting processes for investigation and response to indications of unlawful, unauthorized, suspicious, or unusual activity.
- AU.L2-3.3.6 - Reduction & Reporting -- Provide audit record reduction and report generation to support on-demand analysis and reporting
- AU.L2-3.3.8 - Audit Protection -- Protect audit information and audit logging tools from unauthorized access, modification, and deletion.

Many log management systems and security information and event management (SIEM) solutions will meet these requirements. Some are more friendly to small organizations regarding pricing and complexity (most small businesses can't afford an engineer just to run the SIEM). There are a lot of products available, including some with "starter" plans designed for small businesses (hoping you will grow and pay them money as you out-grow their low-end plan). In addition, there are some free systems, like NX Log Community Edition, where you sacrifice some capabilities and the support structure to be able to get started for free.

The price of buying or subscribing to a SIEM system is just part of the cost. Few of these systems are set-it-and-forget-it. Many of these systems need a lot of attention. In a perfect world, a log analysis system would be easily installed and then need no attention except alerting you in the event of an actual attack; this is not the reality.

Some of these log analysis systems are cloud-based (as opposed to on-premise systems). When utilizing a cloud-based system, care should be taken to ensure that the system meets the current security expectations for containing your security data. This may include their own CMMC, Level 2, certification or FedRAMP Moderate equivalency.

Many systems have extensive capabilities that add unnecessary complexity. While it seems exciting to have tons of bell-and-whistles, the goal of compliance with the standard should be kept in mind. If the complexity of a system designed for a much larger company keeps you from being successfully certified, it is a failure. Keep the system as simple as possible to help achieve certification. Although it would be optimal to have a robust, broad-ranging system that monitors for all known cybersecurity threats and suspicious behaviors, it is not necessary to have all of that to demonstrate compliance for certification. Your auditing of system information can start simple and basic. Minimally, you must demonstrate how each requirement has been addressed. With that minimal system set up as a foundation, it is possible to grow from there as you have the resources available or needs arise.

Assessment Stats

- Assessment Points: 5
- Assessment POAM Eligible: No

Keys

- Process Creation – Implement a system that can correlate the logging data from across systems and determine activities that pose a risk. Furthermore, the implemented system should be selected based on the ability to meet multiple requirements across the Audit & Accountability section of the CMMC standard.
- Plan – Develop a plan for your response to incidents to include review, analysis, and reporting. Both the plan and the results should be documented.

- Documentation – Be prepared to demonstrate which unlawful, unauthorized, suspicious, or unusual activities are being actively monitored for.

Audit & Accountability

AU.L2-3.3.6

Reduction & Reporting

Provide audit record reduction and report generation to support on-demand analysis and reporting.

Impact

If you were handed a printout of a day's worth of all the client transactions at JP Morgan Chase Bank and asked to hunt for any suspicious transactions, that would be an impossible task to perform manually. The number of transactions at the largest US bank is staggering, so to pick out anything specific would be nearly impossible. As our network systems generate data from all of the logged activities, we run into a similar situation because there is too much data to assess manually. To do that requires tools that can aid the process.

Official Interpretation*

Raw audit log data is difficult to review, analyze, and report because of the volume of data. Audit record reduction is an automated process that interprets raw audit log data and extracts meaningful and relevant information without altering the original logs. An example of log reduction for files to be analyzed would be the removal of details associated with nightly backups. Report generation on reduced log information allows you to create succinct customized reports without the need to burden the reader with unimportant information. In addition, the security-relevant audit information must be made available to personnel on demand for immediate review, analysis, reporting, and event investigation support. Performing audit log reduction and providing on-demand reports may allow the analyst to take mitigating action before an adversary completes its malicious actions.

(CMMC Assessment Guide, Level 2, Copyright 2020, 2021 Carnegie Mellon University and The Johns Hopkins University Applied Physics Laboratory LLC and/or CMMC Assessment Guide, Level 2, Version 2.11 - DRAFT, November 2023)

Assessment Focus

Also known as Assessment Objectives, these are the checklist items that an assessor will seek to verify. Each one must be addressed in your implementation and documentation:

1. an audit record reduction capability that supports on-demand analysis is provided; and
2. a report generation capability that supports on-demand reporting is provided.

(CMMC Assessment Guide, Level 2, Copyright 2020, 2021 Carnegie Mellon University and The Johns Hopkins University Applied Physics Laboratory LLC and/or CMMC Assessment Guide, Level 2, Version 2.11 - DRAFT, November 2023)

Implementation

This is another area not supported within the native Windows OS system and, therefore, another element that must be considered when planning for an audit log system for CMMC compliance. This requires that the organization has the capability to mine through the accumulated audit data and pull out those tidbits that apply to a specific investigation.

This requirement says that your system must be capable of taking the mass of raw log data, hiding the insignificant, and allowing focus on the portions of interest for analysis. Then, it must have report-generation capabilities based on those focused searches. It is necessary that this processing and reporting does not alter the audit records in any way.

The implementation of this requirement is specific to the logging system your organization is using.

Assessment Stats

- Assessment Points: 1
- Assessment POAM Eligible: Yes

Keys

- See section AU.L2-3.3.5 for information about creating a log handling system that will address a range of these requirements.
- Specifications – A log handling system must be capable of aiding investigations through filtered searches and the creation of reports from those searches.

AU.L2-3.3.7

Authoritative Time Source

Provide a system capability that compares and synchronizes internal system clocks with an authoritative source to generate time stamps for audit records.

Impact

As a hacker moves through your network, they gain control of more resources and seek to increase their privilege. As they "touch" each system, it is essential to be able to trace their footsteps in the correct sequence. Each machine will be recording events that occur, and it becomes necessary for each of those computers to report event times precisely, and that the time on one system exactly aligns with the time on another.

Official Interpretation*

Each system must synchronize its time with a central time server to ensure that all systems are recording audit logs using the same time source. Reviewing audit logs from multiple systems can be a difficult task if time is not synchronized. Systems can be synchronized to a network device or directory service or configured manually.

(CMMC Assessment Guide, Level 2, Copyright 2020, 2021 Carnegie Mellon University and The Johns Hopkins University Applied Physics Laboratory LLC and/or CMMC Assessment Guide, Level 2, Version 2.11 - DRAFT, November 2023)

Assessment Focus

Also known as Assessment Objectives, these are the checklist items that an assessor will seek to verify. Each one must be addressed in your implementation and documentation:

1. internal system clocks are used to generate time stamps for audit records;
2. an authoritative source with which to compare and synchronize internal system clocks is specified; and
3. internal system clocks used to generate time stamps for audit records are compared to and synchronized with the specified authoritative time source.

(CMMC Assessment Guide, Level 2, Copyright 2020, 2021 Carnegie Mellon University and The Johns Hopkins University Applied Physics Laboratory LLC and/or CMMC Assessment Guide, Level 2, Version 2.11 - DRAFT, November 2023)

Implementation

Your Windows domain member machines will automatically synchronize with your domain controller because time synchronization is essential to Windows's Kerberos authentication system. Having a domain controller set to synchronize with an Internet time server will ensure that your network is synchronized, not just internally but also with the rest of the world.

> **HANDY LINK**
>
> For more information about how Windows synchronizes time, go to:
> https://tinyurl.com/CMMC4SMB-949

To set a specific Internet Time Server (NTP) through Group Policy, you can use:

Computer Configuration > Administrative Templates > System > Windows Time Service > Time Providers and enable the policy Configure Windows NTP Client

Assessment Stats

- Assessment Points: 1
- Assessment POAM Eligible: Yes

Keys

- Assure that your domain controller has the default setting of synchronizing the time automatically with an authoritative time source like time.nist.gov or time.windows.com.
- Assure that your domain member computers have the default setting of synchronizing their time with the domain controller.

Audit & Accountability

AU.L2-3.3.8

Audit Protection

Protect audit information and audit logging tools from unauthorized access, modification, and deletion.

Impact

Rarely does a person committing a serious crime not know they risk getting caught. They are motivated to avoid detection and hide evidence of their actions to prevent a conviction. In network security, you may not have people trying to hide a body, but hackers are trying to destroy the evidence of their illicit activities. For hackers, the primary evidence of their activities are the logs of the systems they penetrate. Those logs must be protected against any unauthorized person making any changes or deletions from those logs.

Official Interpretation*

Audit information is a critical record of what events occurred, the source of the events, and the outcomes of the events; this information needs to be protected. The logs must be properly secured so that the information may not be modified or deleted, either intentionally or unintentionally. Only those with a legitimate need-to-know should have access to audit information, whether that information is being accessed directly from logs or from audit tools.

(CMMC Assessment Guide, Level 2, Copyright 2020, 2021 Carnegie Mellon University and The Johns Hopkins University Applied Physics Laboratory LLC and/or CMMC Assessment Guide, Level 2, Version 2.11 - DRAFT, November 2023)

Assessment Focus

Also known as Assessment Objectives, these are the checklist items that an assessor will seek to verify. Each one must be addressed in your implementation and documentation:

1. audit information is protected from unauthorized access;
2. audit information is protected from unauthorized modification;
3. audit information is protected from unauthorized deletion;

4. audit logging tools are protected from unauthorized access;
5. audit logging tools are protected from unauthorized modification; and
6. audit logging tools are protected from unauthorized deletion.

(CMMC Assessment Guide, Level 2, Copyright 2020, 2021 Carnegie Mellon University and The Johns Hopkins University Applied Physics Laboratory LLC and/or CMMC Assessment Guide, Level 2, Version 2.11 - DRAFT, November 2023)

Implementation

Windows makes an effort to protect log data in the individual computer. However, by the time a hacker has compromised a computer, they are potentially in a position to alter the log files on that computer to hide their activities. So, the only real hope of finding accurate records of an attack is on the central logging server. Each computer will have copied all event logs to the central logging server as the events occur. So, if the data on this server is adequately protected, it should provide an unadulterated view of the events on each individual computer.

This requirement is focused on providing adequate protection for the logging data and tools on both systems, on the local machine and the central logging server.

On the local machine, the best protection for the log files is implemented when the user has restricted privileges. A user with local administrator privileges typically has the authority to access, modify, and delete log records on their computer. To conform with this requirement, those privileges must be restricted.

The records on the central logging server are the most defensible. All access to the resources of the central logging server should be restricted as much as possible while still allowing the system to be functional. A security group should be created on the domain, and all files and executables should be limited to the members of this group. Nobody outside this group should be able to access, modify, or delete log data. In addition, the ability to use, modify, or delete any of the "audit logging tools" should also be restricted to this group of users.

This does not have to be an all-or-none situation; you may have another security group that is permitted to use specific tools, to perform analysis, for example, but may not have access to modify the raw data.

It should be noted that Event Viewer on each computer is an Audit Logging Tool and should be restricted accordingly. Even the Event Viewer should be "protected from unauthorized access." For many organizations, this might look like disabling it for all users outside of IT. Few users outside of IT even know what the Event Viewer is and will never miss it.

Access to the Event Viewer can be restricted using Group Policy. The controls can be found at:

Computer Configuration => Policies => Administrative Templates => Windows Components => Event Log Service => Configure Log Access

Setting this Group Policy control requires using SDDL syntax. SDDL is a relatively complex method of communicating security permissions.

HANDY LINK

Article explaining SDDL syntax https://tinyurl.com/CMMC4SMB-399

There are a few other methods of restricting access to the log files. Most of these focus on restricting access to the Event Viewer. One of the most simple methods of blocking access to the event viewer through Group Policy can be managed through:

User Configuration -> Policies -> Administrative Templates -> System -> Don't run specified Windows applications

That block can be set on eventvwr.exe and eventvwr.msc to block running of the Event Viewer.

If your logging data is being collected in the cloud, then you will have to evaluate the security of that product and take the necessary steps (like multi-factor authentication) to ensure that the data is protected.

To satisfy an assessor, you will want the following documentation to describe your protections:

	Unauthorized Access	**Unauthorized Modification**	**Unauthorized Deletions**
Audit Information	[Your System Protections]	[Your System Protections]	[Your System Protections]
Audit Logging Tools	[Your System Protections]	[Your System Protections]	[Your System Protections]

Although many of these items will potentially be the same control, all six control categories must be addressed.

Assessment Stats

- Assessment Points: 1
- Assessment POAM Eligible: Yes

Keys

- Documentation – Describe how your audit information and audit tools are protected from unauthorized access, modification, or deletion.
- System Implementation – As a log management system is configured, ensure that careful consideration is given to who is permitted to access, modify, or delete data and who has access to the audit logging tools (both on the client systems and also the Log Management server).
- System Modification – Assure that any third-party application for audit data collection has restrictions for access, including any help application that may exist on the client machine.

Audit & Accountability

AU.L2-3.3.9

Audit Management

Limit management of audit logging functionality to a subset of privileged users.

Impact

"How could anybody be so stupid?" thought the burglar as she discovered the home's alarm system controls mounted on the outside of the house in an unlocked box. From that box, it was easy to turn off the alarms and go right into the house. In our networks, all the audit settings and tools are equivalent to the alarm system control box. These need to be secured so only authorized personnel can manage them.

Official Interpretation*

Companies should restrict access to audit logging functions to a limited number of privileged users who can modify audit logs and audit settings. General users should not be granted permissions to perform audit management. All audit managers should be privileged users, but only a small subset of privileged users will be given audit management responsibilities. Functions performed by privileged users must be distinctly separate from the functions performed by users who have audit-related responsibilities to reduce the potential of fraudulent activities by privileged users not being detected or reported. When possible, individuals who manage audit logs should not have access to other privileged functions.

(CMMC Assessment Guide, Level 2, Copyright 2020, 2021 Carnegie Mellon University and The Johns Hopkins University Applied Physics Laboratory LLC and/or CMMC Assessment Guide, Level 2, Version 2.11 - DRAFT, November 2023)

Assessment Focus

Also known as Assessment Objectives, these are the checklist items that an assessor will seek to verify. Each one must be addressed in your implementation and documentation:

1. a subset of privileged users granted access to manage audit logging functionality is defined; and
2. management of audit logging functionality is limited to the defined subset of privileged users.

(CMMC Assessment Guide, Level 2, Copyright 2020, 2021 Carnegie Mellon University and The Johns Hopkins University Applied Physics Laboratory LLC and/or CMMC Assessment Guide, Level 2, Version 2.11 - DRAFT, November 2023)

Implementation

Anybody who performs an action that is illegal or might threaten their job would like to have the evidence linking them to the action to be eliminated. This results in the log files being of great interest to anyone who wants to hide their network activities. This CMMC requirement mandates that the ability to manage audit logging functionality be carefully restricted.

Windows has some default restrictions because only users with the Manage Auditing and Security user-right will have access. Consciously giving that right only where it is needed will meet this requirement.

However, if you have any third-party log management tools, they might be enabled to modify the configuration of logging activities. If that is the case, then the restrictions applied to those tools should mimic the permissions granted through Windows.

This requirement is focused on the idea that the people allowed to access auditing controls should be a subset of the privileged users. Under CMMC assessment, there might be trouble if no privileged users are blocked for the administration of audit logging. In a larger organization, it makes perfect sense that not all privileged users would have access to logging settings; however, in a smaller organization, this might prove challenging.

In a small organization with a one or 2-person IT department, it is entirely possible that everybody needs to have access to everything. However, this requirement clearly says the ability to control the logging process should only be given to "a subset of privileged users." So, an organization with only one privileged user CANNOT be compliant with this requirement! Clearly, nobody was thinking of this small of an organization when this requirement was written.

...a subset of privileged users		
Number of privileged users with audit logging capability	<	Number of privileged users

Under this circumstance, it might be advisable to find someone who can be trusted with an alternate privileged logon (but without log administration). Even if this person is non-technical, they aren't expected to really USE that logon, but just to hang onto it. In a CMMC assessment, they can be listed as a privileged user that does not have access to logging administration, thus satisfying the requirement. (You never know when this other privileged user might prove valuable in an unforeseen emergency.)

To satisfy an assessor, you should compile a list of your privileged users and identify which users (not all) are permitted to manage audit logging functionality.

Where Group Policy controls auditing, this provides a greater level of restriction because of the controllable restrictions allowed within the Group Policy environment.

Assessment Stats

- Assessment Points: 1
- Assessment POAM Eligible: Yes

Keys

- User Management – Have at least one privileged user who does not have access to audit logging functionality.
- Documentation – Compile a list of all privileged users and identify which of those have access to the logging functionality
- System Configuration – Assure that only authorized users are allowed to access the controls for auditing.

Configuration Management

CM.L2-3.4.1

System Baselining

Establish and maintain baseline configurations and inventories of organizational systems (including hardware, software, firmware, and documentation) throughout the respective system development life cycles.

Impact

Dexter is in charge of the network security at ABC Company. A few months ago, a new computer appeared on the network. This new device would have confused him since he had no idea where it came from, but he had no visibility of changes to his network inventory. The software installed on the unauthorized system would have raised more than a few eyebrows. However, Dexter did not have any way to identify the difference between what was supposed to be on his network and what was actually on his network. So, the activities on this rogue system remain undetected. If only Dexter had a running inventory that he could monitor for changes…

Official Interpretation*

An effective cybersecurity program depends on consistent, secure system and component configuration and management. Build and configure systems from a known, secure, and approved configuration baseline. This includes:

- documenting the software and configuration settings of a system;
- placement within the network; and
- other specifications as required by the organization.

(CMMC Assessment Guide, Level 2, Copyright 2020, 2021 Carnegie Mellon University and The Johns Hopkins University Applied Physics Laboratory LLC and/or CMMC Assessment Guide, Level 2, Version 2.11 - DRAFT, November 2023)

Assessment Focus

Also known as Assessment Objectives, these are the checklist items that an assessor will seek to verify. Each one must be addressed in your implementation and documentation:

1. a baseline configuration is established;
2. the baseline configuration includes hardware, software, firmware, and documentation;
3. the baseline configuration is maintained (reviewed and updated) throughout the system development life cycle;
4. a system inventory is established;
5. the system inventory includes hardware, software, firmware, and documentation; and
6. the inventory is maintained (reviewed and updated) throughout the system development life cycle.

(CMMC Assessment Guide, Level 2, Copyright 2020, 2021 Carnegie Mellon University and The Johns Hopkins University Applied Physics Laboratory LLC and/or CMMC Assessment Guide, Level 2, Version 2.11 - DRAFT, November 2023)

Implementation

Compliance with this requirement would be much easier if it merely needed an inventory of what devices were connected to the network. This requirement goes beyond just looking at the hardware; it must also look at the software and firmware installed on those devices. This level of detail goes way beyond the typical passive IP scanner.

Because this information is not available to a simple scanner external to the target computer, special accommodations are required to make that information available. Typically, this will require either administrator credentials or an agent installed on each device that can report on what is within the device.

Before investing in new software, you should look closely at the existing software. This network inventorying capability may be found within software whose primary focus might seem unrelated. A Mobile Device Management (MDM) system, vulnerability scanner, or even an antivirus system might have the capability to perform assessments of what is inside your computers. Some software may require local administrator credentials for the computers they are scanning. Installing a local admin account on all your computers (adding accounts can be scripted in PowerShell) may be what it takes to elevate some inventory software to the point that it complies with this requirement.

Currently, Lansweeper is free to scan and inventory networks with less than 100 devices. Remember that every printer, managed switch, VOIP phone, or anything else with an IP address counts. However, devices on VLANs in different address ranges do not count toward that 100.

You must establish a baseline configuration of "hardware, software, firmware, and documentation." While this doesn't mean that every computer has to be exactly the same as every other, it prohibits every system from being randomly set up. If every employee has their computer set up as their wims lead them, it becomes impossible to tell the difference between what is supposed to be there and what isn't. Similarly, if each different computer brand comes with a bunch of bloatware, this will not be standardized. You can use an imaging tool like SmartDeploy to standardize each system. You may have several different configurations (Engineering needs different tools than accounting does) that would be variations on a standard set of software. You will need a list of what should be in the standard configuration(s). If you have any exceptions to the standard configuration, but one person needs special software, that should be documented. The goal is to know what is expected.

The expectation is that you will have a baseline showing what you say should be on each system and an inventory. The inventory would show what is actually found on the systems. The inventory needs to be performed periodically and the results need to be reviewed. There should be evidence of the inventory being run and the review being done.

There is an implication that the review of inventory data will involve a comparison to the baseline. Although the requirement does not explicitly say this must be done, assessors may expect it.

Assessment Stats

- Assessment Points: 5
- Assessment POAM Eligible: No

Keys

- Network Standardization – Establish standard configurations for your network.
- System Change – Establish a system for taking inventory of hardware and software on your system.
- Procedure Change – Establish a procedure that defines the frequency with which the system inventory will be taken and how it will be reviewed and monitored.

Configuration Management

CM.L2-3.4.2

Security Configuration Enforcement

Establish and enforce security configuration settings for information technology products employed in organizational systems.

Impact

As Angela got settled into her new job at your company, she found she was being inconvenienced by the need to re-enter her password every time she stopped using her computer for a few minutes. Because she is independent and clever, she Googled the issue and figured out how to "fix" her computer so it no longer had that annoying problem. As quickly as you can say "Google," settings critical to maintaining a secure environment can be ditched unless there are protections in place that prevent tampering with those settings.

Official Interpretation*

Information security is an integral part of a company's configuration management process. Security-related configuration settings are customized to satisfy the company's security requirements and are applied them *[sic]* to all systems once tested and approved. The configuration settings must reflect the most restrictive settings that are appropriate for the system. Any required deviations from the baseline are reviewed, documented, and approved.

(CMMC Assessment Guide, Level 2, Copyright 2020, 2021 Carnegie Mellon University and The Johns Hopkins University Applied Physics Laboratory LLC and/or CMMC Assessment Guide, Level 2, Version 2.11 - DRAFT, November 2023)

Assessment Focus

Also known as Assessment Objectives, these are the checklist items that an assessor will seek to verify. Each one must be addressed in your implementation and documentation:

1. security configuration settings for information technology products employed in the system are established and included in the baseline configuration; and
2. security configuration settings for information technology products employed in the system are enforced.

(CMMC Assessment Guide, Level 2, Copyright 2020, 2021 Carnegie Mellon University and The Johns Hopkins University Applied Physics Laboratory LLC and/or CMMC Assessment Guide, Level 2, Version 2.11 - DRAFT, November 2023)

Implementation

Active Directory is your friend here. You can simultaneously push the security configuration out to computers and users while enforcing those settings. If a user attempts to modify any security settings that Group Policy controls, their attempts are denied.

The security configurations are not limited to Windows settings. By downloading Administrative Templates and applying those to Group Policy, it is possible to set security configurations for many non-windows products like Chrome, VMware, Adobe Acrobat, or Firefox. This allows you to take the power of Group Policy and expand it significantly.

Security configurations should be deployed using Active Directory Group Policies. This assures uniformity and prevents the setting from being tampered with by users or unauthorized parties.

Configuration auditing and enforcement can be greatly enhanced by using Microsoft Intune, but for many organizations this would be an additional expense.

The security configurations you send to your computers should be added to the baseline configuration you created as part of CM.L2-3.4.1.

Assessment Stats

- Assessment Points: 5
- Assessment POAM Eligible: No

Keys

- System Change – Makes security configurations in group policy.
- Documentation –Documentation of the Security Configuration that Group Policy is deploying should be added to the baseline configuration document.

Configuration Management

CM.L2-3.4.3

System Change Management

Track, review, approve, or disapprove, and log changes to organizational systems.

Impact

Zach and Zeke comprise the entire IT staff at a small company. They are both knowledgeable and skilled and often work independently. One Monday, Zach was working with the DHCP server and decided to enable MAC address filtering. However, that was one of the last things that Zach did before he went home with a stomach bug that kept him out for several days. The next day, Zeke is setting up a couple of new user workstations. Not knowing about the MAC address filtering, he is pulling his hair out, trying to get the new computers to attach to the network. This requirement assures everybody is on the same page concerning system changes.

Official Interpretation*

You must track, review, and approve configuration changes before committing to production. Changes to computing environments can create unintended and unforeseen issues that can affect the security and availability of the systems, including those that process CUI. Relevant experts and stakeholders must review and approve proposed changes. They should discuss potential impacts before the organization puts the changes in place. Relevant items include changes to the physical environment and to the systems hosted within it.

(CMMC Assessment Guide, Level 2, Copyright 2020, 2021 Carnegie Mellon University and The Johns Hopkins University Applied Physics Laboratory LLC and/or CMMC Assessment Guide, Level 2, Version 2.11 - DRAFT, November 2023)

Assessment Focus

Also known as Assessment Objectives, these are the checklist items that an assessor will seek to verify. Each one must be addressed in your implementation and documentation:

1. changes to the system are tracked;
2. changes to the system are reviewed;

3. changes to the system are approved or disapproved; and
4. changes to the system are logged.

(CMMC Assessment Guide, Level 2, Copyright 2020, 2021 Carnegie Mellon University and The Johns Hopkins University Applied Physics Laboratory LLC and/or CMMC Assessment Guide, Level 2, Version 2.11 - DRAFT, November 2023)

Implementation

In an SMB with a tiny IT department, this won't look anything like it would in a big company. The CMMC Assessment Guide says, "Relevant experts and stakeholders must review and approve proposed changes." In a small organization, the "Relevant experts and stakeholders" may only be the person who thought of the change and would be implementing it. However, assessors seem to agree that nobody can approve their own changes. So, it will require that somebody else be found to approve or disapprove the system changes, even if their technical skills are lacking.

Tracking of changes may look like a paper log or spreadsheet. Entries in the log can be accompanied by initials, indicating that the work was reviewed and approved. Any record that shows that the changes were evaluated and approved would be acceptable.

In a larger organization, technical people would evaluate changes before they are implemented. In a small organization, this is not always possible. Often, the person who proposes the change is the only person with the technical knowledge to evaluate the impact of the change.

There is a risk that your CMMC assessor will only have experience in larger organizations, and they might find it difficult to accept a non-technical person making approvals. The only other alternative to a nontechnical approver may be to utilize somebody outside the organization, but that may carry some challenges, too. A small organization often must be creative to make the CMMC requirements work in their environment.

This documentation is close to the continuous improvement purpose of the POAM system. If your POAM system has approvals fields, it can fulfill the documentation requirement.

Assessment Stats

- Assessment Points: 1
- Assessment POAM Eligible: Yes

Keys

🔧 Policy Change – System changes should be tracked, reviewed, and approved (or disapproved) before implementation. The tracking, reviewing, and approvals should be clearly documented. This documentation may be a log, an email chain, or even a paper system.

Configuration Management

CM.L2-3.4.4

Security Impact Analysis

Analyze the security impact of changes prior to implementation.

Impact

The sales staff has requested that Microsoft Remote Desktop Protocol (RDP) be made visible via the Internet so they can access their desktop while on the road. While this might be useful for making their job easier, it would potentially be a disaster from a security standpoint. This is precisely the sort of systems change that requires some analysis to evaluate the security impact.

Official Interpretation*

Changes to complex environments are reviewed for potential security impact before implemented. Changes to IT systems can cause unforeseen problems and have unintended consequences for both users and the security of the operating environment. Analyze the security impact of changes prior to implementing them. This can uncover and mitigate potential problems before they occur.

(CMMC Assessment Guide, Level 2, Copyright 2020, 2021 Carnegie Mellon University and The Johns Hopkins University Applied Physics Laboratory LLC and/or CMMC Assessment Guide, Level 2, Version 2.11 - DRAFT, November 2023)

Assessment Focus

Also known as Assessment Objectives, these are the checklist items that an assessor will seek to verify. Each one must be addressed in your implementation and documentation:

1. the security impact of changes to the system is analyzed prior to implementation.

(CMMC Assessment Guide, Level 2, Copyright 2020, 2021 Carnegie Mellon University and The Johns Hopkins University Applied Physics Laboratory LLC and/or CMMC Assessment Guide, Level 2, Version 2.11 - DRAFT, November 2023)

Implementation

This requirement says we must evaluate the security implications before changing the system. While this seems pretty basic, it can be challenging when systems are down or the boss is on your back about finishing something yesterday.

CMMC doesn't mandate that you run through complex analysis but instead leaves it up to the practitioner to exercise an appropriate level of evaluation, considering the risks and the nature of the change. They do mandate that some analysis is performed and that it happens before making the change.

To provide an assessor with evidence that the analysis has been performed, there should be some documentation of the performance and nature of the evaluation. Avoid a "security analysis performed" checkbox sort of documentation. Assessors will be looking for more details about the risks that were evaluated. This process can be approached as a risk/benefit analysis. Jot down the risks associated with the change and the benefits expected to be achieved, then make a judgment, that would be suitable documentation.

If CM.L2-3.4.3 is documented within the POAM system, then it would not be much of a stretch to consider this also happening within that same system.

Assessment Stats

- Assessment Points: 1
- Assessment POAM Eligible: Yes

Keys

- Procedure – Create a procedure of how this will be performed and documented.
- Documentation – Document how each system change is examined for security implications before implementation.

Configuration Management

CM.L2-3.4.5

Access Restrictions for Change

Define, document, approve, and enforce physical and logical access restrictions associated with changes to organizational systems.

Impact

Lucy was new to the company. Her only previous IT work had been with a casino. As she began this job, her manager realized that the challenge would be to convince Lucy that not every organization needs to be as tightly locked down as the casino had been. Soon after she started working independently, she spotted what she thought must be an oversight in group policy and fixed it.

It didn't take long for the complaints to start rolling in as employees found they could not access the information needed to do their jobs. This was caused by Lucy taking it upon herself to fix what she thought was a problem. This happened because the organization lacked adequate restrictions about who could make these changes and under what circumstances.

If these changes can be made accidentally, then there is a clear opportunity for changes with malicious intent.

Official Interpretation*

Define, identify, and document qualified individuals authorized to make physical and logical changes to the organization's hardware, software, software libraries, or firmware components. Control of configuration management activities may involve:

- physical access control that prohibits unauthorized users from gaining physical access to an asset (e.g., requiring a special key card to enter a server room);
- logical access control that prevents unauthorized users from logging onto a system to make configuration changes (e.g., requiring specific credentials for modifying configuration settings, patching software, or updating software libraries);
- workflow automation in which configuration management workflow rules define human tasks and data or files are routed between people authorized to do configuration management based on pre-defined

business rules (e.g., passing an electronic form to a manager requesting approval of configuration change made by an authorized employee);

- an abstraction layer for configuration management that requires changes be made from an external system through constrained interface (e.g., software updates can only be made from a patch management system with a specific IP address); and
- utilization of a configuration management change window (e.g., software updates are only allowed between 8:00 AM and 10:00 AM or between 6:00 PM and 8:00 PM).

(CMMC Assessment Guide, Level 2, Copyright 2020, 2021 Carnegie Mellon University and The Johns Hopkins University Applied Physics Laboratory LLC and/or CMMC Assessment Guide, Level 2, Version 2.11 - DRAFT, November 2023)

Assessment Focus

Also known as Assessment Objectives, these are the checklist items that an assessor will seek to verify. Each one must be addressed in your implementation and documentation:

1. physical access restrictions associated with changes to the system are defined;
2. physical access restrictions associated with changes to the system are documented;
3. physical access restrictions associated with changes to the system are approved;
4. physical access restrictions associated with changes to the system are enforced;
5. logical access restrictions associated with changes to the system are defined;
6. logical access restrictions associated with changes to the system are documented;
7. logical access restrictions associated with changes to the system are approved; and
8. logical access restrictions associated with changes to the system are enforced.

(CMMC Assessment Guide, Level 2, Copyright 2020, 2021 Carnegie Mellon University and The Johns Hopkins University Applied Physics Laboratory LLC and/or CMMC Assessment Guide, Level 2, Version 2.11 - DRAFT, November 2023)

Implementation

This requirement is focused on the restrictions controlling system changes. It has two big families of restrictions, physical and logical. In both cases, the restrictions limiting system changes are to be defined, documented, approved, and enforced.

This requirement is specifically focused on the controls that limit making changes to system access. So, for example, instead of looking at the controls in Active Directory that limit access to directories containing CUI, this requirement looks at how making changes to those Active Directory controls is restricted.

This focuses on the restrictions to things that allow system changes to be made. System access changes can be made in Active Directory, servers, switches, DNS, DHCP, anti-virus, firewalls, etc. So, this requirement looks at how those are protected.

You will want to create a list of those authorized to make or approve changes to access. You might consider creating a procedure for how these changes will be made.

Example of records of the protections for system change (one logical and one physical):

Definition	Documentation	Approval	Enforcement
The logical controls on Active Directory on DOM01	To access the AD, a user must be a member of the Domain Administrator security group.	These logical controls were approved by the IT manager on 4/1/2024.	Attempts to access AD from users not in the Domain Administrator group are denied and logged.
SERV01 which contains the DOM01 Active Directory is kept in a locked room.	The server room door lock is a STRATTEC RTS-PZ digital lock.	The door lock was approved by the IT manager on 4/1/2024.	The lock logs the entries and failed attempts.

Assessment Stats

- Assessment Points: 5
- Assessment POAM Eligible: No

Keys

- Define – Create a list of those users authorized to approve changes to the protections around the tools of system change.
- Documentation – For each point of system change, you must develop documentation showing how access to the tools of system change are protected. The documentation should show how each protection is defined, documented, approved, and enforced.

Configuration Management

CM.L2-3.4.6

Least Functionality

Employ the principle of least functionality by configuring organizational systems to provide only essential capabilities.

Impact

All Malcomb wanted to do was make his honeymoon photos available to his co-workers. He didn't want them on the server where management might discover them, so he went online and followed instructions about how to do this. What he succeeded in doing was to turn on IIS on his workstation computer. There was absolutely no reason why he needed a webserver for his job. His actions increased the security risk for his computer.

Official Interpretation*

You should customize organizational systems to remove non-essential applications and disable unnecessary services. Systems come with many unnecessary applications and settings enabled by default including unused ports and protocols. Leave only the fewest capabilities necessary for the systems to operate effectively.

(CMMC Assessment Guide, Level 2, Copyright 2020, 2021 Carnegie Mellon University and The Johns Hopkins University Applied Physics Laboratory LLC and/or CMMC Assessment Guide, Level 2, Version 2.11 - DRAFT, November 2023)

Assessment Focus

Also known as Assessment Objectives, these are the checklist items that an assessor will seek to verify. Each one must be addressed in your implementation and documentation:

1. essential system capabilities are defined based on the principle of least functionality; and
2. the system is configured to provide only the defined essential capabilities.

(CMMC Assessment Guide, Level 2, Copyright 2020, 2021 Carnegie Mellon University and The Johns Hopkins University Applied Physics Laboratory LLC and/or CMMC Assessment Guide, Level 2, Version 2.11 - DRAFT, November 2023)

Implementation

This requirement is almost identical to CM.L2-3.4.7, Nonessential Functionality. The critical difference between the two requirements is that this one focuses on the "least functionality" concept in capabilities. Looking at each user (or group of similar users), computer, server, or device, it is important to determine the lowest level of functionality for them to perform their intended job.

While CM.L2-3.4.7 looks at unnecessary functionality generally, this requirement looks at the capabilities necessary to perform the needed tasks. So, while CM.L2-3.4.7 requires determining what is generally unnecessary, this requirement needs an examination of the minimum functionality necessary for the actions the system needs to perform as intended.

It will be necessary to assemble a list of "essential system capabilities." An assessor will not usually be able to complain about the items you include on this list as long as it does not include items that are obviously non-business, like games. Individual departments may need specialized capabilities, like the marketing department's need for video editing or the engineering group's need for design tools, so the list does not have to be one-size-fits-all. Assure that the list allows a clear view of the essential capabilities for any given system.

Then, deleting or restricting access to the capabilities not on your list of essential capabilities is necessary. Group policy can be the tool that pushes these restrictions out to individual systems. Alternately, non-essential capabilities can be disabled or uninstalled.

In a CMMC assessment, the assessor will not know what functions are essential for the organization. So, it will be critical that you provide them with evidence that you have made a good-faith effort to determine your organization's "essential system capabilities."

You will note that the language in the requirement and the method of implementation are backward from one another. The standard says you should identify and limit functionality to the essential capabilities, but in Windows group policy implementation, you have to disable non-essential functions. This difference in approach could create some risk. If an assessor was determined to find a nonconformance, all they would have to do is to find any capability on your systems that is not on your essential functions list. So, approach this with care.

Assessment Stats

- Assessment Points: 5
- Assessment POAM Eligible: No

Keys

- Documentation – Create a list of essential capabilities. This list may be broken down by role or department.
- Group Policy Change – Turn off, disable, or uninstall the capabilities that are not the essential capabilities for each system.

Configuration Management

CM.L2-3.4.7

Nonessential Functionality

Restrict, disable, or prevent the use of nonessential programs, functions, ports, protocols, and services.

Impact

When Beth started her job as an AR/AP entry clerk, she inherited a computer that had previously been used elsewhere in the company. On one slow day, she started looking around on the computer and found it had several things that went beyond the ERP and Office she had been using every day. She found something called TeamViewer. She quickly realized that it was a ticket into any computer in the building. She asked a coworker about this software on her computer and that gal's response confirmed for Beth that a serious error had occurred. She reported this to IT, who was most grateful and promptly cleaned up her system.

Official Interpretation*

Organizations should only use the minimum set of programs, services, ports, and protocols required for to accomplish the organization's mission. This has several implications:

- All unnecessary programs and accounts are removed from all endpoints and servers.
- The organization makes a policy decision to control the execution of programs through either whitelisting or blacklisting. Whitelisting means a program can only run if the software has been vetted in some way, and the executable name has been entered onto a list of allowed software. Blacklisting means any software can execute as long it is not on a list of known malicious software. Whitelisting provides far more security than blacklisting, but the organization's policy can direct the implementation of either approach. Control of execution applies to both servers and endpoints.
- The organization restricts the use of all unnecessary ports, protocols, and system services in order to limit entry points that attackers can use. For example, the use of the FTP service is eliminated from all computers, and the associated ports are blocked unless a required service utilizes those ports. The elimination of nonessential functionality on the network and systems provides a smaller attack surface for an attacker to gain access and take control of your network or systems.

This requirement, CM.L2-3.4.7, which requires limiting functionality to essential programs, ports, protocols, and services, extends CM.L2-3.4.6, which requires adherence to the principle of least functionality but does not specifically address which elements of a system should be limited.

(CMMC Assessment Guide, Level 2, Copyright 2020, 2021 Carnegie Mellon University and The Johns Hopkins University Applied Physics Laboratory LLC and/or CMMC Assessment Guide, Level 2, Version 2.11 - DRAFT, November 2023)

Assessment Focus

Also known as Assessment Objectives, these are the checklist items that an assessor will seek to verify. Each one must be addressed in your implementation and documentation:

1. essential programs are defined;
2. the use of nonessential programs is defined;
3. the use of nonessential programs is restricted, disabled, or prevented as defined;
4. essential functions are defined;
5. the use of nonessential functions is defined;
6. the use of nonessential functions is restricted, disabled, or prevented as defined;
7. essential ports are defined;
8. the use of nonessential ports is defined;
9. the use of nonessential ports is restricted, disabled, or prevented as defined;
10. essential protocols are defined;
11. the use of nonessential protocols is defined;
12. the use of nonessential protocols is restricted, disabled, or prevented as defined;
13. essential services are defined;
14. the use of nonessential services is defined; and
15. the use of nonessential services is restricted, disabled, or prevented as defined.

(CMMC Assessment Guide, Level 2, Copyright 2020, 2021 Carnegie Mellon University and The Johns Hopkins University Applied Physics Laboratory LLC and/or CMMC Assessment Guide, Level 2, Version 2.11 - DRAFT, November 2023)

Implementation

This requirement is similar to CM.L2-3.4.6. This requirement limits what functionality is essential to the organization as a whole, while CM.L2-3.4.6 is pointed at specific roles.

Removing unneeded functionality in any computer system is always a good security practice. This requires that information systems have those extra functions disabled or removed. This simultaneously reduces your attack profile while making your computers more productive.

To be compliant with this requirement, it will be necessary to compile lists of:

- Essential programs,
- Essential functions,
- Essential ports,

- Essential protocols, and
- Essential services

From there, it will be necessary to define the nonessential items in each category. Then, you must outline how those nonessential items are restricted, disabled, or prevented.

Group Policy can be used to apply many restrictions. Windows applications can be disabled, and settings can be applied to the Windows firewall. The firewall can prevent computers that should normally never be communicating directly, from connecting. Through Group Policy, ports that have no reason ever to be used can be nailed shut.

If you are standardizing a common build to all computers, it is much easier to ensure that specific Windows programs are uninstalled from the golden image applied to all other computers. There are Windows elements that cannot be effectively disabled through Group Policy but can be removed when working with hands-on the keyboard.

From a practical (seeking CMMC) standpoint, it may be advantageous to work this backward. Determine what you are capable of disabling or removing, then work through your lists so those items get pointed out as the nonessential functions that need to be addressed. While this isn't how this process is intended, your assessor doesn't need to know how you produced the results.

PLEASE NOTE: The following items are just suggestions of how this requirement might be addressed. Every organization is different. While many organizations might be able to make these restrictions without problems, you should test carefully to ensure that the suggested changes are appropriate for your organization.

PROGRAMS

Antivirus provides blacklisting of unsafe programs.

FUNCTIONS

System Configuration, Event Viewer, Registry Editor, Firewall, Task Scheduler, Computer Management, and Device Manager can usually be disabled for standard users.

PORTS

There are only a few ports open in a basic Windows installation. As software is added and configuration changes are made, additional ports may be opened. Group policy can be used to forcibly close down some ports in each computer's Windows firewall. Non-essential ports can be disabled by Windows Defender Firewall with Advanced Security.

These are the ports that are most frequently scanned by hackers:

21: ftp	80: http	143: imap	1723: pptp
22: ssh	110: pop3	443: https	3306: mysql
23: telnet	111: rpcbind	445: microsoft-ds	3389: ms-wbt-server
25: smtp	135: msrpc	993: imaps	5900: vnc
53: DNS	139: netbios-ssn	995: pop3s	8080: http-proxy

Several of these ports are in active use by your systems, so blocking them would cause problems. The challenge is to determine the ports that are not essential to your organization's operations.

You can create firewall rules for ports at: Computer Configuration -> Policies -> Windows Settings -> Security Settings -> Windows Firewall with Advanced Security.

PROTOCOLS

FTP and Peer-to-peer networking can typically be disabled

SERVICES

The following is a list of Windows 10 services that are typically not required within business environments. This list is extracted from CIS Microsoft Windows 10 Enterprise (Release 2004) Benchmark (an excellent resource).

<table>
<tr><td>Disable 'Downloaded Maps Manager (MapsBroker)'</td><td>Mapping technologies can unwillingly reveal your location to attackers and other software that picks up the information. In addition, automatic downloads of data from 3rd-party sources should be minimized when not needed. Therefore, this service should not be needed in high-security environments.</td></tr>
<tr><td colspan="2">In Group Policy, ensure that the following is set to Disabled.

Computer Configuration -> Policies -> Windows Settings -> Security Settings -> System Services -> Downloaded Maps Manager</td></tr>
</table>

<table>
<tr><td>Disable 'Infrared monitor service (irmon)'</td><td>Infrared connections can potentially be a source of data compromise - especially via the automatic "file transfer application" functionality. Enterprise-managed systems should utilize a more secure method of connection than infrared.</td></tr>
<tr><td colspan="2">In Group Policy, ensure that the following is set to Disabled or ensure the service is not installed.

Computer Configuration -> Policies -> Windows Settings -> Security Settings -> System Services -> Infrared monitor service</td></tr>
</table>

<table>
<tr><td>Disable 'Internet Connection Sharing (ICS) (SharedAccess)</td><td>Internet Connection Sharing (ICS) is a feature that allows someone to "share" their Internet connection with other machines on the network - it was designed for home or small office environments where only one machine has Internet access - it effectively turns that machine into an Internet router. This feature causes the bridging of networks and likely bypassing other, more secure pathways. It should not be used on any enterprise-managed system.</td></tr>
<tr><td colspan="2">In Group Policy, ensure that the following is set to Disabled.

Computer Configuration -> Policies -> Windows Settings -> Security Settings -> System Services -> Internet Connection Sharing (ICS)</td></tr>
</table>

<table>
<tr><td>Disable 'Remote Procedure Call (RPC) Locator (RpcLocator)'</td><td>This is a legacy service that has no value or purpose other than application compatibility for very old software. It should be disabled unless there is a specific old application still in use on the system that requires it.</td></tr>
<tr><td colspan="2">In Group Policy, ensure that the following is set to Disabled.</td></tr>
</table>

Computer Configuration -> Policies -> Windows Settings -> Security Settings -> System Services -> Remote Procedure Call (RPC) Locator

Disable 'SSDP Discovery (SSDPSRV)'	Universal Plug n Play (UPnP) is a real security risk - it allows automatic discovery and attachment to network devices. Note that UPnP is different than regular Plug n Play (PnP). Workstations should not be advertising their services (or automatically discovering and connecting to networked services) in a security-conscious enterprise-managed environment.
In Group Policy, ensure that the following is set to Disabled. Computer Configuration -> Policies -> Windows Settings -> Security Settings -> System Services -> SSDP Discovery	

Disable 'UPnP Device Host (upnphost)'	Universal Plug n Play (UPnP) is a real security risk - it allows automatic discovery and attachment to network devices. Notes that UPnP is different than regular Plug n Play (PnP). Workstations should not be advertising their services (or automatically discovering and connecting to networked services) in a security-conscious enterprise-managed environment.
In Group Policy, ensure that the following is set to Disabled. Computer Configuration -> Policies -> Windows Settings -> Security Settings -> System Services -> UPnP Device Host	

Disable 'Windows Media Player Network Sharing Service (WMPNetworkSvc)'	Network sharing of media from Media Player has no place in an enterprise-managed environment.
In Group Policy, ensure that the following is set to Disabled or ensure the service is not installed. Computer Configuration -> Policies -> Windows Settings -> Security Settings -> System Services -> Windows Media Player Network Sharing Service	

Disable 'Windows Mobile Hotspot Service (icssvc)'	The capability to run a mobile hotspot from a domain-connected computer could easily expose the internal network to wardrivers or other hackers.
In Group Policy, ensure that the following is set to Disabled. Computer Configuration -> Policies -> Windows Settings -> Security Settings -> System Services -> Windows Mobile Hotspot Service	

Disable 'Xbox Accessory Management Service (XboxGipSvc)'	Xbox Live is a gaming service and has no place in an enterprise-managed environment (perhaps unless it is a gaming company).
In Group Policy, ensure that the following is set to Disabled. Computer Configuration -> Policies -> Windows Settings -> Security Settings -> System Services -> Xbox Accessory Management Service	

Disable 'Xbox Live Auth Manager (XblAuthManager)'	Xbox Live is a gaming service and has no place in an enterprise-managed environment (perhaps unless it is a gaming company).
In Group Policy, ensure that the following is set to Disabled. Computer Configuration -> Policies -> Windows Settings -> Security Settings -> System Services -> Xbox Live Auth Manager	

Disable 'Xbox Live Game Save (XblGameSave)'	Xbox Live is a gaming service and has no place in an enterprise-managed environment (perhaps unless it is a gaming company).
In Group Policy, ensure that the following is set to Disabled. Computer Configuration -> Policies -> Windows Settings -> Security Settings -> System Services -> Xbox Live Game Save	

Disable 'Xbox Live Networking Service (XboxNetApiSvc)'	Xbox Live is a gaming service and has no place in an enterprise-managed environment (perhaps unless it is a gaming company).
In Group Policy, ensure that the following is set to Disabled. Computer Configuration -> Policies -> Windows Settings -> Security Settings -> System Services -> Xbox Live Networking Service	

To demonstrate compliance with this requirement, you will need to individually address unnecessary functionality in each of these five areas: programs, functions, ports, protocols, and services. It is strongly recommended that you identify at least a couple of items in each category to demonstrate the category was addressed. Your lists should also include what measures are being taken to block unnecessary functionalities.

Assessment Stats

- Assessment Points: 5
- Assessment POAM Eligible: No

Keys

- Documentation – Assemble lists of unnecessary functionalities for each category: programs, functions, ports, protocols, and services. Each identified unnecessary functionality should list the method by which these functionalities are made unusable.
- System change -- Implement & verify all of the measures to limit these unnecessary functionalities.

Configuration Management

CM.L2-3.4.8

Application Execution Policy

Apply deny-by-exception (blacklisting) policy to prevent the use of unauthorized software or deny-all, permit-by-exception (whitelisting) policy to allow the execution of authorized software.

Impact

Anton discovered he had an unauthorized software problem when it came out that the users in several departments were installing an Instant Messenger application without authorization. Anton had been watching security newsletters and had seen several articles about the security and privacy issues with this particular piece of software.

At the same time, an engineering intern had gone to a website that claimed that a special viewer was required to access their data. The intern easily installed the viewer, which did not help him with the website but instead gave remote access to his computer from some people in Eastern Europe.

Whether intentionally or not, users can install unsafe software unless there are safeguards to prevent that from happening.

Official Interpretation*

Organizations should determine their blacklisting or whitelisting policy and configure the system to manage software that is allowed to run. Blacklisting or deny-by-exception allows all software to run except if on an unauthorized software list such as what is maintained in antivirus solutions. Whitelisting or permit-by-exception does not allow any software to run except if on an authorized software list. The stronger policy of the two is whitelisting.

This requirement, CM.L2-3.4.8, requires the implementation of allow-lists and deny-lists for application software. It leverages CM.L2-3.4.1, which requires the organization to establish and maintain software inventories.

This requirement, CM.L2-3.4.8, also extends CM.L2-3.4.9, which only requires control and monitoring of any user installed software.

(CMMC Assessment Guide, Level 2, Copyright 2020, 2021 Carnegie Mellon University and The Johns Hopkins University Applied Physics Laboratory LLC and/or CMMC Assessment Guide, Level 2, Version 2.11 - DRAFT, November 2023)

Assessment Focus

Also known as Assessment Objectives, these are the checklist items that an assessor will seek to verify. Each one must be addressed in your implementation and documentation:

1. a policy specifying whether whitelisting or blacklisting is to be implemented is specified;
2. the software allowed to execute under whitelisting or denied use under blacklisting is specified; and
3. whitelisting to allow the execution of authorized software or blacklisting to prevent the use of unauthorized software is implemented as specified.

(CMMC Assessment Guide, Level 2, Copyright 2020, 2021 Carnegie Mellon University and The Johns Hopkins University Applied Physics Laboratory LLC and/or CMMC Assessment Guide, Level 2, Version 2.11 - DRAFT, November 2023)

Implementation

A good endpoint anti-virus can be considered to be a blacklist software restriction. So, this tool that you likely have in place will "check the box" for this requirement. Other security software, such as EDR, may have a blacklisting element.

However, greater security effectiveness can be found by utilizing whitelisting. The essence of whitelisting is that it identifies every possible executable that the system is allowed to run. While there is maintenance to keeping a whitelist current, this configuration will stop anything unknown, whereas a blacklist will accept anything unknown.

Whitelisting has been proven to be a more effective tool for security, and there are some excellent products for the enterprise. However, many major whitelist providers will not consider installing in a smaller organization. Some of the earlier offerings were very labor-intensive to support the whitelisting process. Application whitelisting is a rapidly evolving market. The future will improve the offerings that make sense in a small organization. Reputation-based application whitelisting is one vehicle that will allow the SMB to gain many of the benefits without incurring the arduous support overhead.

Environments with Windows Server 2008 R2+ and Windows 7+ clients can use the Windows native application, AppLocker, for whitelisting. While AppLocker may not be the most streamlined and easiest-to-manage system for application whitelisting, it has the advantage of being effective and (basically) free. While AppLocker can technically run on clients that are Windows 10 Pro, many versions cannot be managed with GroupPolicy. From the Microsoft website, "You can only manage AppLocker with Group Policy on devices running Windows 10 and Windows 11 Enterprise, Windows 10 and Windows 11 Education, and Windows Server 2016." Not having Group Policy as a management tool adds much more complexity to AppLocker. It is likely that migration to clients running Enterprise can be achieved at a lower cost than purchasing another whitelisting application.

Similarly, Microsoft's latest whitelisting tool, Windows Defender Application Control (WDAC) is provided in your existing systems, but the ability to effectively control it requires additional expense. The WDAC package offers a form of reputation-based whitelisting. The ability to control WDAC is severely limited unless you have Microsoft Intune, a feature of the more expensive Microsoft 365 packages. So, Intune adds a significant per-user-per-month fee if you do not already have it available.

As you consider the application control tool to be used in your organization, you should note that there will inevitably be a time when whitelisting will be mandated. At this time this is written, the requirements of CMMC come from NIST SP 800-171 r2 (that's revision 2). However, NIST SP 800-171 r3 is already written. In the third revision, whitelisting is the only approved method for application control. At some point in the future, CMMC will be redesigned around revision 3. For now, either whitelisting or blacklisting is OK, but that is unlikely to always be the case.

Your documentation will need to outline the blacklisting or whitelisting tool that is used in your organization to protect it from unsafe software.

Assessment Stats

- Assessment Points: 1
- Assessment POAM Eligible: Yes

Keys

- System Configuration - Implement an endpoint antivirus solution or an application whitelisting application.
- Documentation – Identify and describe the blacklisting/whitelisting application in use and how the disallowed/allowed executables are defined.

CM.L2-3.4.9

User-Installed Software

Control and monitor user-installed software.

Impact

All Chris wanted was a game to play on his computer during his lunch breaks. However, he inadvertently installed a pathway for the network to be hacked, the company secrets to be exfiltrated, and the bank accounts to be emptied. Chris figured that software couldn't get on the internet unless it was safe (he read that on the internet, so it must be true). This simple download and installation was the downfall of the company. They were never able to recover from the losses experienced. These included financial losses, intellectual property losses, and losses to their reputation in the marketplace. Chris now has lots of time to play computer games on his home computer until he finds a new job.

Official Interpretation*

Software that users have the ability to install is limited to items that the organization approves. When not controlled, users could install software that can create unnecessary risk. This risk applies both to the individual machine and to the larger operating environment. Policies and technical controls reduce risk to the organization by preventing users from installing unauthorized software.

(CMMC Assessment Guide, Level 2, Copyright 2020, 2021 Carnegie Mellon University and The Johns Hopkins University Applied Physics Laboratory LLC and/or CMMC Assessment Guide, Level 2, Version 2.11 - DRAFT, November 2023)

Assessment Focus

Also known as Assessment Objectives, these are the checklist items that an assessor will seek to verify. Each one must be addressed in your implementation and documentation:

1. a policy for controlling the installation of software by users is established;
2. installation of software by users is controlled based on the established policy; and
3. installation of software by users is monitored.

(CMMC Assessment Guide, Level 2, Copyright 2020, 2021 Carnegie Mellon University and The Johns Hopkins University Applied Physics Laboratory LLC and/or CMMC Assessment Guide, Level 2, Version 2.11 - DRAFT, November 2023)

Implementation

In a perfect environment, there would be no user-installed software, but this is one of the places where the less structured environment of the SMB is a disadvantage.

The requirement does not specify that users can never install software. If your specific situation necessitates that users may need particular pieces of software, there are ways that can ensure that this is performed in a controlled and safe manner. You would want a specific list of permitted products with links so the users get the code from safe places. However, disallowing user-installed software is the best choice in most situations.

Your control of user-installed software will likely consist of multiple layers of imperfect controls. Like most aspects of cybersecurity, perfect protection is impossible to achieve.

1. While it does not block every form of software installation, there is a Group Policy setting that will block the installation of many programs. This is found at Computer Configurations → Administrative Templates → Windows Components → Windows Installer.
2. Users cannot install most software if they do not have local machine administrator rights. Still, many people (especially the bosses) may believe they need the ability to install software. You may also have business-essential software that requires administrator rights to install updates. However, limiting local administrator rights is important for many security reasons.
3. If you are using an application whitelisting system, it can restrict software that a user might install. While it is optimal to make it impossible for users to install unauthorized software, a total ban is not essential to conformance.
4. If you have antivirus controls on the user's devices, this prevents the installation of unsafe software.
5. Your computer use policy should outline restrictions/policies on user-installed software. This is an essential element of this requirement.

The requirement requires a clear policy with regard to user-installed software. Their expectation is that this policy DOES control user behavior. While everybody is aware of some policy that is universally ignored, this cannot be one of those. When the CMMC assessor interviews users, it should be clear that this policy does control what the users do and don't do.

This requirement also calls for the monitoring of user-installed software. The software inventory solution that helps meet the requirements of CM.L2-3.4.1 can potentially provide the monitoring mechanism for user-installed software. If your monitoring solution identifies policy violations and the violations have even minor consequences, then that will drive behavior in conformance with the policy.

If you have access to Microsoft Intune, it is a good tool to assist with monitoring and control of user installed software.

Assessment Stats

- Assessment Points: 1
- Assessment POAM Eligible: Yes

Keys

- Documentation – List out the controls that restrict user-installed software.
- Policy – You will want to be sure that your computer use policy explicitly prohibits the installation of unauthorized software. If there are some exceptions to this rule, those exceptions should be expressly stated in the policy.
- System Change – You must monitor for user-installed software by utilizing the hardware/software inventory system or some other tool.

Identification & Authentication

IA.L1-3.5.1

Identification

Identify system users, processes acting on behalf of users, and devices.

Impact

The sales manager asked Emmett to make a set of training videos available to the sales team. Emmett created a share on a NAS that required a username and password to access it. He then circulated this single set of credentials to all sales personnel. This worked just fine until, one day, it was discovered that all of the training videos had been replaced by "Sailor Moon" videos. While this was likely performed as a joke, and backup copies of the videos existed, the sales manager was still furious. Emmett realized that since everybody was logging in using the same credentials, he didn't have any easy way to figure out who had perpetrated the joke. This was when Emmett learned that shared credentials could be a bad thing.

Official Interpretation*

Make sure to assign individual, unique identifiers (e.g., user names) to all users and processes that access company systems. Authorized devices also should have unique identifiers. Unique identifiers can be as simple as a short set of alphanumeric characters (e.g., SW001 could refer to a network switch, SW002 could refer to a different network switch).

This requirement, IA.L2-3.5.1, provides a vetted and trusted identity that supports the access control mechanism required by AC.L2-3.1.1.

(CMMC Assessment Guide, Level 2, Copyright 2020, 2021 Carnegie Mellon University and The Johns Hopkins University Applied Physics Laboratory LLC and/or CMMC Assessment Guide, Level 2, Version 2.11 - DRAFT, November 2023)

Assessment Focus

Also known as Assessment Objectives, these are the checklist items that an assessor will seek to verify. Each one must be addressed in your implementation and documentation:

1. system users are identified;
2. processes acting on behalf of users are identified; and

3. devices accessing the system are identified.

(CMMC Assessment Guide, Level 2, Copyright 2020, 2021 Carnegie Mellon University and The Johns Hopkins University Applied Physics Laboratory LLC and/or CMMC Assessment Guide, Level 2, Version 2.11 - DRAFT, November 2023)

Implementation

This is another area where the security practice is built into Windows. However, this depends on the Active Directory being properly configured. There must be a one-to-one correspondence between human users and the Active Directory users. Active Directory provides unique identification of users and devices based on their login credentials. This functionality can be undermined by any practice that breaks that one-to-one correspondence. These may include:

- Having a shared set of logon credentials used by multiple people. This may be a conference room or specialized workstation.
- Having employees that tell other employees their passwords.
- Users that log onto the local machine, instead of using domain authentication.
- Having credentials that are recycled for use by temporary folks or contractors.

If a CMMC assessor can identify a single shared logon, then the implementation of this requirement will appear unsuccessful.

Attempt to minimize the number of devices on the network that are not joined to the domain. A printer may sit on the network for multiple users to access, but not be a member of the domain. Although it is likely to fly under the radar, it would be far better if the printer was joined to the domain, so it could reap the security benefits of being a domain member.

Windows will take care of the identification of processes spawned by the logged-in user. Windows also uniquely identifies the devices that log onto the domain.

Assessment Stats

- Assessment Points: 1
- Assessment POAM Eligible: Yes

Keys

- Network Configuration – Assure that all users have unique authentication credentials in Active Directory
- Training – Assure that users understand the issues associated with letting others know their network password.

Identification & Authentication

IA.L1-3.5.2

Authentication

Authenticate (or verify) the identities of users, processes, or devices, as a prerequisite to allowing access to organizational systems.

Impact

Erin wasn't that concerned when she put the confidential customer data into a network share. After all, it was supposed to be a quick, short-term method to distribute the data to sales team members. Although that was the plan, the data remained on the share for months. To make matters worse, the share was set up to be accessible to any device connected to the network. After the information turned up on the Internet and they started digging into what happened, it appeared that none of the company workstations were responsible. Another device, by an unknown user, was used to gather the data and remove it from the company.

Official Interpretation*

Before a person or device is given system access, verify that the user or device is who or what it claims to be. This verification is called authentication. The most common way to verify identity is using a username and a hard-to-guess password.

Some devices ship with default usernames and passwords. Some devices ship with a default username (e.g., admin) and password. A default username and password must be immediately changed to something unique. Default passwords may be well known to the public, easily found in a search, or easy to guess, allowing an unauthorized person to access the system.

(CMMC Assessment Guide, Level 2, Copyright 2020, 2021 Carnegie Mellon University and The Johns Hopkins University Applied Physics Laboratory LLC and/or CMMC Assessment Guide, Level 2, Version 2.11 - DRAFT, November 2023)

Assessment Focus

Also known as Assessment Objectives, these are the checklist items that an assessor will seek to verify. Each one must be addressed in your implementation and documentation:

1. the identity of each user is authenticated or verified as a prerequisite to system access;

2. the identity of each process acting on behalf of a user is authenticated or verified as a prerequisite to system access; and
3. the identity of each device accessing or connecting to the system is authenticated or verified as a prerequisite to system access.

(CMMC Assessment Guide, Level 2, Copyright 2020, 2021 Carnegie Mellon University and The Johns Hopkins University Applied Physics Laboratory LLC and/or CMMC Assessment Guide, Level 2, Version 2.11 - DRAFT, November 2023)

Implementation

Note: This requirement is one of 6 regarding remote access. These requirements should all be considered together when designing controls. The remote-access-related controls are:

AC.L2-3.1.12	control of remote access	AC.L2-3.1.15	privileged commands on remote sessions
AC.L2-3.1.14	remote access control points	IA.L2-3.5.3	multifactor authentication
AC.L2-3.1.13	cryptography for remote sessions	MA.L2-3.7.5	MFA for remote maintenance sessions

The Windows domain environment requires authentication for devices, users, and the resulting processes. That authentication is directly tied to access, permissions, and privileges. The upshot is that the Windows Domain System handles this requirement for the domain members.

However, some things should concern you:

- Devices or users are only members of the domain if you make them members, so there may be users or computers that are not joined to the domain. For example, a network-connected computer with a local user consists of a computer and a user that are not part of the domain. Whenever you have non-domain-joined users or devices on your network, the authentication burden becomes a process that must be managed manually.
- Certain devices, like IoT, are not capable of being domain-managed (AD integration). These devices may be connected to your network but may (1) function as a non-domain user or (2) allow other unauthorized users to connect through them. This is not to say that all IoT devices are automatically bad, but they require careful scrutiny, management, and care.
- Network resources need permissions that restrict their access to domain-authenticated users. The old concept of setting a share to "Full Control" for "Anybody" is extremely risky. Changing the group from "Anybody" to "Authenticated Users" will add significant security and help assure that a CMMC assessor will not have a problem with your compliance with this requirement.

As long as each computer, device, and user is authenticated to Active Directory, Windows will assume responsibility for access, process tracking, and device tracking.

Assessment Stats

- Assessment Points: 1
- Assessment POAM Eligible: Yes

Keys

- Network Configuration – Assure that all devices, users, and computers are domain members so AD can manage the authentication.

Identification & Authentication

IA.L2-3.5.3

Multifactor Authentication

Use multifactor authentication for local and network access to privileged accounts and for network access to non-privileged accounts.

Impact

Jenny always considered herself very cautious in handling the digital treasures that her company had entrusted to her. However, as she logged into her company VPN from the neighborhood coffee shop, she didn't notice a guy using his cell phone to make a video of her every keystroke. Once he used the video to figure out her login credentials, he should have free reign over the company's network, except there is one hurdle that he isn't counting on. The company recently instituted 2-factor authentication. To finish logging in to the network, this hacker needs to have the authenticator app installed on Jenny's phone. This two-factor authentication sucks the value out of a hacker gaining access to the username and password.

Official Interpretation*

Implement a combination of two or more factors of authentication to verify privileged account holders' identity regardless of how the user is accessing the account. Implement a combination of two or more factors for non-privileged users accessing the system over a network.

The implementation of multi-factor authentication will depend on the environment and business needs. Although two-factor authentication directly on the computer is most common, there are situations (e.g., multi-factor identification for a mission system that cannot be altered) where additional technical or physical solutions can provide security. If a mobile device is used to access a system or application containing CUI, multi-factor authentication is required.

This requirement, IA.L2-3.5.3, requires multifactor authentication for network access to non-privileged accounts and complements five other requirements dealing with remote access (AC.L2-3.1.12, AC.L2-3.1.14, AC.L2-3.1.13, AC.L2-3.1.15, and MA.L2-3.7.5:

- AC.L2-3.1.12 requires the control of remote access sessions.
- AC.L2-3.1.14 limits remote access to specific access control points.

- AC.L2-3.1.13 requires the use of cryptographic mechanisms when enabling remote sessions.
- AC.L2-3.1.15 requires authorization for privileged commands executed during a remote.
- Finally, MA.L2-3.7.5 requires the addition of multifactor authentication for remote maintenance sessions.

This requirement, IA.L2-3.5.3, also enhances IA.L2-3.5.2, which is a requirement for a less rigorous form of user authentication.

(CMMC Assessment Guide, Level 2, Copyright 2020, 2021 Carnegie Mellon University and The Johns Hopkins University Applied Physics Laboratory LLC and/or CMMC Assessment Guide, Level 2, Version 2.11 - DRAFT, November 2023)

Assessment Focus

Also known as Assessment Objectives, these are the checklist items that an assessor will seek to verify. Each one must be addressed in your implementation and documentation:

1. privileged accounts are identified;
2. multifactor authentication is implemented for local access to privileged accounts;
3. multifactor authentication is implemented for network access to privileged accounts; and
4. multifactor authentication is implemented for network access to non-privileged accounts.

(CMMC Assessment Guide, Level 2, Copyright 2020, 2021 Carnegie Mellon University and The Johns Hopkins University Applied Physics Laboratory LLC and/or CMMC Assessment Guide, Level 2, Version 2.11 - DRAFT, November 2023)

Implementation

Note: This requirement is one of 6 regarding remote access. These requirements should all be considered together when designing controls. The remote-access-related controls are:

AC.L2-3.1.12	control of remote access	AC.L2-3.1.15	privileged commands on remote sessions
AC.L2-3.1.14	remote access control points	IA.L2-3.5.3	multifactor authentication
AC.L2-3.1.13	cryptography for remote sessions	MA.L2-3.7.5	MFA for remote maintenance sessions

This requirement was the primary reason the big corporate defense contractors needed to extend the NIST SP 800-171 implementation deadline. There is no easy way around this requirement for multifactor authentication.

When is MFA required?

Account Type	Network Authentication*	Local Machine Authentication
Privileged account	Yes	Yes
Standard account	Yes	No

*This includes any domain authentication.

If you choose to use the native Windows option(Windows Hello for Business), you will likely have some hardware costs associated with implementation. If you decide to go with a third-party option, then there will be subscription expenses (per user/per month). Either way, there will likely be expenses associated with implementing this requirement.

Multifactor authentication requires the use of 2 or more factors to achieve authentication.

Factor	Examples
Something you know	a password or a memorized PIN
Something you have	a smartphone or a secure USB key
Something you are	a fingerprint or facial recognition

The CUI FAQ explicitly states that "where you are" does not qualify as a factor for this requirement, so the IP address and the computer you are using do not constitute an additional factor. They want the extra authentication factor to be something that you bring to the transaction.

In understanding the scope of this requirement, the key is in the words "network access." The official documents make it clear that anything other than local authentication is "network access" since the network is required in the authentication process. Effectively, the only time you can have authentication without MFA is when you are logging on to a local (not domain-authenticated) account that is not privileged. All other authentications must have an MFA. So, clearly, this requirement is mandating MFA for all authentications (especially when the implications of IA.L1-3.5.2 are considered).

This certainly includes authentications made remotely.

Windows allows for multifactor authentication through Windows Hello for Business. Windows Hello for Business does not feature a lot of options for factors. It only supports PIN, Fingerprint, Facial Recognition, and Trusted Signal. No options exist for authenticator apps or sending codes to phones within Hello.

Windows Hello for Business is also picky about hardware. While your users may have a webcam mounted on their computer, it generally won't work with Windows Hello for Business unless it is certified for Hello compatibility. The same issue applies to fingerprint readers and other biometric devices.

One of the options within Windows Hello that sounds enticing is to make a Bluetooth connection to a saved cell phone one of the Trusted Signal factors. That way, if the user has their cell phone when they attempt to log on, the Bluetooth signal will be detected, and the second-factor authentication will be invisible to the user. However, many Bluetooth adapters "go to sleep," so the user must still jump through hoops to make that factor work effectively. Test carefully before getting excited about this option.

The other Trusted Signal options include looking for specific IP addresses or specific WiFi signals, which all come down to "where you are" factors that do not apply to CMMC MFA.

There is one more issue with using Hello for Business for the IA.L2-3.5.3 MFA requirement. Multifactor authentication is required whenever a privileged account is used. So, if your processes require occasional use of a local administrator account, Hello for Business won't provide authentication. So, either these local administrator authentications will need to be eliminated or a different MFA tool will be required.

HANDY LINK

More info about using Hello for Business for MFA https://tinyurl.com/CMMC4SMB-275

Obtaining more MFA options requires using a third-party authentication app that integrates with Active Directory. Duo Security produces the most popular product in this area. Using a third-party product will be an ongoing expense, but offers more options over Windows Hello for Business.

Multifactor authentication is an obvious example of how there is potential to become highly unpopular with the users when implementing security practices. The users, including those in top management, will not be happy if they have to jump through crazy hoops to use their computers. So, in determining the appropriate application of MFA for your organization, you should not just look at the security and compliance but also think about the burden it puts on the user and the support burden that might land on IT. Users who refuse to buy into an implementation will find ways to work around it. If the users become focused on bypassing the MFA (and threatening you with bodily harm), then you have not succeeded in producing a productive and secure environment.

Assessment Stats

- Assessment Points: 3 or 5*
- Assessment POAM Eligible: No

* Three points are subtracted from the maximum score if MFA is implemented only for remote and privileged users and 5 points are subtracted from the maximum score if MFA is not implemented for any users.

Keys

- System Configuration – Establish a multifactor authentication for all logins except those using unprivileged local accounts (non-domain). Be prepared to demonstrate this for an assessor.

IA.L2-3.5.4

Replay-Resistant Authentication

Employ replay-resistant authentication mechanisms for network access to privileged and non-privileged accounts.

Impact

Brent had a huge desire to poke around in an application used in his office, but there was no business purpose why he should be granted authorization to access that application. First, he set up a rogue promiscuous packet sniffer. He was convinced he would have the username and password if he could capture the packets transmitted between his boss and this application. However, all he captured was garbage. He was pretty disappointed. Sometime in the middle of the night, a solution came to him. If this bunch of garbage was what it took to log in, then all he would have to do would be to send it back to the app from his machine, and he would be logged in! Although Brent was disappointed, the application used an authentication method that couldn't be fooled by simply replaying a prior authentication.

Official Interpretation*

When insecure protocols are used for access to computing resources, an adversary may be able to capture login information and immediately reuse (replay) it for other purposes. It is important to use mechanisms that resist this technique.

(CMMC Assessment Guide, Level 2, Copyright 2020, 2021 Carnegie Mellon University and The Johns Hopkins University Applied Physics Laboratory LLC and/or CMMC Assessment Guide, Level 2, Version 2.11 - DRAFT, November 2023)

Assessment Focus

Also known as Assessment Objectives, these are the checklist items that an assessor will seek to verify. Each one must be addressed in your implementation and documentation:

1. replay-resistant authentication mechanisms are implemented for network account access to privileged and non-privileged accounts.

(CMMC Assessment Guide, Level 2, Copyright 2020, 2021 Carnegie Mellon University and The Johns Hopkins University Applied Physics Laboratory LLC and/or CMMC Assessment Guide, Level 2, Version 2.11 - DRAFT, November 2023)

Implementation

Windows Kerberos domain authentication system is not subject to replay attacks because the encrypted communication between server and client contains a timestamp. If that same encrypted stream of data is sent again to the server, then the system will not accept it because the timestamp is wrong.

Because this security is built into Windows, no further action is required relative to Windows authentication.

If you have other applications that are used with CUI, meet t the criteria of "authentication mechanisms for network access to privileged and non-privileged accounts," and have their own authentication, those apps will need evaluation for their replay resistance capabilities. If these applications can be set to apply Single Sign On (SSO) based on the user's domain authentication, then concerns about replay are alleviated.

Assessment Stats

- Assessment Points: 1
- Assessment POAM Eligible: Yes

Keys

- No action required for domain authentication.
- Evaluate other applications for replay resistance.

Identification & Authentication

IA.L2-3.5.5

Identifier Reuse

Prevent the reuse of identifiers for a defined period.

Impact

Harry is frustrated about all the employee turnover in his office because continually issuing new usernames drives him crazy. Finally, he decides to create a bunch of generic employee usernames and just hand those out. When somebody leaves the office, he will simply assign the username to their replacement. This plan should save him loads of work. This goes along just fine until the day comes when one of the users attempts to access the restricted share containing the company secrets. Suddenly, Harry is stumped because he isn't sure who might have been using that username.

Official Interpretation*

Identifiers uniquely associate a user ID to an individual, group, role, or device. Establish guidelines and implement mechanisms to prevent identifiers from being reused for the period of time established in the policy.

(CMMC Assessment Guide, Level 2, Copyright 2020, 2021 Carnegie Mellon University and The Johns Hopkins University Applied Physics Laboratory LLC and/or CMMC Assessment Guide, Level 2, Version 2.11 - DRAFT, November 2023)

Assessment Focus

Also known as Assessment Objectives, these are the checklist items that an assessor will seek to verify. Each one must be addressed in your implementation and documentation:

1. a period within which identifiers cannot be reused is defined; and
2. reuse of identifiers is prevented within the defined period.

(CMMC Assessment Guide, Level 2, Copyright 2020, 2021 Carnegie Mellon University and The Johns Hopkins University Applied Physics Laboratory LLC and/or CMMC Assessment Guide, Level 2, Version 2.11 - DRAFT, November 2023)

Implementation

Internally to Windows Active Directory, all users, groups, roles, and devices are assigned unique identifiers. These identifiers are long and random and might not see duplications for centuries. Even if an admin assigns "jack" as a username, then deletes that user and re-assigns the username "jack," then Active Directory automatically gives the user a new internal identifier so that none of the information associated with the prior "jack" gets attached to the new person given that same username.

This security assumes only one user will use a given account. If the existing account (logon credentials) is simply renamed to another user, then the new user will inherit all of the history and permissions of the prior user. The simplest control is a policy to always delete a user in Active Directory when the account is no longer needed. This assures that the account cannot be re-used.

Assessment Stats

- Assessment Points: 1
- Assessment POAM Eligible: Yes

Keys

- Policy – Establish a policy for handling user accounts when an individual leaves the company or their account is no longer needed for any other reason.

Identification & Authentication

IA.L2-3.5.6
Identifier Handling

Disable identifiers after a defined period of inactivity.

Impact

Sergey is working hard to gain access to some valuable digital assets within the network of a particular small business. He used a phishing attack to gain a toe-hold, but the user's account he has appropriated does not have adequate permissions to access the assets he desires. By poking around, he found a long-disused account that appears to have greater permissions. As he accessed the old account, he chuckled softly to himself because he suspected that the network owners probably had no idea that this account still existed, but it was like the account had been left there just for him to use.

Official Interpretation*

Identifiers are uniquely associated with an individual, account, process, or device. An inactive identifier is one that has not been used for a defined extended period of time. For example, a user account may be needed for a certain time to allow for transition of business processes to existing or new staff. Once use of the identifier is no longer necessary, it should be disabled as soon as possible. Failure to maintain awareness of accounts that are no longer needed yet still active could allow an adversary to exploit IT services.

(CMMC Assessment Guide, Level 2, Copyright 2020, 2021 Carnegie Mellon University and The Johns Hopkins University Applied Physics Laboratory LLC and/or CMMC Assessment Guide, Level 2, Version 2.11 - DRAFT, November 2023)

Assessment Focus

Also known as Assessment Objectives, these are the checklist items that an assessor will seek to verify. Each one must be addressed in your implementation and documentation:

1. a period of inactivity after which an identifier is disabled is defined; and
2. identifiers are disabled after the defined period of inactivity.

(CMMC Assessment Guide, Level 2, Copyright 2020, 2021 Carnegie Mellon University and The Johns Hopkins University Applied Physics Laboratory LLC and/or CMMC Assessment Guide, Level 2, Version 2.11 - DRAFT, November 2023)

Implementation

It is easy to create or enroll computers, and users in Active Directory, but it is harder to identify and purge those that are unused by using the standard AD interface. However, tools like PowerShell provide tools to accomplish this. For example, this PowerShell code sample will export a list of user accounts that are active but have not been used in the last 90 days:

```
$Days = 90
$Time = (Get-Date).Adddays(-($Days))
Get-ADUser -Filter {LastLogonTimeStamp -lt $Time} -Properties * | Where-Object {$_.Enabled -like "true"} |
Select Name, LastLogonDate, Enabled | Export-CSV "C:\Temp\UsersSubjectToInactivate.CSV" -
NoTypeInformation
```

This PowerShell code will find those user accounts that have been deactivated and not used in 180 days:

```
$Days = 180
$Time = (Get-Date).Adddays(-($Days))
Get-ADUser -Filter {LastLogonTimeStamp -lt $Time} -Properties * | Where-Object {$_.Enabled -like "false"} |
Select Name, LastLogonDate, Enabled | Export-CSV "C:\Temp\UsersSubjectToDelete.CSV" -NoTypeInformation
```

Finally, this sample finds computer accounts that have not been utilized in 180 days:

```
$Days = 180
$Time = (Get-Date).Adddays(-($Days))
Get-ADComputer -Filter {LastLogonTimeStamp -lt $Time} -Properties * | Select Name, LastLogonDate, Enabled |
Export-CSV "C:\Temp\ComputersSubjectToDelete.CSV" -NoTypeInformation
```

HANDY LINK

The code samples can be found at https://tinyurl.com/CMMC4SMB-727

There are scripts available on the Internet that can be used to automate the process of purging unused accounts. The scripts can be set to run periodically without any operator intervention. However, it is recommended that before considering any automation, you manually evaluate what accounts might be affected, as there may be some accounts that are intentionally designed to be only rarely used.

A common methodology is to inactivate unused accounts for a period of time, then delete the accounts if nothing is broken and there are no complaints. For example, accounts might be inactivated after 60 days without activity. Then, accounts that are inactivated for 60 more days can be deleted.

The last thing you want to see is to have deleted some accounts that people need. Inactivated accounts can be recovered, but deleted accounts cannot.

Whether the process you design is manual, semi-automatic, or fully automatic, the process should be clearly documented, and the results of each purge should be recorded. This provides clarity of the process as well as a record of whether the account purging causes problems.

If you have any accounts (for instance, an intentionally rarely used account) that will not be treated according to these standard rules of deactivation and deletion, then those exceptions should also be documented and explained. You would want to ensure that a CMMC assessor finds all accounts purged following your documented process, even if your documented process contains some exceptions.

Assessment Stats

- Assessment Points: 1
- Assessment POAM Eligible: Yes

Keys

- Create Policy – Define the procedure for inactivating and deleting accounts not being used, clearly identifying the age when accounts without activity are deactivated and then how long before they are deleted.
- System – Define the mechanics of an inactive account purging process. For any process that has to be manually initiated, a schedule of when it will be performed should be created.
- Documentation – Generate records associated with the process being conducted.

IA.L2-3.5.7

Password Complexity

Enforce a minimum password complexity and change of characters when new passwords are created.

Impact

Drake was sure that his dog's name spelled backward was a terrific password. He did not recognize the speed with which brute force hacks can generate passwords. Considering the technology, his password of "selbbep" wasn't very secure. Using standard available technology, every possible seven-character password (lowercase only, no numbers or special characters) can be generated in less than 10 minutes.

Official Interpretation*

Password complexity means using different types of characters as well as a specified number of characters. This applies to both the creation of new passwords and the modification of existing passwords. Characters to manage complexity include numbers, lowercase and uppercase letters, and symbols. Minimum complexity requirements are left up to the organization to define. Define the lowest level of password complexity required. Define the number of characters that must be changed when an existing password is changed. Enforce these rules for all passwords. Salting passwords adds a string of random characters (salt) to a password prior to hashing. This ensures the randomness of the resulting hash value.

(CMMC Assessment Guide, Level 2, Copyright 2020, 2021 Carnegie Mellon University and The Johns Hopkins University Applied Physics Laboratory LLC and/or CMMC Assessment Guide, Level 2, Version 2.11 - DRAFT, November 2023)

Assessment Focus

Also known as Assessment Objectives, these are the checklist items that an assessor will seek to verify. Each one must be addressed in your implementation and documentation:

1. password complexity requirements are defined;
2. password change of character requirements are defined;
3. minimum password complexity requirements as defined are enforced when new passwords are created; and

4. minimum password change of character requirements as defined are enforced when new passwords are created.

(CMMC Assessment Guide, Level 2, Copyright 2020, 2021 Carnegie Mellon University and The Johns Hopkins University Applied Physics Laboratory LLC and/or CMMC Assessment Guide, Level 2, Version 2.11 - DRAFT, November 2023)

Implementation

Password hacking tools are readily available and become more sophisticated each day. Combine this with the increasing processing speed of off-the-shelf computers, and the acceptable passwords of years past are no longer adequate. This trend will continue until passwords become obsolete and are no longer in use.

One of the available tools for making brute force hacking more difficult is increasing the number of possible characters the hacker needs to try. This can be illustrated with a simple example: the number of possible 4-character all-lower-case passwords is 456,976 (26^4). If you include numbers and capital letters, that number of possibilities grows to 14,776,336 (62^4). The password is still 4 characters long, but the number of possibilities has increased 32 times!

Password complexity is a double-edged sword. If a user has a password so complex that they cannot remember it, they will be forced to write it down and leave that note handy. There is little security in a computer with the password on a sticky note.

Password complexity can be controlled through group policy. This is controlled in Computer Configuration → Windows Settings → Security Settings → Account Policies → Password Policy.

Within that Password Policy section, you would want to set several items, but the one that satisfies this requirement is "Passwords Must Meet Complexity Requirements." This prevents users from using simple passwords.

The other part of this requirement revolves around the process of changing passwords. The requirement says you should define how much of the previous password should be changed to be accepted as a new one. Within native Windows, only a single character needs to be different. So, "SolvorTok1" can be changed to "SolvorTok2" acceptably within Windows. While some might find this behavior unacceptable, changing it requires a 3rd party "password filter" DLL. In evaluating the risk associated with users potentially changing only a single character, consider that the password is only a single factor in the required multifactor authentication process. CMMC doesn't specify the number of change characters, only that a policy must be in place and enforced. Based upon that, your policy can be for one or more characters to be changed.

Your documentation for this requirement must contain a description of the complexity requirements being implemented, so the following description of Microsoft's complexity requirements should be included:

Passwords must meet these criteria:

- Not contain the user's account name or parts of the user's full name that exceed two consecutive characters
- Contain characters from 3 of the following four categories:
    - English uppercase characters (A through Z)
    - English lowercase characters (a through z)
    - Base 10 digits (0 through 9)
    - Non-alphabetic characters (for example, !, $, #, %)

HANDY LINK

This text can be downloaded at https://tinyurl.com/CMMC4SMB-655

While working in the password policy section, setting the Minimum Password Length to at least 9 is an excellent idea. Otherwise, Windows will accept 6-character passwords, an unacceptable defense against today's password-hacking technology. The password length can be included in the description of password complexity.

Assessment Stats

- Assessment Points: 1
- Assessment POAM Eligible: Yes

Keys

- Group Policy – Set password complexity parameters at Computer Configuration → Windows Settings → Security Settings → Account Policies → Password Policy.
- Documentation – Document the (1) password complexity and (2) character change parameters that are being enforced in your system.

Identification & Authentication

IA.L2-3.5.8

Password Reuse

Prohibit password reuse for a specified number of generations.

Impact

Daphne loves her password. She does not love that her employer forces her to change her password. For years, when the system asked her to change her password, she would change it to her same beloved password. Now, the system is suddenly prohibiting her from recycling that same password. She was complaining to her coworker about this. Her coworker shared that the system only remembered your last password, so the solution is simple. She advised Daphne to change her password to something new and immediately change it to the old password she wanted to use. By doing this, she could work around this annoying demand from the system. Of course, in doing so, she was bypassing this security control and leaving her employer less protected.

Official Interpretation*

Individuals may not reuse their passwords for a defined period of time and a set number of passwords generated.

(CMMC Assessment Guide, Level 2, Copyright 2020, 2021 Carnegie Mellon University and The Johns Hopkins University Applied Physics Laboratory LLC and/or CMMC Assessment Guide, Level 2, Version 2.11 - DRAFT, November 2023)

Assessment Focus

Also known as Assessment Objectives, these are the checklist items that an assessor will seek to verify. Each one must be addressed in your implementation and documentation:

1. the number of generations during which a password cannot be reused is specified
2. reuse of passwords is prohibited during the specified number of generations.

(CMMC Assessment Guide, Level 2, Copyright 2020, 2021 Carnegie Mellon University and The Johns Hopkins University Applied Physics Laboratory LLC and/or CMMC Assessment Guide, Level 2, Version 2.11 - DRAFT, November 2023)

Implementation

Group Policy allows you to set a specific number of passwords that the system "remembers," so the user cannot re-use those passwords. There is no downside to setting this to a high value. Users will try different tricks to avoid making real changes to their password. Some may simply tack a single digit to the end of their password and increment that value when forced to make a password change. This user hack becomes more difficult if this Enforce Password History is set to more than 10.

This can be controlled through group policy. This is controlled in Computer Configuration → Windows Settings → Security Settings → Account Policies → Password Policy as the Enforce Password History option. The number of remembered passwords can be as high as 24.

For additional encouragement for the users to really change passwords when they are supposed to, you can also set the Minimum Password Age in the same section of Group Policy. This value can be set as the number of days between password changes. This prevents the user from performing multiple password changes, one after another, to get back to their original password. This step is not required under CMMC.

Assessment Stats

- Assessment Points: 1
- Assessment POAM Eligible: Yes

Keys

- Documentation – you must define the number of passwords remembered to prevent password reuse.
- Group Policy Configuration – Enable Enforce Password History and set a value identical to what is specified in your documentation.

Identification & Authentication

IA.L2-3.5.9

Temporary Passwords

Allow temporary password use for system logons with an immediate change to a permanent password.

Impact

Chuck is a bit of a control freak in all aspects of his life. This need for control definitely applies to how he controls his employer's network. For years, he has given each new employee a network access password that he assigned so he could be positive that the passwords met his approval for randomness. He then made it impossible for the users to change their own password. One day, a horrible event brought his password satisfaction crashing down around him. An employee back in the operations area was arrested for downloading child pornography on his work computer, which was appalling enough. Still, at the trial, it came out that Chuck had copies of everybody's password. This employee faced no criminal conviction because it couldn't be proven that he was using the computer for these illicit activities. Since the employee wasn't the only person who knew his password, it couldn't be proved that he had logged into the computer. If only Chuck had issued single-use passwords requiring the employee to create his own password, then it would have been legally clear that the user was guilty.

Official Interpretation*

Users must change their temporary passwords the first time they log in. Temporary passwords often follow a consistent style within an organization and can be more easily guessed than passwords created by the unique user. This approach to temporary passwords should be avoided.

(CMMC Assessment Guide, Level 2, Copyright 2020, 2021 Carnegie Mellon University and The Johns Hopkins University Applied Physics Laboratory LLC and/or CMMC Assessment Guide, Level 2, Version 2.11 - DRAFT, November 2023)

Assessment Focus

Also known as Assessment Objectives, these are the checklist items that an assessor will seek to verify. Each one must be addressed in your implementation and documentation:

1. an immediate change to a permanent password is required when a temporary password is used for system logon.

(CMMC Assessment Guide, Level 2, Copyright 2020, 2021 Carnegie Mellon University and The Johns Hopkins University Applied Physics Laboratory LLC and/or CMMC Assessment Guide, Level 2, Version 2.11 - DRAFT, November 2023)

Implementation

This simple step will ensure that your employees have no (as the lawyers say) "plausible deniability" in the event of a problem.

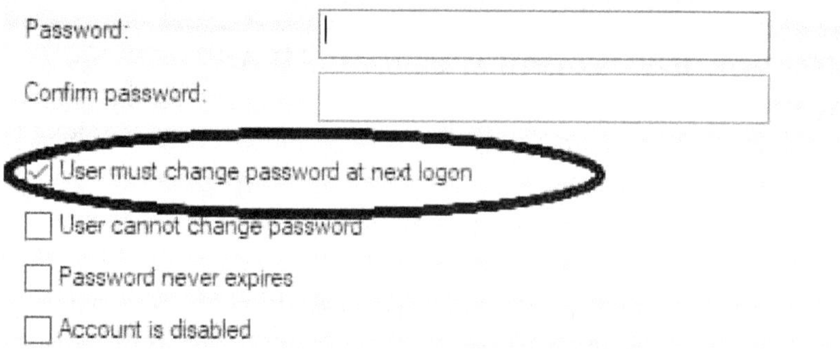

When performing a password reset in Active Directory, the administrator enters a temporary password and should check the box that forces the user to change the password upon first logon (which is checked by default). This mechanism cannot be made mandatory but should be set as a policy for all new users and password resets for all user standard accounts. There might be some special-purpose accounts where it makes sense for the admins to know the password, but it poses risks for the admins to know the password for a user's logon.

Assessment Stats

- Assessment Points: 1
- Assessment POAM Eligible: Yes

Keys

- Create Policy -- Establish a policy that requires admins to use the "User must Change password at next logon" option for new users and user password resets.

Identification & Authentication

IA.L2-3.5.10

Cryptographically-Protected Passwords

Store and transmit only cryptographically-protected passwords.

Impact

Sophia wanted access to her employer's accounting software even though accounting had nothing to do with her job. She saw this access as a means toward financial gain. The company never knew that one of the users was using a packet sniffer to examine network traffic. She wanted to capture a set of logon credentials to the application. This did not prove to be a challenge. With those credentials, she was able to log on and make a wire transfer to an off-shore bank. By the time the loss was identified, the culprit had vanished, headed off to enjoy her profits. Because this software sent the username and password over the network in an unencrypted state, capturing the packets and locating the needed information was simple.

Official Interpretation*

All passwords must be cryptographically protected using a one-way function for storage and transmission. This type of protection changes passwords into another form, or a hashed password. A one-way transformation makes it theoretically impossible to turn the hashed password back into the original password, but inadequate complexity (IA.L2-3.5.7) may still facilitate offline cracking of hashes.

(CMMC Assessment Guide, Level 2, Copyright 2020, 2021 Carnegie Mellon University and The Johns Hopkins University Applied Physics Laboratory LLC and/or CMMC Assessment Guide, Level 2, Version 2.11 - DRAFT, November 2023)

Assessment Focus

Also known as Assessment Objectives, these are the checklist items that an assessor will seek to verify. Each one must be addressed in your implementation and documentation:

1. passwords are cryptographically protected in storage; and
2. passwords are cryptographically protected in transit.

(CMMC Assessment Guide, Level 2, Copyright 2020, 2021 Carnegie Mellon University and The Johns Hopkins University Applied Physics Laboratory LLC and/or CMMC Assessment Guide, Level 2, Version 2.11 - DRAFT, November 2023)

Implementation

Windows logon protocols transmit only non-reversible hashes of passwords. This Windows process prevents any domain authentication password from being stored or ever leaving the user's computer.

> When a digital item is "hashed," the process generates a digital fingerprint of the item. The tiniest change to the item produces a completely different hash value. Just as an unknown fingerprint left at a crime scene can't be decoded to find out information about the human that left it, the hash value cannot be decoded to reveal anything about the original item that was hashed. However, every time the same item is hashed, it will produce the same hash value.

Here is what happens with authentication to a domain:

The password is run through a one-way hashing function, and the actual text of the password is discarded and cannot be recovered.

The domain controller runs a service called the Key Distribution Center (KDC). The user's client machine sends a request to the KDC Authentication Service (AS). The request includes details like the user's username and the date and time. All information except the username is encrypted (an encryption that can be decoded with the correct key) using the hash of the user's password as the encryption key.

The KDC AS uses the username to look up its copy of the user's password hash and uses it to decrypt the rest of the request. If the decryption is successful, that shows the client used the correct password hash and the user has successfully authenticated.

So, the password is not stored or transmitted for this process to work.

However, there is a configuration that messes up this nice, clean implementation. In the Active Directory user properties is a checkbox for "Store password using reversible encryption." This checkbox should <u>never</u> be marked. If it were marked, this IA.L2-3.5.10 requirement would not be met, and security would be much worse.

Windows authentication meets this requirement, if there are other applications, associated with CUI in your system that perform their own authentication, then the authentication process of those should be examined for conformance to this requirement.

Assessment Stats

- Assessment Points: 5
- Assessment POAM Eligible: No

Keys

- No action required for Windows domain authentication. Windows takes care of this.
- Documentation – Provide your assessor a description of how Active Directory and Kerberos handle passwords.
- Policy – Forbid marking the user properties or group policy, "Store password using reversible encryption." This reversible encryption is always a bad idea.
- Examine the authentication process of other CUI processes to ensure they meet the requirement.

Identification & Authentication

IA.L2-3.5.11

Obscure Feedback

Obscure feedback of authentication information.

Impact

Figuring out a user's password is the easiest way for an unauthorized user to access a system. If your system is configured such that a user's password is visible on the screen as they type it, it is simple for somebody behind the user to see the password used to log in.

Official Interpretation*

Authentication information includes passwords. When users enter a password, the system displays a symbol, such as an asterisk, to obscure feedback preventing others from seeing the actual characters. Feedback is obscured based on a defined policy (e.g., smaller devices may briefly show characters before obscuring).

(CMMC Assessment Guide, Level 2, Copyright 2020, 2021 Carnegie Mellon University and The Johns Hopkins University Applied Physics Laboratory LLC and/or CMMC Assessment Guide, Level 2, Version 2.11 - DRAFT, November 2023)

Assessment Focus

Also known as Assessment Objectives, these are the checklist items that an assessor will seek to verify. Each one must be addressed in your implementation and documentation:

1. authentication information is obscured during the authentication process.

(CMMC Assessment Guide, Level 2, Copyright 2020, 2021 Carnegie Mellon University and The Johns Hopkins University Applied Physics Laboratory LLC and/or CMMC Assessment Guide, Level 2, Version 2.11 - DRAFT, November 2023)

Implementation

Windows will inherently hide a user's password. No further effort is required to assure conformance to this requirement. However, if there is concern that some over-zealous assessor will want to see action, it is possible to use Group Policy to disable the button that allows the password to be revealed. That control is located at Computer Configuration-> Administrative Templates-> Windows Components -> Credential User Interface -> Do not display the password reveal button.

Confirm that any other CUI-related applications hide their passwords.

Assessment Stats

- Assessment Points: 1
- Assessment POAM Eligible: Yes

Keys

- No action is required. Windows does this natively.
- Configuration - Optionally, the password reveal button can be disabled.
- Confirm other applications hide the password.

IR.L2-3.6.1

Incident Handling

Establish an operational incident-handling capability for organizational systems that includes preparation, detection, analysis, containment, recovery, and user response activities.

Impact

Lucy is a one-person IT department at a small company. She does it all. One spring Tuesday morning, Lucy checks her email on her phone as she brushes her teeth and finds that her inbox is full of alerts from her antivirus system, the event log analyzer, and freaked-out night-shift users. In the middle of the night, everything went down the tubes. She realizes she has a major security incident within minutes of opening her email. She has no idea what to do. She always figured they were a small company and generally safe. Lucy's stress level just shot through the roof. Although she recognizes this is serious, she wishes she had a better idea of how she should handle this situation.

Official Interpretation*

Incident handling capabilities prepare your organization to respond to incidents and may:

- identify people inside and outside your organization you may need to contact during an incident;
- establish a way to report incidents, such as an email address or a phone number;
- establish a system for tracking incidents; and
- determine a place and a way to store evidence of an incident.

Software and hardware may be required to analyze incidents when they occur. Incident prevention activities are also part of an incident-handling capability. The incident-handling team provides input for such things as risk assessments and training.

OSAs detect incidents using different indicators. Indicators may include:

- alerts from sensors or antivirus software;
- a filename that looks unusual; and
- log entries that raise concern.

After detecting an incident, an incident response team performs analysis. This requires some knowledge of normal network operations. The incident should be documented including all the log entries associated with the incident.

Containment of the incident is a critical step to stop the damage the incident is causing to your network. Containment activities should be based on previously defined organizational priorities and assessment of risk.

Recovery activities restore systems to pre-incident functionality and address its underlying causes. Organizations should use recovery activities as a means of improving their overall resilience to future attacks.

(CMMC Assessment Guide, Level 2, Copyright 2020, 2021 Carnegie Mellon University and The Johns Hopkins University Applied Physics Laboratory LLC and/or CMMC Assessment Guide, Level 2, Version 2.11 - DRAFT, November 2023)

Assessment Focus

Also known as Assessment Objectives, these are the checklist items that an assessor will seek to verify. Each one must be addressed in your implementation and documentation:

1. an operational incident-handling capability is established;
2. the operational incident-handling capability includes preparation;
3. the operational incident-handling capability includes detection;
4. the operational incident-handling capability includes analysis;
5. the operational incident-handling capability includes containment;
6. the operational incident-handling capability includes recovery; and
7. the operational incident-handling capability includes user response activities.

(CMMC Assessment Guide, Level 2, Copyright 2020, 2021 Carnegie Mellon University and The Johns Hopkins University Applied Physics Laboratory LLC and/or CMMC Assessment Guide, Level 2, Version 2.11 - DRAFT, November 2023)

Implementation

You must establish incident response capabilities that include all 6 of the following areas. For the sake of your organization's systems, it is important to figure these procedures out before the crisis occurs.

It should be noted that CISA offers free incident response training for government contractors.

Preparation

This is an important step. It has inherent challenges because you cannot prepare for all possibilities. Your primary goal is to create preparations for the elements that you know you will need for any cyber incident. Beyond that, you will want to prepare for the most common attacks.

It should be noted that your Incident Response documentation should be available in a form that does not require access to your system computers, just in case your systems are unavailable. So, putting your incident response documents on paper or into a phone, tablet, or other isolated computing device may make them available when other systems are not.

One of the key elements here is a listing of who needs to be informed in the event of an incident. This contact listing may include company management or board members. In addition, authorities may need to be notified, including local police, the FBI, or the Department of Defense. This aspect of incident response preparation is covered in more detail in IR.L2-3.6.2.

Your preparation documents should address the three aspects of cybersecurity: confidentiality, integrity, and access. The confidentiality element refers to protecting against the loss of information that should be secret. The need for data integrity is the prevention of alteration of data. The final area is the need to retain access to your data. Organizations have different levels of risk in these different areas.

Detection

Cyber incidents can take many different forms. In most cases, the incident's perpetrators seek to avoid detection. This can make detection challenging. You will want to list out your tools of detection. This might include your employees, antivirus, EDR/XDR, or log-analysis systems.

Analysis

For the small organization, this is likely to look very similar to your detection list but with a little more detail about the information provided by the various tools to help you understand what you are dealing with.

Containment

Your incident response plans need to consider how you can isolate an incident. If you find a couple of computers have been encrypted with ransomware, what steps can you take to prevent the malware from spreading throughout the network? These containment steps may include disconnecting Ethernet cables, powering down network switches, or using some software approaches to isolate computers. This planning is crucial because you have options already thought through.

Remember that inconveniencing your users is not nearly as bad as a major cyber incident. Just as a doctor might amputate a limb to keep the patient from dying, you might find yourself having to take some drastic measures to protect the organization. It is critically important that your management understand the hard decisions that must be made very quickly in the event of an incident. It is helpful if management has seen and signed off on your incident response plan. They might be disturbed about a business interruption, but they can't be too upset if it follows the approved plan. Correspondingly, your management should not believe that the steps they take and the money they spend on cybersecurity can ever provide 100% protection.

Recovery

In most cases of modern cyber attacks, recovery will require drastic measures like scrubbing the systems, reinstating the BIOS, the OS, and applications, and then recovering the data from backups. It is common for attackers to install many different tools on a single computer. If the cleanup is incomplete, the attack may resume when the systems return online.

User Response

This planning requirement refers to the roles and responsibilities of various employees concerning incident response. Regular users may be responsible for watching for evidence of issues and knowing who should be informed when they experience these signs. Others may be responsible for performing notifications across a clear channel (like text messaging or a cloud-based system like Slack). Specific individuals might be handling different aspects of the incident response. All of these roles and responsibilities should be defined. In addition, alternate individuals should be defined in case the primary person is unavailable.

It should go without saying that this list should be kept current. I cannot imagine a CMMC assessor would be impressed if critical roles were assigned to someone the organization no longer employed there.

For organizations that need to develop an Incident Response Plan for the first time, you can find some basic templates on the Internet (see below for a link to templates). None of these will allow you to put your name at the top and expect it to pass a CMMC assessment. This document must contain organization-specific information.

To make this document have value in the event of an actual incident, it will be necessary to involve many company stakeholders in the planning phase to understand their needs and expectations relative to an incident. Different individuals may focus on legal aspects, data confidentiality, cost, or continuity. Walking company management through incident scenarios can be a win-win proposition.

HANDY LINK

Here is a link to several incident handling templates: https://tinyurl.com/CMMC4SMB-610

Assessment Stats

- Assessment Points: 5
- Assessment POAM Eligible: No

Keys

Procedure – You must create a written procedure that includes details concerning preparation, detection, analysis, containment, recovery, and user response activities for a cyber incident. This must be specific to your organization.

Incident Response

IR.L2-3.6.2

Incident Reporting

Track, document, and report incidents to designated officials and/or authorities both internal and external to the organization.

Impact

Antonio was sweating this new attack on the company network. His efforts to contain and eradicate the scourge were unsuccessful. Despite his optimism that the resolution was right around the corner, new problems were popping up faster than his team could address them. Although he didn't want to admit it, the attack was completely out of control. Although Antonio and his team had been wrestling with this incident for three days, he had never informed management of the challenge that the company was undergoing. He kept hoping he could be successful and simply report the issue in the context of an effective defense.

When the CEO's computer was incapacitated, the entire story came out. Management was mighty ticked off. They were convinced that Antonio was so proud that he wasn't allowing the company management to be involved in making essential decisions. They likened his performance during this crisis to somebody who keeps trying to put out a fire themselves and refusing to call the fire department. They made up their mind that Antonio needed to be replaced as soon as possible, assuming the company was able to survive.

Official Interpretation*

Incident handling is the actions the organization takes to prevent or contain the impact of an incident to the organization while it is occurring or shortly after it has occurred. The majority of the process consists of incident identification, containment, eradication, and recovery. During this process, it is essential to track the work processes required in order to effectively respond. Designate a central hub to serve as the point to coordinate, communicate, and track activities. The hub should receive and document information from system administrators, incident handlers, and others involved throughout the process. As the incident process moves toward eradication, executives, affected business units, and any required external stakeholders should be kept aware of the incident in order to make decisions affecting the business. Report to designated authorities, taking into account applicable laws, directives, regulations, and other guidance. Specify staff responsible for communicating about the incident to internal and external stakeholders.

(CMMC Assessment Guide, Level 2, Copyright 2020, 2021 Carnegie Mellon University and The Johns Hopkins University Applied Physics Laboratory LLC and/or CMMC Assessment Guide, Level 2, Version 2.11 - DRAFT, November 2023)

Assessment Focus

Also known as Assessment Objectives, these are the checklist items that an assessor will seek to verify. Each one must be addressed in your implementation and documentation:

1. incidents are tracked;
2. incidents are documented;
3. authorities to whom incidents are to be reported are identified;
4. organizational officials to whom incidents are to be reported are identified;
5. identified authorities are notified of incidents; and
6. identified organizational officials are notified of incidents.

(CMMC Assessment Guide, Level 2, Copyright 2020, 2021 Carnegie Mellon University and The Johns Hopkins University Applied Physics Laboratory LLC and/or CMMC Assessment Guide, Level 2, Version 2.11 - DRAFT, November 2023)

Implementation

This requirement is much more challenging in a small organization. When you have just one or two people responsible for incident response, it is much harder for them to stop fighting the incident for long enough to track, document, and report the ongoing and changing status of the incident. However, these steps are also essential responses.

It would be easy to believe that you need special software to comply with this requirement's tracking, documenting, and reporting aspects. However, this doesn't have to be anything special. The tracking and reporting can be accomplished with paper or Office. The reporting will potentially be conducted by some mode external to your network systems, like a cell phone.

To meet the tracking requirements, you will want some method of periodically recording what has been seen, what you have learned, what actions have been taken, and the progress made. To meet the need for documenting, you might have a specific repository for all the documentation elements about the incident. The tracking data becomes part of the documentation. Your incident response plan should define the details of how this tracking and documenting will be conducted. Although nothing requires a moment-by-moment accounting of what has occurred, there must be some documentation of the incident. You should remember that your standard network resources may not be available during the mitigation of an attack.

Determine who is to notify whom, how, and under what circumstances. If a user observes something suspicious, they would likely contact an internal entity that would perform a preliminary investigation. Then, that person would need to know who to inform if they find evidence of an incident. The incident continues escalating until it is discounted or reported to external bodies. The process must be planned (written) and tracked.

External authorities to notify include your local police department. It might include the FBI, CISA, or the DoD. Many states have reporting requirements or offices that can provide active assistance.

HANDY LINK

State cyberincident reporting requirements can be found here:
https://tinyurl.com/CMMC4SMB-799

DFARS 252.204-7012 contains explicit reporting requirements associated with a security incident. Your policy should include this need for any company where the DFARS is called out in contracts. If you have this requirement, you should look closely at it because it requires applying for a security key, which takes time and cannot be accomplished on the fly.

The plan and tracking can be combined into a checklist containing full contact info for each entity that needs to be informed, including multiple contact methods. Only having an email address does no good if the email system has failed.

If you have DFARS 252.204-7012 on contracts, you must obtain a Medium Assurance Certificate. Without this, you cannot perform your legally required reporting to https://dibnet.dod.mil in the event of a security incident! This must be done in preparation.

Assessment Stats

- Assessment Points: 5
- Assessment POAM Eligible: No

Keys

- Procedure – Your process and tools for Tracking and Documentation should be defined. Also, develop a plan that defines who should be contacted and at what point they should be informed. This should include both internal and external entities.
- Records – If you have experienced any incidents, then you should have records of tracking reporting and documentation to show to CMMC assessors.

IR.L2-3.6.3

Incident Response Testing

Test the organizational incident response capability.

Impact

When Brad started his new job, he inherited a notebook labeled "Incident Response Plan." Brad had never opened that book because he never needed it. But, on this particular day, he found himself in a serious security incident. With his heart pounding and hands shaking, he opened the notebook, hoping the solution to his stress would be found within those pages. However, what he found was a series of web pages that had been printed out. This "plan" was essentially useless for his current situation. It contributed nothing to help him deal with the crisis.

Official Interpretation*

Testing incident response capability validates existing plans and highlights potential deficiencies. The test should address questions such as what happens during an incident; who is responsible for incident management; what tasks are assigned within the IT organization; what support is needed from legal, public affairs, or other business components; how resources are added if needed during the incident; and how law enforcement is involved. Any negative impacts to the normal day-to-day operations when responding to an incident should also be identified and documented.

(CMMC Assessment Guide, Level 2, Copyright 2020, 2021 Carnegie Mellon University and The Johns Hopkins University Applied Physics Laboratory LLC and/or CMMC Assessment Guide, Level 2, Version 2.11 - DRAFT, November 2023)

Assessment Focus

Also known as Assessment Objectives, these are the checklist items that an assessor will seek to verify. Each one must be addressed in your implementation and documentation:

1. the incident response capability is tested.

(CMMC Assessment Guide, Level 2, Copyright 2020, 2021 Carnegie Mellon University and The Johns Hopkins University Applied Physics Laboratory LLC and/or CMMC Assessment Guide, Level 2, Version 2.11 - DRAFT, November 2023)

Implementation

It is not adequate to simply pull an incident response plan off the Internet because your system must be tested to ensure that it works for your organization. Incident response testing can take many different forms. Some acceptable methods include checklists, walk-throughs, tabletop exercises, and more involved simulations. Whatever testing methods are utilized, the testing and the corresponding results should be documented.

This testing aims to determine if the incident response plan is current, applicable to the organization's needs, and contains all the necessary information. A simple tabletop exercise might reveal that people with Incident Response responsibilities haven't even read the Incident Response Plan!

This requirement is vague on exactly how involved the process should be. I suggest that you approach it as an opportunity. If you use this requirement as an excuse to walk your management through the organization's risks, you have much to gain. While management may be acutely aware of many business risks, they may be oblivious to cybersecurity risks. Management that is blind to cyber risks will not be very sympathetic or supportive in the event of an incident.

Effective Incident Response Plan testing will generally generate changes that need to be made. These changes may be due to personnel changes, business changes, security incidents, and changes to the threat landscape. The necessary changes to your Incident Response Plan should be identified in your testing documentation.

The generally accepted standard is that these tests of the Incident Response Plans would occur at least annually. Annual testing is probably the most common frequency.

HANDY LINK

Guidance for performing a tabletop Incident Response Plan test:
https://tinyurl.com/CMMC4SMB-734

Assessment Stats

- Assessment Points: 1
- Assessment POAM Eligible: Yes

Keys

- Procedure – Your Incident Response Plan must include how and when periodic tests of the incident response plan will be conducted. The plan should include who will be involved, the records that will be generated, and what will be done with the results.
- Records – Records of the conduct of this testing should be available as evidence that the procedure is being followed.

Maintenance

MA.L2-3.7.1

Perform Maintenance

Perform maintenance on organizational systems.

Impact

Troy might have been a good Emergency Room employee because he thrives on the adrenaline of each day's crises. He is responsible for keeping his employer's computer network running. He accomplishes this by responding to every cry for help. Lately, there have been a lot of issues related to the workstation computers behaving very strangely. He often had to nuke a system to get it back into running condition. But Troy didn't have time to recognize the trends; he was too busy putting out fires. Troy isn't a planning kind of guy. Instead, his focus was on a single issue at a time. His philosophy is to deal with one thing at a time, and then move on to the next. Troy has never taken broad steps to protect his network from hackers, nor was he able to recognize that his network has become full of malware.

Official Interpretation*

One common form of computer security maintenance is regular patching of discovered vulnerabilities in software and operating systems, though there are others that require attention.

- System maintenance includes:
- corrective maintenance (e.g., repairing problems with the technology);
- preventative maintenance (e.g., updates to prevent potential problems);
- adaptive maintenance (e.g., changes to the operative environment); and
- perfective maintenance (e.g., improve operations).

(CMMC Assessment Guide, Level 2, Copyright 2020, 2021 Carnegie Mellon University and The Johns Hopkins University Applied Physics Laboratory LLC and/or CMMC Assessment Guide, Level 2, Version 2.11 - DRAFT, November 2023)

Assessment Focus

Also known as Assessment Objectives, these are the checklist items that an assessor will seek to verify. Each one must be addressed in your implementation and documentation:

1. system maintenance is performed.

(CMMC Assessment Guide, Level 2, Copyright 2020, 2021 Carnegie Mellon University and The Johns Hopkins University Applied Physics Laboratory LLC and/or CMMC Assessment Guide, Level 2, Version 2.11 - DRAFT, November 2023)

Implementation

Maintenance is essential to a high-functioning system. That maintenance should combine those needs that scream for attention and those that make things better over the long haul. This particular requirement is a simple "Do maintenance" statement. As long as maintenance is done, this requirement is being met. However, for example, if the same proverbial fire needs to be put out over and over, then that could be evidence that preventive maintenance is lacking.

Records become essential when demonstrating to an assessor that a particular activity is happening. The maintenance on your car is according to a schedule. Similarly, some network maintenance tasks could also be placed on a schedule, so if a schedule and records of performed maintenance corresponded to the schedule, that provides excellent evidence of conformance.

Some maintenance tasks may be scripted to run automatically. Just like operations performed manually, these are also maintenance, and you should use them as evidence of conformance to this requirement. So, don't forget to take credit for the automatic maintenance tasks.

Some improvement projects could come under the umbrella of "perfective maintenance." These projects should be tracked and documented in your POAM system.

The manual maintenance records may be as simple as a paper periodic (monthly or quarterly) checklist where the person performing the work would signify the performance with a date and initials.

Start small. Improve your maintenance program over time. The requirement does not demand all-encompassing perfection.

Assessment Stats

- Assessment Points: 3
- Assessment POAM Eligible: No

Keys

- Documentation – You should create a maintenance plan so an assessor can see that maintenance is being performed in accordance with a plan.
- Records – Have records of performed maintenance available for CMMC Assessors to review.

Maintenance

MA.L2-3.7.2

System Maintenance Control

Provide controls on the tools, techniques, mechanisms, and personnel used to conduct system maintenance.

Impact

Andrew wanted to do the best possible job of supporting his users and protecting his network. One of the ways he protected his network was by performing regular vulnerability scans. The tool he uses for this is Kali Linux. He doesn't know it, but a hacker had used phishing to gain a foothold in his network. As the hacker moved laterally through the network, he came across the Kali Linux machine, which was inadequately controlled. For hacking purposes, this machine is a treasure trove of tools and precious data about how to best attack the rest of the network. Protecting the network was the reason this machine existed, but it is being used as a springboard to propel the hacking efforts.

Official Interpretation*

Tools used to perform maintenance must remain secure so they do not introduce viruses or other malware into your system. Controlling your maintenance techniques prevents intentional or unintentional harm to your network and systems. Additionally, the personnel responsible for maintenance activities should be supervised considering their elevated privilege on company assets.

(CMMC Assessment Guide, Level 2, Copyright 2020, 2021 Carnegie Mellon University and The Johns Hopkins University Applied Physics Laboratory LLC and/or CMMC Assessment Guide, Level 2, Version 2.11 - DRAFT, November 2023)

Assessment Focus

Also known as Assessment Objectives, these are the checklist items that an assessor will seek to verify. Each one must be addressed in your implementation and documentation:

1. tools used to conduct system maintenance are controlled;
2. techniques used to conduct system maintenance are controlled;
3. mechanisms used to conduct system maintenance are controlled; and

4. personnel used to conduct system maintenance are controlled.

(CMMC Assessment Guide, Level 2, Copyright 2020, 2021 Carnegie Mellon University and The Johns Hopkins University Applied Physics Laboratory LLC and/or CMMC Assessment Guide, Level 2, Version 2.11 - DRAFT, November 2023)

Implementation

While maintenance is essential for the smooth running of your systems, it also creates some risks. Many tools and techniques used to perform maintenance can also be used by hackers. Maintenance activities are often performed using high levels of privileges, so any error (intentional or not) can cause significant damage.

Each of the following areas should be addressed explicitly in your documentation:

Tools

This is likely the most significant area of this requirement. The tools used for maintenance should not be "lying around" for anybody to use or abuse. Remember that "control" of these tools does not necessarily mean making it completely impossible for any user ever to access them; you merely need to have some elements of control that you can point to. Technically, having a folder on a share labeled "FOR IT MAINTENANCE ONLY" is a form of control (unadvisable, but the contents are technically controlled).

Many of the same tools that are used to maintain the network can also be used for nefarious purposes. While Kali Linux, for example, might be a great suite of tools for analyzing the security of your information systems, if it resides on your network, it could potentially be accessed and used by a hacker to compromise the network it is supposed to protect.

Infrequently used tools should not reside on the network. They should only be connected as necessary. This may mean that tools are used from a USB key used as needed or a VM that is only loaded for official purposes. A retired computer may be repurposed as a network maintenance machine, and it lives in a storage closet, unplugged and disconnected, when not in use.

Certain tools accessible in the default configuration of Windows workstations can be abused. The Windows command line provides access to "ping" and "ipconfig," which are useful for maintenance but most users do not need. Access to the command line can be disabled in Group Policy at User Configuration → Administrative Templates → System.

In addition, your tools need to be patched appropriately to ensure they are not introducing unnecessary problems into the system. Care should be taken in downloading tools to ensure that maliciously tampered copies are not introduced to the system. Remember, these tools generally operate with higher permissions and risk causing significant damage.

Document the way your maintenance tools are controlled.

Techniques

The documentation associated with system maintenance can be helpful to an individual with malicious intent. Procedures, instructions, notes, and other documentation should be given some level of control.

Document the controls that are applied to your maintenance techniques.

Mechanisms

When your maintenance processes use automated scripts and scheduled jobs, those scripts can inadvertently be left accessible for use or abuse by others. A malicious user could modify a script that runs nightly so it reinstalls malware that might otherwise be subject to removal by IT personnel.

It is best if scripts are located in controlled folders and digitally signed so changes cannot be made.

Document the controls to be applied to your maintenance mechanisms.

Personnel

The maintenance personnel have significant power to do good or do evil. There should be control over who performs these duties. In performing certain high-risk activities, having a second person present may be appropriate to help ensure that errors are not made.

Document the controls applied to the personnel that are authorized to perform maintenance.

Assessment Stats

- Assessment Points: 5
- Assessment POAM Eligible: No

Keys

- Documentation -- Outline the controls applied to maintenance tools, techniques, mechanisms, and personnel. Consider performing audits to verify that the controls remain in place.

Maintenance

MA.L2-3.7.3

Equipment Sanitization

Ensure equipment removed for off-site maintenance is sanitized of any CUI.

Impact

Tom is a computer equipment repair technician by day and a thief by night. Today, a printer from the engineering department of a local business had come in for repairs. As usual, nobody at the company considered security when they sent this device out. Tom was assigned to work on this printer. Tom was delighted because he loved these high-tech printers since they fed his after-hours ambition. He extracted images of all of the recently printed documents onto his personal USB drive. After work, he reviewed the documents to see what he had obtained. While he saw most of the documents as useless junk, a few items could be turned into some cash. Tom loved treasure hunting through the files on computers, printers, and network equipment. Nobody ever suspected anything.

Official Interpretation*

Sanitization is a process that makes access to data infeasible on media such as a hard drive. The process may overwrite the entire media with a fixed pattern such as binary zeros. In addition to clearing the data an organization could purge (e.g., degaussing, secure erasing, or disassembling) the data, or even destroy the media (e.g., incinerating, shredding, or pulverizing). Performing one of these activities ensures that the data is extremely hard to recover, thus ensuring its confidentiality.

For additional guidance on which specific sanitization actions should be taken on any specific type of media, review the description of the Purge actions given in NIST SP 800-88 Revision 1 – Guidelines for Media Sanitization.

(CMMC Assessment Guide, Level 2, Copyright 2020, 2021 Carnegie Mellon University and The Johns Hopkins University Applied Physics Laboratory LLC and/or CMMC Assessment Guide, Level 2, Version 2.11 - DRAFT, November 2023)

Assessment Focus

Also known as Assessment Objectives, these are the checklist items that an assessor will seek to verify. Each one must be addressed in your implementation and documentation:

1. equipment to be removed from organizational spaces for off-site maintenance is sanitized of any CUI.

(CMMC Assessment Guide, Level 2, Copyright 2020, 2021 Carnegie Mellon University and The Johns Hopkins University Applied Physics Laboratory LLC and/or CMMC Assessment Guide, Level 2, Version 2.11 - DRAFT, November 2023)

Implementation

This requires developing and implementing a policy that addresses any data processing equipment that exits your facility for repair or maintenance. An evaluation must be performed to determine if any CUI is present, then a course of action should be prescribed to outline the actions that will be taken to remove all traces of the CUI. Ensuring that maintenance performed does not interfere with any security controls is important.

See MP.L1-3.8.3 for approved methods of equipment sanitization.

Assessment Stats

- Assessment Points: 1
- Assessment POAM Eligible: Yes

Keys

- Documentation – Develop a procedure to include information about the circumstances that would necessitate media sanitization, the methods and tools to be used, who would be responsible, and what records would be created when the actions are performed.

Maintenance

MA.L2-3.7.4

Media Inspection

Check media containing diagnostic and test programs for malicious code before the media are used in organizational systems.

Impact

Charity needed to perform some network analysis. She shopped for a tool but was appalled at the price asked, considering her plans for it. After searching around, she found a source for the software she wanted at a significantly reduced price. She later learned that she got both a copy of the software she wanted plus a load of malware. The software had been modified to install the malware as it installed the intended program. She had many challenges getting everything back to normal after that simple installation.

Official Interpretation*

As part of troubleshooting, a vendor may provide a diagnostic application to install on a system. As this is executable code, there is a chance that the file is corrupt or infected with malicious code. Implement procedures to scan any files prior to installation. The same level of scrutiny must be made as with any file a staff member may download.

This requirement, MA.L2-3.7.4, extends both SI.L2-3.14.2 and SI.L2-3.14.4. SI.L2-3.14.2 and SI.L2-3.14.4 require the implementation and updating of mechanisms to protect systems from malicious code, and MA.L2-3.7.4 extends this requirement to diagnostic and testing tools.

(CMMC Assessment Guide, Level 2, Copyright 2020, 2021 Carnegie Mellon University and The Johns Hopkins University Applied Physics Laboratory LLC and/or CMMC Assessment Guide, Level 2, Version 2.11 - DRAFT, November 2023)

Assessment Focus

Also known as Assessment Objectives, these are the checklist items that an assessor will seek to verify. Each one must be addressed in your implementation and documentation:

1. media containing diagnostic and test programs are checked for malicious code before being used in organizational systems that process, store, or transmit CUI.

(CMMC Assessment Guide, Level 2, Copyright 2020, 2021 Carnegie Mellon University and The Johns Hopkins University Applied Physics Laboratory LLC and/or CMMC Assessment Guide, Level 2, Version 2.11 - DRAFT, November 2023)

Implementation

At times, technical people can be the most sloppy from a security standpoint. It is possible that, in performing maintenance and diagnostics, the technician says, "Oh, I know just the tool," then downloads and runs something under a high-privilege account.

Anything downloaded might contain malware. Careful attention should be taken to the source of the executable, but beyond that, even the most reputable site can be hacked. Most anti-malware programs can scan removable media or a specific file. There should be a policy in place that requires a malware scan before using any downloaded maintenance and diagnostic tools before they are used.

Assessment Stats

- Assessment Points: 3
- Assessment POAM Eligible: No

Keys

- Policy – A policy should require all downloaded diagnostic and test programs to be scanned for malware before use. The policy should define the circumstances that require the scanning and the scanning tools to be used.

MA.L2-3.7.5

Nonlocal Maintenance

Require multifactor authentication to establish nonlocal maintenance sessions via external network connections and terminate such connections when nonlocal maintenance is complete.

Impact

Devon has contracted much of the maintenance burden for his network. For years, this activity has been getting done like clockwork by Todd, his contractor. Recently, Todd went through an ugly divorce. Without Todd's knowledge, his ex had taken copies of all the logon credentials for Todd's various client companies. Using these high-level remote-access credentials, she could remote into Devon's company, and others of Todd's clients, to download files and sometimes even empty bank accounts. However, a few client companies required multi-factor authentication before establishing remote access, and she could not access those networks with the improperly acquired credentials.

Official Interpretation*

Nonlocal maintenance activities must use multifactor authentication. Multifactor authentication requires at least two factors, such as:

- something you know (e.g., password, personal identification number [PIN]);
- something you have (e.g., cryptographic identification device, token); or
- something you are (e.g., biometric fingerprint or facial scan).

Requiring two or more factors to prove your identity increases the security of the connection. Nonlocal maintenance activities are activities conducted from external network connections such as over the internet. After nonlocal maintenance activities are complete, shut down the external network connection.

This requirement, MA.L2-3.7.5 specifies the addition of multifactor authentication for remote maintenance sessions and complements five other requirements dealing with remote access (AC.L2-3.1.12, AC.L2-3.1.14, AC.L2-3.1.13, AC.L2-3.1.15, and IA.L2-3.5.3):

- AC.L2-3.1.12 requires the control of remote access sessions.

- AC.L2-3.1.14 limits remote access to specific access control points.
- AC.L2-3.1.13 requires the use of cryptographic mechanisms when enabling remote sessions.
- AC.L2-3.1.15 requires authorization for privileged commands executed during a remote session.
- Finally, IA.L2-3.5.3 requires multifactor authentication for network access to non-privileged accounts.

Assessment Focus

Also known as Assessment Objectives, these are the checklist items that an assessor will seek to verify. Each one must be addressed in your implementation and documentation:

1. multifactor authentication is used to establish nonlocal maintenance sessions via external network connections; and
2. nonlocal maintenance sessions established via external network connections are terminated when nonlocal maintenance is complete.

Implementation

Note: This requirement is one of 6 regarding remote access. These requirements should all be considered together when designing controls. The remote-access-related controls are:

AC.L2-3.1.12	control of remote access	AC.L2-3.1.15	privileged commands on remote sessions
AC.L2-3.1.14	remote access control points	IA.L2-3.5.3	multifactor authentication
AC.L2-3.1.13	cryptography for remote sessions	MA.L2-3.7.5	MFA for remote maintenance sessions

Using outside IT services is a common situation for an SMB that doesn't have a large IT staff. Also, in a multiple-location organization, remote access provides many advantages. However, it must be remembered that these sessions poke a big hole through many layers of your security structure. There are many ways to accomplish these remote sessions, but security has to be a prime consideration in the selection of a tool for remote access.

When vetting a remote access tool for remote maintenance, it is essential that you only permit the use of secure tools. A significant part of security on any remote access is multifactor authentication. When high-privilege system maintenance activities are performed using remote access, security becomes even more critical. Multifactor authentication can help ensure that designated users only perform these high-risk operations.

In addition to requiring MFA, this requirement says that connections must be terminated when the maintenance work is complete. This disconnection may be built into the remote access software or accomplished through a policy that requires logging off the remote system before disconnecting.

Assessment Stats

- Assessment Points: 5
- Assessment POAM Eligible: No

Keys

- Procedure – Document the process used for remote maintenance operations, clearly defining the remote access tools and assuring that all the access enforces multifactor authentication.
- Policy -- Any remote access user for maintenance purposes must understand that the connection must be terminated when the maintenance work is finished.

MA.L2-3.7.6

Maintenance Personnel

Supervise the maintenance activities of maintenance personnel without required access authorization.

Impact

Tabitha had been struggling with a group policy object that had not been doing what she intended. She called in a consultant to help her get this up and running. She was watching the guy work, hoping to learn as she watched, but she had to leave for a meeting before he was finished. After she was gone, the consultant pulled out a USB drive and loaded a bit of code (while he was logged in as network administrator) to assist him in accessing materials remotely. Whether his intentions were good, or not, setting up this remote access without permission was unethical and potentially illegal.

Official Interpretation*

Individuals without proper permissions must be supervised while conducting maintenance on organizational machines. Consider creating temporary accounts with short-term expiration periods rather than regular user accounts. Additionally, limit the permissions and access these accounts have to the most restrictive settings possible.

(CMMC Assessment Guide, Level 2, Copyright 2020, 2021 Carnegie Mellon University and The Johns Hopkins University Applied Physics Laboratory LLC and/or CMMC Assessment Guide, Level 2, Version 2.11 - DRAFT, November 2023)

Assessment Focus

Also known as Assessment Objectives, these are the checklist items that an assessor will seek to verify. Each one must be addressed in your implementation and documentation:

1. maintenance personnel without required access authorization are supervised during maintenance activities.

(CMMC Assessment Guide, Level 2, Copyright 2020, 2021 Carnegie Mellon University and The Johns Hopkins University Applied Physics Laboratory LLC and/or CMMC Assessment Guide, Level 2, Version 2.11 - DRAFT, November 2023)

Implementation

This supervision requirement only applies to "maintenance personnel without required access authorization." As long as maintenance is being performed by persons granted access permission in Active Directory, whether those are employees of your organization or outside consultants, this requirement is not applicable.

However, circumstances can change in unpredictable ways. While it would be easy to say that maintenance will only be performed by individuals with the required authorization, that may not always be true. Unforeseen circumstances may force you to allow a previously unauthorized person to perform some maintenance tasks (like a server manufacturer's service technician).

So, the best course is to develop a policy that requires supervision for maintenance performed by someone different than your typical staff. This circumstance may not arise very often, but having the policy will provide coverage when it does come up.

Assessment Stats

- Assessment Points: 1
- Assessment POAM Eligible: Yes

Keys

- Policy – The policy should require that whenever somebody other than your normally authorized maintenance personnel performs system maintenance tasks, that work should be supervised by one of your employees.
- Documentation – It would be helpful if there were some clear definitions of who possesses the "required access authorization" for performing system maintenance. This might be members of a specific AD group.

Media Protection

MP.L2-3.8.1

Media Protection

Protect (i.e., physically control and securely store) system media containing CUI, both paper and digital.

Impact

At Wellington Defense, they were never too worried about security. After all, they are a tiny company. They keep their records in the office. Only four people work there, so anybody different stands out like a sore thumb. They had been working in this same casual way for years without any problems…until last weekend. Last Saturday, Chelsey, who does their accounting, came in to close the month. That morning, Chelsey's sister unexpectedly dropped off Chelsey's 15-year-old nephew. Chelsey wasn't happy since she knew she had to go into the office. Chelsey decided that her nephew would have to tag along. After all, he had his phone for entertainment, so he should be fine. This plan might not have been a problem, but the nephew had an ongoing curiosity about the defense products made by Wellington. After Chelsey got busy, the nephew started opening file drawers to see what he could find. He quickly found a drawer of product drawings. While he couldn't make sense of the drawings, he knew they looked cool and could see their basic form. He took some pictures and posted them on Instagram without realizing there were issues with his actions. Since the boy's mom monitors her son's Instagram, she sees the part drawings come through. She forwarded them back to Chelsey. Wellington Defense imagined terrifying scenarios of DoD security personnel showing up on their doorstep. This was the point at which Wellington Defense began to get more serious about controlling their data on all forms of media.

Official Interpretation*

CUI can be contained on two types of physical media:

- hardcopy (e.g., CD drives, USB drives, magnetic tape); and
- digital devices (e.g., CD drives, USB drives, video).

You should store physical media containing CUI in a secure location. This location should be accessible only to those people with the proper permissions. All who access CUI should follow the process for checking it out and returning it.

(CMMC Assessment Guide, Level 2, Copyright 2020, 2021 Carnegie Mellon University and The Johns Hopkins University Applied Physics Laboratory LLC and/or CMMC Assessment Guide, Level 2, Version 2.11 - DRAFT, November 2023)

Assessment Focus

Also known as Assessment Objectives, these are the checklist items that an assessor will seek to verify. Each one must be addressed in your implementation and documentation:

1. paper media containing CUI is physically controlled;
2. digital media containing CUI is physically controlled;
3. paper media containing CUI is securely stored; and
4. digital media containing CUI is securely stored.

(CMMC Assessment Guide, Level 2, Copyright 2020, 2021 Carnegie Mellon University and The Johns Hopkins University Applied Physics Laboratory LLC and/or CMMC Assessment Guide, Level 2, Version 2.11 - DRAFT, November 2023)

Implementation

The requirements, MP.L2-3.8.1, Media Protection, and MP.L2-3.8.2, Media Access, are very similar in scope. While MP.L2-3.8.1 deals with steps to protect the CUI-containing media, MP.L2-3.8.2 is focused on assuring that only authorized individuals can access the CUI-containing media. So, MP.L2-3.8.1 is focused on preventing unauthorized access, while MP.L2-3.8.2 is about the processes for authorized access.

This requirement entails creating controls of access for all media containing CUI. This includes flash drives, removable hard drives, CD/DVD, plus paper and microfilm. Access should be limited to those individuals that are authorized. This policy will look different in every organization. The key to making this policy simple is to minimize the amount of removable (including paper copies) media containing CUI.

In many organizations, paper copies of CUI are used for many things. Much of this is an ingrained habit. Creating a level of control that will satisfy a CMMC assessor will require significant changes to these behaviors. The paper copies offer advantages: notes can be made on them, and they can be easily carried from place to place. So, making the necessary changes may produce pushback.

The goal of media control is to know where all copies are located all the time. The assessment guide says, "Physically controlling system media includes conducting inventories, maintaining accountability for stored media, and ensuring procedures are in place to allow individuals to check out and return media to the media library." Because of these expectations for control, the best thing would be to eliminate the paper copies and media containing CUI altogether, but the staff might riot at the very thought.

An option to consider as an alternative to paper copies would be some large tablets running document-viewing software that allows annotation. This would provide many of the same benefits as paper copies. After an initial adjustment period, many people find using a tablet an acceptable alternative to paper for engineering and inspection purposes. The CUI can be accessed from a secure cloud location. A scheme like this can eliminate the need for any CUI-containing media and render this requirement "not applicable" to your organization. (Having a procedure in place makes sense to prepare for unanticipated future changes.)

HANDY LINK

The author's preferred tool for secure and compliant cloud storage of CUI for the small organization can be found here https://tinyurl.com/CMMC4SMB-938

Many organizations will be unable to eliminate CUI-containing media completely, so it will be necessary to implement a system that fully satisfies this requirement. The two sides of this are "physical controls" and "secure storage" for both digital and paper media. Physical control requires accountability for all CUI-containing media. The secure storage requires that the media be in locked containers when not in active use.

The physical controls aspect will generally be more complex to implement successfully. Having a system that will account for all media at all times will be challenging since it is so easy for individuals to create (or print) new media, hand them off to somebody else, and destroy them. These behaviors must be fully documented to know what media exists and where it is located. Sit down with your people who use the media to hash out a system that will satisfy the requirement.

Secure storage is much easier to satisfy. Nothing in the requirement says that the media needs to be stored in a high-security bank vault. A locked desk drawer or a locking file box will suffice, just so there is some sort of lock between the media and some unauthorized person who might want to pick them up.

Assessment Stats

- Assessment Points: 3
- Assessment POAM Eligible: No

Keys

- Policy – The policy should assign all people who use CUI to take responsibility for doing their part to control and secure media. The policy should describe how both digital and paper media (containing CUI) will be controlled and how they will be securely stored.

Media Protection

MP.L2-3.8.2

Media Access

Limit access to CUI on system media to authorized users.

Impact

Christine needed a USB drive. Her boss was out of the office. She believed there were a few USB drives in his desk. She found one in his pencil drawer and plugged it into her laptop, hoping it was empty. She found that it had a bunch of files on it, including drawings for some of the Defense products they make. As long as she had been working for this company, her boyfriend had been bugging her for details about the products they make, but she was not involved with their products in her job.

She looked around and saw that nobody was paying any attention, so she emailed herself the contents of the USB drive so she could let her boyfriend examine the drawings. After emailing the contents, she returned the USB drive where she found it. She was excited, knowing her boyfriend would love to see what she had obtained.

Official Interpretation*

Limit physical access to CUI to people permitted to access CUI. Use locked or controlled storage areas and limit access to only those allowed to access CUI. Keep track of who accesses physical CUI in an audit log.

(CMMC Assessment Guide, Level 2, Copyright 2020, 2021 Carnegie Mellon University and The Johns Hopkins University Applied Physics Laboratory LLC and/or CMMC Assessment Guide, Level 2, Version 2.11 - DRAFT, November 2023)

Assessment Focus

Also known as Assessment Objectives, these are the checklist items that an assessor will seek to verify. Each one must be addressed in your implementation and documentation:

1. access to CUI on system media is limited to authorized users.

(CMMC Assessment Guide, Level 2, Copyright 2020, 2021 Carnegie Mellon University and The Johns Hopkins University Applied Physics Laboratory LLC and/or CMMC Assessment Guide, Level 2, Version 2.11 - DRAFT, November 2023)

Implementation

The requirements, MP.L2-3.8.1, Media Protection, and MP.L2-3.8.2, Media Access, are very similar in scope. While MP.L2-3.8.1 deals with steps to protect the CUI-containing media, MP.L2-3.8.2 is focused on assuring that only authorized individuals can access the CUI-containing media. So, MP.L2-3.8.1 is focused on preventing unauthorized access, while MP.L2-3.8.2 is about the processes for the authorized accesses.

The key to meeting this requirement is to develop a system through which only authorized users have access to media (including non-digital) containing CUI. Just like with MP.L2-3.8.1, this requirement could essentially go away if you could run your operations avoiding CUI on media (including printing on paper). If the elimination of CUI on media cannot be achieved, then steps must be taken to control the access of that media to authorized users.

This can be as simple as keeping the CUI-containing media in a specific, locked file cabinet except when it is in use by an authorized user. Your procedure should describe how access to the media is limited to authorized people. There must be a way of knowing exactly what media is in the cabinet. If any user has CUI-containing media out of the cabinet, a log or other tool should identify what authorized user has what media items.

Obviously, this log must be maintained current. A CMMC assessor would frown upon the log listing a particular item that isn't there, even if you know that the item was destroyed. So, a log like this might need to be periodically inventoried to minimize possible errors.

Whatever control procedure you implement should be documented in your policy.

Assessment Stats

- Assessment Points: 3
- Assessment POAM Eligible: No

Keys

- Policy – Create a policy for the controlling media that contains CUI so it is only accessible to authorized users. This should include information about how access records will be generated and maintained.

MP.L1-3.8.3

Media Disposal

Sanitize or destroy system media containing CUI before disposal or release for reuse.

Impact

Allen wishes there was a less derogatory-sounding term for how he makes a living. He strongly dislikes the term "Dumpster Diving" because it sounds like he pulls out scraps of days-old food to eat. In truth, his version of dumpster diving is seeking digital media, financial printouts, and passwords. Even after years of doing this, he is astonished by what people throw away. He believes people think that when stuff gets thrown away, it is immediately buried in a landfill. Allen makes a good living off of things people thought were gone entirely.

Official Interpretation*

"Media" refers to a broad range of items that store information, including paper documents, disks, tapes, digital photography, USB drives, CDs, DVDs, and mobile phones. It is important to know what information is on media so that you can handle it properly. If there is CUI, you or someone in your company should either:

- shred or destroy the device before disposal so it cannot be read; or
- clean or purge the information, if you want to reuse the device.

See NIST Special Publication 800-88, Revision 1, Guidelines for Media Sanitization, for more information.

(CMMC Assessment Guide, Level 2, Copyright 2020, 2021 Carnegie Mellon University and The Johns Hopkins University Applied Physics Laboratory LLC and/or CMMC Assessment Guide, Level 2, Version 2.11 - DRAFT, November 2023)

Assessment Focus

Also known as Assessment Objectives, these are the checklist items that an assessor will seek to verify. Each one must be addressed in your implementation and documentation:

1. system media containing CUI is sanitized or destroyed before disposal; and
2. system media containing CUI is sanitized before it is released for reuse.

(CMMC Assessment Guide, Level 2, Copyright 2020, 2021 Carnegie Mellon University and The Johns Hopkins University Applied Physics Laboratory LLC and/or CMMC Assessment Guide, Level 2, Version 2.11 - DRAFT, November 2023)

Implementation

This is best satisfied by creating a procedure that lists specific procedures for use on different media varieties. Physical destruction and recycling methods must be listed for each media type. All methods should render the data completely inaccessible by any method. Don't forget non-digital media, such as paper copies, when considering destruction options.

Deleting files from digital media does not typically remove the data. It just marks the area of the drive as available space. Until something writes over top of that space, the data is still stored there; it just isn't as convenient to access.

Certainly, the less media is used with CUI, then the less this requirement applies. If media containing CUI were eliminated, then this requirement is not applicable. However, even if you had a policy prohibiting CUI on media, under some unforseen future circumstance, someone might put some CUI on media. So, it is advisable to have a procedure in place even if CUI media were prohibited.

The methods listed in NIST Special Publication 800-88 Revision 1 are suited for media containing classified materials. This document is provided as a reference. The methods listed in that document are not required under CMMC. It can be helpful to see the methods they list, but many are not reasonable for CMMC Level 2. Nobody is suggesting that you need to pay to have old hard drives incinerated because they had old government contracts on them.

Here are some sanitization methods to consider:

MEDIA TYPE	REUSE METHOD	DESTROY METHOD
Thumb Drive	EaseUS BitWiper	Crush in vise
Mechanical Hard Drive	DiskWipe or KillDisk	Saw in half
SSD Drive	SSD Manufacturer Secure Erase Tool	Crush in vise
Paper	N/A	Crosscut Shredder
CD/DVD Disk	N/A	Shatter

Assessment Stats

- Assessment Points: 5
- Assessment POAM Eligible: No

Keys

- Policy – Create a policy that requires employees to apply approved destruction or sanitization methods to applicable media. This policy should contain information about who is responsible, what media needs to be addressed, and the acceptable methods of securing the media.

MP.L2-3.8.4

Media Markings

Mark media with necessary CUI markings and distribution limitations.

Impact

It happened during a recent supplier visit. Paula was chatting with the suppliers when the suppliers brought up a document that would be most helpful to Paula. The supplier had the file on his laptop, which was too large to email, so he asked if Paula might have a USB drive he could copy it onto. Paula went and grabbed a USB drive from her desk and gave it to the supplier. The supplier inserted the drive into his laptop and prepared to copy the file onto the drive for Paula, but then he spotted some of the file and folder names on the thumb drive, and they looked so juicy that he couldn't resist. He copied all the data onto his laptop, including some very sensitive files, and then provided Paula with the file she wanted. Looking at the drive in her hand, there was no way to tell that it contained anything sensitive.

Official Interpretation*

All media, hardcopy and digital, must be properly marked to alert individuals to the presence of CUI stored on the media. The National Archives and Records Administration (NARA) has published guidelines for labeling media of different sizes.

MP.L2-3.8.8 requires that media have an identifiable owner, so organizations may find it desirable to include ownership information on the device label as well.

(CMMC Assessment Guide, Level 2, Copyright 2020, 2021 Carnegie Mellon University and The Johns Hopkins University Applied Physics Laboratory LLC and/or CMMC Assessment Guide, Level 2, Version 2.11 - DRAFT, November 2023)

Assessment Focus

Also known as Assessment Objectives, these are the checklist items that an assessor will seek to verify. Each one must be addressed in your implementation and documentation:

1. media containing CUI is marked with applicable CUI markings; and
2. media containing CUI is marked with distribution limitations.

(CMMC Assessment Guide, Level 2, Copyright 2020, 2021 Carnegie Mellon University and The Johns Hopkins University Applied Physics Laboratory LLC and/or CMMC Assessment Guide, Level 2, Version 2.11 - DRAFT, November 2023)

Implementation

Back in the day, when all government materials were on paper, this wasn't an issue because the government had already marked each document with human-readable information concerning the distribution guidelines for that document. In today's world, it is impossible to discern the difference between a thumb drive containing controlled documents and an identical thumb drive containing innocuous documents.

However, do not assume that any entity will always have proper markings on CUI they provide to you. Currently, the Federal Government is working through older materials to apply appropriate CUI markings. You might be provided with materials from the Government or your partner organizations that are clearly CUI (like Distribution Statements B, C, D, E, or F), but not marked as CUI. So, checking and applying CUI markings when documents arrive will often be necessary.

Media with CUI must be marked. The media that needs to be marked includes diskettes, magnetic tapes, external/removable hard disk drives, flash drives, compact disks, digital video disks, and paper. Perhaps the cleanest way to conform to this requirement is to have no CUI on media, but that is not always feasible. So, any media containing CUI must be labeled accordingly.

CUI has very specific guidelines for the marking that should be applied to CUI-containing media. The link provided below shows the marking to be applied for all different sorts of CUI.

For example, a common type of CUI is Controlled Technical Information. These documents include materials like engineering drawings, specifications, and manuals. According to the CUI Registry, the marking code is "CUI//SP-CTI." CTI includes materials the government identifies as technical information with a Distribution statement of B through F. So, any media containing these CTI documents should have that marking.

If the documents or their associated documentation list specific distribution limitations, those should be reflected in the labeling. For example, some Defense documents list "DISTRIBUTION STATEMENT D. Distribution authorized to the Department of Defense and U.S. DoD contractors only." This would need to be referenced in the labeling.

Also, consider that MP.L2-3.8.8 requires that media have an identifiable owner, so organizations may find it desirable to include ownership information on the device/tag label as well.

HANDY LINK

The CUI registry for applicable marking for other forms of CUI at https://tinyurl.com/CMMC4SMB-530

Assessment Stats

- Assessment Points: 1
- Assessment POAM Eligible: Yes

Keys

- Policy – Set a policy for either no CUI on removable media OR to mark the media in accordance with the requirements.

MP.L2-3.8.5

Media Accountability

Control access to media containing CUI and maintain accountability for media during transport outside of controlled areas.

Impact

Charlie is the president of Firmament Weaponry Systems, a defense contractor. He was working on a big RFQ for the government while traveling to visit a prospective customer. He had all the information concerning the new RFQ on a USB drive. After the staff on the aircraft gave permission, he pulled out his laptop to continue working, but he didn't find the USB drive. He had been using it in the Atlanta airport, but now it was nowhere to be found. He could only assume that he had left it at the airport gate. Now, what was he supposed to do? That drive contained loads of drawings, specifications, and other controlled documents. He was at least 3 hours before he could use his cell phone and tell anybody, but he didn't know who he would call and what good it would do, anyway?

Official Interpretation*

CUI is protected in both physical and digital formats. Physical control can be accomplished using traditional concepts like restricted access to physical locations or locking papers in a desk or filing cabinet. The digitization of data makes access to CUI much easier. CUI can be stored and transported on magnetic disks, tapes, USB drives, CD-ROMs, and so on. This makes digital CUI data very portable. It is important for an organization to apply mechanisms to prevent unauthorized access to CUI due to ease of transport.

(CMMC Assessment Guide, Level 2, Copyright 2020, 2021 Carnegie Mellon University and The Johns Hopkins University Applied Physics Laboratory LLC and/or CMMC Assessment Guide, Level 2, Version 2.11 - DRAFT, November 2023)

Assessment Focus

Also known as Assessment Objectives, these are the checklist items that an assessor will seek to verify. Each one must be addressed in your implementation and documentation:

1. access to media containing CUI is controlled; and

2. accountability for media containing CUI is maintained during transport outside of controlled areas.

(CMMC Assessment Guide, Level 2, Copyright 2020, 2021 Carnegie Mellon University and The Johns Hopkins University Applied Physics Laboratory LLC and/or CMMC Assessment Guide, Level 2, Version 2.11 - DRAFT, November 2023)

Implementation

This requirement applies explicitly when CUI-containing media leaves the normal controlled areas of your facility. As with other requirements in this section, this requirement becomes immaterial if you can configure operating procedures to avoid storing any CUI on media.

Note: the requirement partners with MP.L2-3.8.6 to define controls over media transported outside your facility.

According to this requirement, the CUI-containing media must be controlled and accountable when it goes outside your facility. These controls may include:

- Transporting the media in locked containers (see MP.L2-3.8.6),
- Having the CUI files encrypted* on the media (see MP.L2-3.8.6),
- Selection of traceable, reputable carriers of the media is to be shipped,
- Accountability records of who has responsibility for specific media,
- Systems to detect loss, tampering, or destruction during transport.

The requirement does not provide a specific listing of what these controls must include, so you must create and adhere to a policy that defines what controls you will be applying.

When CUI is on media outside of controlled areas, then there needs to be accountability of the media. This accountability system needs to know who is responsible for the media, where they are taking it, and what CUI is on it. When assessed, the expectation should be that the system would have current information concerning all CUI on media and outside controlled areas.

It is possible to avoid this requirement entirely. If you have cloud storage that meets the necessary security requirements, users can access the CUI where needed and avoid transport controls. This secure cloud storage can be considered part of your controlled area.

HANDY LINK

The author's preferred tool fwor secure and compliant cloud storage of CUI for the small organization can be found here https://tinyurl.com/CMMC4SMB-938

*When encryption protects CUI, then SC.L2-3.13.11 applies, so the encryption implementation must be FIPS-validated.

Assessment Stats

- Assessment Points: 1
- Assessment POAM Eligible: Yes

Keys

- Policy - Outline the controls your organization will apply to CUI-containing media outside your facility to achieve the necessary accountability.

MP.L2-3.8.6

Portable Storage Encryption

Implement cryptographic mechanisms to protect the confidentiality of CUI stored on digital media during transport unless otherwise protected by alternative physical safeguards.

Impact

Gary has heard about all the ransomware attacks and wanted to ensure that his company's most valuable data is stored offline and off-site, so it absolutely cannot be maliciously encrypted. He has 5 USB drives. Daily, he performs a backup routine to copy the most critical data onto a USB drive. That evening, he takes that drive home and picks up the next in the sequence. He typically has four prior copies of the data at home and one he is taking to work to get the updated data. Thankfully, he never had to use this backup to deal with a ransomware attack. However, one day, he went to the gym right after work, and while changing clothes, the USB drive fell out of his pocket. He panicked because he knew the drive contained CUI, personnel, and financial data. There was a ton of stuff on the drive that should not be public. He suddenly found that his method for protecting the company data was a way to lose control of that data.

Official Interpretation*

CUI can be stored and transported on a variety of portable media, which increases the chance that the CUI can be lost. When identifying the paths CUI flows through your company, identify devices to include in this requirement.

To mitigate the risk of losing or exposing CUI, implement an encryption scheme to protect the data. Even if the media are lost, proper encryption renders the data inaccessible. When encryption is not an option, apply alternative physical safeguards during transport.

Because the use of cryptography in this requirement is to protect the confidentiality of CUI, the cryptography used must meet the criteria specified in requirement SC.L2-3.13.11.

This requirement, MP.L2-3.8.6, provides additional protections to those provided by MP.L2-3.8.5. This requirement is intended to protect against situations where control of media access fails, such as through the loss of the media.

(CMMC Assessment Guide, Level 2, Copyright 2020, 2021 Carnegie Mellon University and The Johns Hopkins University Applied Physics Laboratory LLC and/or CMMC Assessment Guide, Level 2, Version 2.11 - DRAFT, November 2023)

Assessment Focus

Also known as Assessment Objectives, these are the checklist items that an assessor will seek to verify. Each one must be addressed in your implementation and documentation:

1. the confidentiality of CUI stored on digital media is protected during transport using cryptographic mechanisms or alternative physical safeguards.

(CMMC Assessment Guide, Level 2, Copyright 2020, 2021 Carnegie Mellon University and The Johns Hopkins University Applied Physics Laboratory LLC and/or CMMC Assessment Guide, Level 2, Version 2.11 - DRAFT, November 2023)

Implementation

When CUI goes onto media and leaves controlled areas, it can end up in the wrong hands. Therefore, it is necessary that there would be another line of defense for the data beyond simple possession. The requirement MP.L2-3.8.5, Media Accountability, also addresses the security of CUI on media outside your controlled areas.

The first step is to perform an analysis of how CUI moves in your organization so that you can determine what media devices are subject to these controls.

How you will protect the data on the portable media must be determined. It is fairly obvious from the way the requirement is written that the CMMC authors strongly prefer the data's encryption. Most encryption methods are more convenient than keeping media under lock and key. Greater convenience often leads to greater compliance.

Searching "FIPS encrypted USB drives" will reveal many products where the encryption is built into the thumb drive, and a tiny keypad allows key entry. When CUI is provided on one of these drives, it clearly emphasizes that the data requires special handling. These USB drives generally cost four to ten times more than their unencrypted counterparts. You would want to ensure that the encryption used is FIPS-compliant and listed on the CMVP list (see SC.L2-3.13.11 for more information on FIPS requirements).

Windows (not the Home version) has a method of encrypting a standard thumb drive. To do this, insert the drive, right-click the drive in File Explorer, and select Turn on BitLocker. You can then set a password that will apply to this thumb drive. This drive cannot be used on a Mac or a Windows machine of an incompatible version.

Beyond encryption, there are always other options. The requirement says, "unless otherwise protected by alternative physical safeguards," so it is clear that media protected by physical means also meets the requirements.

Keep in mind that this requirement can be avoided altogether if CUI is on a cloud service of adequate security. This makes all the issues associated with the transport of media moot.

HANDY LINK

The author's preferred tool for secure and compliant cloud storage of CUI for the small organization can be found here https://tinyurl.com/CMMC4SMB-938

Assessment Stats

- Assessment Points: 1
- Assessment POAM Eligible: Yes

Keys

- Policy – Determine the procedure that should be followed to assure that any media containing CUI will be protected by encryption or other means during transport.

Personnel Security

MP.L2-3.8.7

Removable Media

Control the use of removable media on system components.

Impact

Only Jack knew that he would be quitting his job in 3 weeks. He was trying to make the best use of his remaining time. He had been collecting a big folder of special files. He had customer lists, financial information, procedures, and forms and even had a copy of this company's equivalent to the "secret sauce." Today, he brought in a brand-new USB drive to remove the documents from the company. In about 2 minutes, all those valuable files were in his shoe where nobody could find them, and he was headed out to his car. He had successfully gotten away with 215 GB of valuable data, and nobody suspected a thing.

Official Interpretation*

Removable media are any type of media storage that you can remove from your computer or machine (e.g., CDs, DVDs, diskettes, and USB drives). Write a specific policy for removable media. The policy should cover the various types of removable media (e.g., write-once media and rewritable media) and should discuss the company's approach to removable media. Ensure the following controls are considered and included in the policy:

- limit the use of removable media to the smallest number needed; and
- scan all removable media for viruses.

(CMMC Assessment Guide, Level 2, Copyright 2020, 2021 Carnegie Mellon University and The Johns Hopkins University Applied Physics Laboratory LLC and/or CMMC Assessment Guide, Level 2, Version 2.11 - DRAFT, November 2023)

Assessment Focus

Also known as Assessment Objectives, these are the checklist items that an assessor will seek to verify. Each one must be addressed in your implementation and documentation:

1. the use of removable media on system components is controlled.

(CMMC Assessment Guide, Level 2, Copyright 2020, 2021 Carnegie Mellon University and The Johns Hopkins University Applied Physics Laboratory LLC and/or CMMC Assessment Guide, Level 2, Version 2.11 - DRAFT, November 2023)

Implementation

With the ever-expanding variety of network and cloud storage options, the demand for removable storage devices has reduced but generally refuses to go away completely. The risks associated with the devices include the introduction of malware from outside the network and the exfiltration of data from network systems. While the devices have associated risks, many users still demand them. Because of the risks around USB devices, it is good that their usage can be addressed simply and easily.

The best implementation option is to prohibit the use of all removable storage, but this is often not practical for organizational reasons. However, with the magic of Group Policy scope, prohibitions on USB use can be applied to specific computers or users.

For computers:

> Computer Configuration -> Policies -> Administrative Templates -> System -> Removable Storage Access -> All Removable Storage classes: Deny all access

For users:

> User Configuration -> Policies -> Administrative Templates -> System -> Removable Storage Access -> All Removable Storage classes: Deny all access

Although maintenance can carry a more significant burden, an option will be to issue "company-approved" USB devices and disallow everything else. This can be done through Group Policy.

When a USB storage device is inserted, an installation process occurs. Group Policy can be set to allow specific devices (the definition of a device can range from a particular model or a general class of devices) to install and prohibit the installation of all others.

1. You need to find the hardware ID of the device. Go to "Device Manager" to find the device. By going into the device properties, Details tab, and selecting Hardware ID, you will see a list of various hardware IDs that describe the device. These are listed from most specific to most general.

2. Enter USB key Hardware ID into the Group Policy Setting Computer Configuration –> Administrative Templates –> System –>Device Installation –> Device Installation Restrictions -> "Allow installation of devices that match any of these device IDs."

3. Within this policy, you will want to set it to Enable, and then click on the "Show" button to enter your USB key hardware ID.

4. The other related policy is the Group Policy Setting Computer Configuration –> Administrative Templates –> System –>Device Installation –> Device Installation Restrictions -> "Prevent installation of devices not described by other policy settings," set that to Enable.

This method will occasionally catch devices that are not removable storage, so you may have, for example, a keyboard that refuses to be acknowledged by a system because it got caught in this filter. In this case, it is necessary to perform the same procedure to determine the Hardware ID and put it into the group policy.

Because of the burden of keeping the master list of hardware IDs current, it is the best idea to prohibit removable storage devices for those users that have no business use for them and only apply the filtering to those users that have a business need.

Applying a restriction to USB storage devices will likely uncover many unexpected uses of USB storage devices, so you can assume that there will be a flurry of support inquiries when these restrictions are applied.

Assessment Stats

- Assessment Points: 5
- Assessment POAM Eligible: No

Keys

- Policy – Develop a policy that defines your controls for removable storage devices
- Group Policy – Implement a plan that will ensure control of removable storage devices

Media Protection

MP.L2-3.8.8

Shared Media

Prohibit the use of portable storage devices when such devices have no identifiable owner.

Impact

Robert wanted to break into the computer systems at this particular company. He had attempted to use some phishing attacks but hadn't had any nibbles. His next plan was to create special USB drives to auto-load a remote access trojan (RAT). He then put enticing labels on the drives, like "Personnel Records" and "Executive Background Checks." He took them to the company and left these drives scattered in the parking lot and on the grounds. He was counting on somebody picking one up, carrying it into the office, and plugging it into their computer. The following day, he started to get notifications on new installations of his RAT shortly after the office employees began to arrive. Robert thought to himself, "Bingo, I've got you!"

Official Interpretation*

A portable storage device is a system component that can be inserted into and removed from a system and is used to store data or information. It typically plugs into a laptop or desktop port (e.g., USB port). These devices can contain malicious files that can lead to a compromise of a connected system. Therefore, use should be prohibited if the device cannot be traced to an owner who is responsible and accountable for its security.

This requirement, MP.L2-3.8.8, furthers the protections provided by MP.L2-3.8.7 by prohibiting unidentified media use even if that media type is allowable.

(CMMC Assessment Guide, Level 2, Copyright 2020, 2021 Carnegie Mellon University and The Johns Hopkins University Applied Physics Laboratory LLC and/or CMMC Assessment Guide, Level 2, Version 2.11 - DRAFT, November 2023)

Assessment Focus

Also known as Assessment Objectives, these are the checklist items that an assessor will seek to verify. Each one must be addressed in your implementation and documentation:

1. the use of portable storage devices is prohibited when such devices have no identifiable owner.

(CMMC Assessment Guide, Level 2, Copyright 2020, 2021 Carnegie Mellon University and The Johns Hopkins University Applied Physics Laboratory LLC and/or CMMC Assessment Guide, Level 2, Version 2.11 - DRAFT, November 2023)

Implementation

If any portable storage devices will be used in your organization, they need to be labeled. When the controls of MP.L2-3.8.7 are implemented, there will be restrictions on all USB storage devices, whether they hold CUI or not. It is easiest if the only allowed devices are company-owned because all of them can be labeled as belonging to the company. If employee-owned devices are permitted, it will still be necessary to identify the ownership clearly, and the employees may not like that being done to their devices.

Purchase a small quantity of "permanent waterproof labels" sized small enough to be applied to USB "thumb" drives that identify them as property of your organization. Then, order a second set in an alternate color with CUI markings and the company property statement. In this way, the USB storage devices for mundane use and the devices for CUI transport (encrypted*) can all be labeled to conform to this requirement while also satisfying the need for CUI markings (MP.L2-3.8.4). General advice: You will be surprised how many labels you need, so order more than you anticipate needing.

Getting labels on the devices is just part of compliance with this requirement. The second part is to train employees never to attempt to use any device that doesn't have a label showing the company, or an authorized employee owns it. If you have uniformly labeled company-owned USB storage devices, it is easier for an employee to decide if it is acceptable than when evaluating a thumb drive that has "TOM" written on it in Sharpie.

Evaluating this training will be an easy check for a CMMC assessor. All they have to do is find one user willing to insert an unlabeled USB stick, and they have discovered a non-conformance. So, your restrictions implemented to satisfy MP.L2-3.8.7 can serve to supplement the training, since people are unreliable.

*When encryption protects CUI, then SC.L2-3.13.11 applies, so the encryption implementation must be FIPS-validated.

Assessment Stats

- Assessment Points: 3
- Assessment POAM Eligible: No

Keys

- System - Assure that all authorized portable storage devices have their ownership clearly labeled.
- Training – Assure that all of your employees understand that they should never attempt to use any portable storage device unless it has the ownership clearly labeled.
- Records – Have training records available.

Media Protection

MP.L2-3.8.9

Protect Backups

Protect the confidentiality of backup CUI at storage locations.

Impact

The company had a big problem. Jeremy was getting the brunt of the blame because he could not seem to explain or fix it. The company had a significant information leakage problem. Data from customers, vendors, or consultants was all being leaked. Soon after they received data, it was posted on the Internet. Jeremy had been through everything he could think of and could find nothing that could explain the leakage. Then, one day, he had a user accidentally delete a network file, which Jeremy was able to restore from backup when he started thinking about his data backups. Sure enough, his data backups were being compromised. Jeremy had been paying great attention to the security of his servers and workstations but wasn't even thinking about his backups.

Official Interpretation*

You protect CUI to ensure that it remains private (confidentiality) and unchanged (integrity). Methods to ensure confidentiality may include:

- encrypting files or media;
- managing who has access to the information; and
- physically securing devices and media that contain CUI.

Storage locations for information are varied, and may include:

- external hard drives;
- USB drives;
- magnetic media (tape cartridge);
- optical disk (CD, DVD);
- Networked Attached Storage (NAS);

- servers; and
- cloud backup.

This requirement, MP.L2-3.8.9, requires the confidentiality of backup information at storage locations.

(CMMC Assessment Guide, Level 2, Copyright 2020, 2021 Carnegie Mellon University and The Johns Hopkins University Applied Physics Laboratory LLC and/or CMMC Assessment Guide, Level 2, Version 2.11 - DRAFT, November 2023)

Assessment Focus

Also known as Assessment Objectives, these are the checklist items that an assessor will seek to verify. Each one must be addressed in your implementation and documentation:

1. the confidentiality of backup CUI is protected at storage locations.

(CMMC Assessment Guide, Level 2, Copyright 2020, 2021 Carnegie Mellon University and The Johns Hopkins University Applied Physics Laboratory LLC and/or CMMC Assessment Guide, Level 2, Version 2.11 - DRAFT, November 2023)

Implementation

To protect your data, it is essential to implement data backups. However, those backups that contain CUI are required to have additional controls to ensure that the CUI data remains protected. From a real-world business standpoint, there is likely other data in your organization important enough to protect from possible leakage through the backups.

Backups that contain CUI should be protected with the same vigilance as the original CUI (See SC.L2-3.13.16). They should be encrypted* or stored in ways that have access limited to authorized users only. The procedure for this should be documented.

The trend in backups is to rely increasingly upon cloud storage of data backups. However, not all cloud storage is the same from a security standpoint. In an audit, it would be best to show that you performed due diligence in assuring that your cloud provider had adequate security. To have the lowest probability of issues in your CMMC assessment, your cloud backup provider should be FedRAMP certified and using FIPS 140-2 encryption.

If your backups are local or cloud, it should be remembered that they are CUI if any CUI files are in the backup scope. Based upon this, an assessor could potentially attempt to apply any CMMC control applicable to CUI might be applied to these backups.

*When encryption protects CUI, then SC.L2-3.13.11 applies, so the encryption implementation must be FIPS-validated.

Assessment Stats

- Assessment Points: 1
- Assessment POAM Eligible: Yes

Keys

🔧 Policy – Define the controls that will be placed upon backup copies of CUI to assure their protection.

PS.L2-3.9.1

Screen Individuals

Screen individuals prior to authorizing access to organizational systems containing CUI.

Impact

The company was in a hiring phase. They had just hired Charlene as a project coordinator. They did not know that Charlene had a criminal history and was working for their competitor. While Charlene was working on maintaining the project data for their research and development, she also sent regular updates to the competition. Her manager thought Charlene was doing a wonderful job.

Official Interpretation*

Ensure all employees who need access to CUI undergo organization-defined screening before being granted access. Base the types of screening on the requirements for a given position and role.

The effective screening of personnel provided by this requirement, PS.L2-3.9.1, improves upon the effectiveness of authentication performed in IA.L2-3.5.2.

(CMMC Assessment Guide, Level 2, Copyright 2020, 2021 Carnegie Mellon University and The Johns Hopkins University Applied Physics Laboratory LLC and/or CMMC Assessment Guide, Level 2, Version 2.11 - DRAFT, November 2023)

Assessment Focus

Also known as Assessment Objectives, these are the checklist items that an assessor will seek to verify. Each one must be addressed in your implementation and documentation:

1. individuals are screened prior to authorizing access to organizational systems containing CUI.

(CMMC Assessment Guide, Level 2, Copyright 2020, 2021 Carnegie Mellon University and The Johns Hopkins University Applied Physics Laboratory LLC and/or CMMC Assessment Guide, Level 2, Version 2.11 - DRAFT, November 2023)

Implementation

This requirement is quite vague about what constitutes an adequate employee screening. However, there is an expectation within much of the Defense community that employees will receive a pre-employment background check before working in a security capacity, like handling CUI.

Performing a criminal background check is not an expensive process (starting around $30 per employee) and might reveal important information while providing compliance with this requirement. The requirements that your organization determines to be necessary should be documented. The procedure might have different requirements depending on the employee's role, but there should be minimum steps for each employee who deals with CUI.

This is also an opportunity to take credit for other pre-employment screening steps in your documented hiring process which might include:

- Drug tests
- Checking references
- Checking social media

Since people change roles during their employment, you might consider applying the screening process to all employees. This reduces the likelihood of an employee transferring into a position handling CUI that has never received the screening.

Assessment Stats

- Assessment Points: 3
- Assessment POAM Eligible: No

Keys

- Policy – Determine what screening steps will be required for all employees given access to CUI.
- Documentation – The assessor should be able to see documentation generated by the screening process.

PS.L2-3.9.2

Personnel Actions

Ensure that organizational systems containing CUI are protected during and after personnel actions such as terminations and transfers.

Impact

When Jacob was fired, he was fuming mad. He was convinced that he had been doing a good job and that the company was targeting him. As he stormed out of the building, his mind turned toward revenge. He wanted to make the company feel pain for doing this to him. When he got home, he checked whether his VPN connection was still active. As it connected through, he was elated. He started downloading data, and then when he thought he had the juiciest stuff, he proceeded to delete whole directories from the company network. He then turned his mind toward taking all the material he had downloaded and posting it on the Internet for all the world to see.

Official Interpretation*

Employee access to CUI is removed when they change jobs or leave the company. When employment or program access is terminated for any reason, the following actions may occur within the defined time frame:

- all company IT equipment (e.g., laptops, cell phones, storage devices) is returned;
- all identification, access cards, and keys are returned; and
- an exit interview is conducted to remind the employee of their obligations to not discuss CUI, even after employment.

Additionally, perform the following:

- remove access to all accounts granting access to CUI or modify access to CUI as appropriate for a new work role;
- disable or close employee accounts for departing employees; and
- limit access to physical spaces with CUI for departing employees or those who transition to a work role that does not require access to CUI.

This requirement, PS.L2-3.9.2, leverages the identification of system users required by IA.L2-3.5.1 in order to ensure that all accesses are identified and removed.

(CMMC Assessment Guide, Level 2, Copyright 2020, 2021 Carnegie Mellon University and The Johns Hopkins University Applied Physics Laboratory LLC and/or CMMC Assessment Guide, Level 2, Version 2.11 - DRAFT, November 2023)

Assessment Focus

Also known as Assessment Objectives, these are the checklist items that an assessor will seek to verify. Each one must be addressed in your implementation and documentation:

1. a policy and/or process for terminating system access and any credentials coincident with personnel actions is established
2. system access and credentials are terminated consistent with personnel actions such as termination or transfer
3. the system is protected during and after personnel transfer actions.

(CMMC Assessment Guide, Level 2, Copyright 2020, 2021 Carnegie Mellon University and The Johns Hopkins University Applied Physics Laboratory LLC and/or CMMC Assessment Guide, Level 2, Version 2.11 - DRAFT, November 2023)

Implementation

Former employees whose network access credentials have not been revoked have been an issue for many companies in many unpleasant ways. Your organization should create a separation checklist, ensuring everything gets done correctly when an employee leaves the company. This should include disabling or deleting the user in Active Directory, removing any remote access (VPN and WiFi), disabling the user's access to company email, and removing any local users on the user's computer. In the event of a termination, it may be especially prudent to archive an image of the user's computer, including the user's email, just in case of litigation.

In a Windows environment, disabling the user in Active Directory will revoke all access privileges to domain resources. If you have any remote access that does not use Active Directory for authentication (GoToMyPC, for example), then that will need to be disabled in a separate action.

Physical access instruments like keys, hardware authentication tokens, ID cards, and RFID access tokens must also be addressed. Your procedure for addressing the security needs of employee separations should be addressed in the procedure.

Changes in role/department also need to be addressed. Consider a person who moves from IT to sales. As an IT employee, they likely had network permissions far beyond what any sales staff member would typically be granted. When this change in role occurs, the individual would need to have their permissions adjusted accordingly. While the specific adjustments might differ from one transfer to another, it would be good to have a checklist of all the things that need to be considered. Then, the addressed items will be recorded, and those that do not require any action will also be documented as not applicable.

If a separation checklist is created, it may include a list of immediate items (like disabling remote access and email) and another list of items that need to be addressed without urgency (like archiving email history).

Assessment Stats

- Assessment Points: 5
- Assessment POAM Eligible: No

Keys

- Procedure – Define the procedure that will be followed for an employee who leaves or is reassigned.
- Documentation - Records showing the termination of access and invalidation of credentials should be created as employees are terminated or reassigned.
- Evidence of Conformance – The assessor should be able to see where the process has been followed.

Physical Protection

PE.L1-3.10.1

Limit Physical Access

Limit physical access to organizational systems, equipment, and the respective operating environments to authorized individuals.

Impact

Brad was ready. He was wearing his generic deliveryman uniform and had his clipboard in hand. He was going in the door at precisely 9:59 in the morning. He knew several distracting phone calls would come in just before he opened the front door (because they were from his friends). He stepped through the door and gave an I-don't-have-time-to-chat half-wave to the receptionist, who was busy with the phone, and headed down the hall toward the room where the servers were located. Nobody paid him any attention. He "accidentally" dropped his pen right under the servers. As he bent down to get the pen, he slipped a USB drive into a server. After a few seconds, he pulled the USB drive back out, knowing it had already done its job. He strolled back out the front door, knowing that he had now compromised the server. As he returned to his car, he was astonished at how easy the whole thing had been.

Official Interpretation*

This addresses the company's physical space (e.g., office, testing environments, equipment rooms), technical assets, and non-technical assets that need to be protected from unauthorized physical access. Specific environments are limited to authorized employees, and access is controlled with badges, electronic locks, physical key locks, etc.

Output devices, such as printers, are placed in areas where their use does not expose data to unauthorized individuals. Lists of personnel with authorized access are developed and maintained, and personnel are issued appropriate authorization credentials.

(CMMC Assessment Guide, Level 2, Copyright 2020, 2021 Carnegie Mellon University and The Johns Hopkins University Applied Physics Laboratory LLC and/or CMMC Assessment Guide, Level 2, Version 2.11 - DRAFT, November 2023)

Assessment Focus

Also known as Assessment Objectives, these are the checklist items that an assessor will seek to verify. Each one must be addressed in your implementation and documentation:

1. authorized individuals allowed physical access are identified;
2. physical access to organizational systems is limited to authorized individuals;
3. physical access to equipment is limited to authorized individuals; and
4. physical access to operating environments is limited to authorized individuals.

(CMMC Assessment Guide, Level 2, Copyright 2020, 2021 Carnegie Mellon University and The Johns Hopkins University Applied Physics Laboratory LLC and/or CMMC Assessment Guide, Level 2, Version 2.11 - DRAFT, November 2023)

Implementation

Physical security can mean many different things depending upon many factors. For the purposes of this specific requirement, the focus must be on the "information systems, equipment, and the respective operating environments," which might be quite different from how company management looks at security.

Compliance with this requirement doesn't have to be razor-wire fences and armed guards. Consider the physical defenses already in place and take credit for those access-limiting factors. These controls may include door locks, alarm systems, a receptionist at the front door, cameras, or ID cards. Equipment that is kept in locked rooms or in areas that are visible to many people should be referenced as controls.

However, because this must pass muster with an auditor, they might come into your facility with certain expectations about what constitutes physical security. In a small company, putting a computer in the middle of a room where only four people ever come in would be pretty good security because any other individual would be extremely obvious. Still, an auditor might not see that as secure. For this reason, some investment into creating the "appearance of security" might be justified.

Identify the individuals or groups that have the authorization to access the systems. Assure that you have controls that limit access to only those authorized persons.

The requirement says that access limits should be applied to "organizational information systems, equipment, and the respective operating environments." It will be essential to ensure that all 3 of these areas are appropriately controlled (and addressed in your documentation).

- Organizational Information Systems – This is the broad view of information systems of those aspects that are not equipment. This would include aspects like cabling and paper documents.
- Equipment – Equipment includes "computing devices, external disk drives, networking devices, monitors, printers, copiers, scanners, facsimile machines, and audio devices."
- Operating Environments – These would include general facility security that may not be directly related to information security. This might also consider risk mitigation for appropriate environmental risks, like earthquakes, tornadoes, hurricanes, or forest fires.

Look closely at your assets that are "in scope." You will want to ensure that only the individuals on your authorized access list can access these assets. However, access does NOT have to be limited to individuals authorized to work with CUI. For example, you can limit CUI to a small group but have physical access limited to all employees. Although it is implied that those would be the same lists, nothing says that. If your assessor objects to non-CUI-authorized persons having physical access, ask them to show you where the requirements say that.

If you are accustomed to having exterior doors that are unlocked and unmonitored during business hours, then that will have to change. There MUST be physical safeguards between your in-scope assets and the outside world.

You must be prepared to show an assessor a list of people authorized to enter the area physically. This list is likely the same as those who have been issued door keys or fobs. You may have different areas with different authorization lists. For example, access to your server room might be much more limited than access to your workstations.

You will then need to document the physical security of (1) organizational information systems, (2) equipment, and (3) respective operating environments. CMMC isn't telling you what your physical security needs to look like, only that there must be documented physical security.

Assessment Stats

- Assessment Points: 5
- Assessment POAM Eligible: No

Keys

- Assignment – Create a list of those individuals or groups authorized to access systems.
- Policy – Define what physical security controls are being applied to address risk in the areas of organizational information systems, equipment, and the respective operating environments.

PE.L2-3.10.2

Monitor Facility

Protect and monitor the physical facility and support infrastructure for organizational systems.

Impact

Just inside their visitor entrance was a waiting area. A few chairs and a display of the company's products were in this area. It was necessary to push a doorbell button to notify somebody that you were in the waiting area. For Nathan, while he was interested in the necessity of announcing your presence so that employees knew anyone was out there, he was more interested in the Ethernet port on the wall. He quickly set up his laptop and used a cable to connect to that open port, and, as easy as pie, he was connected to their network. This enabled him to begin a hacking process.

Official Interpretation*

The infrastructure inside of a facility, such as power and network cables, is protected so that visitors and unauthorized employees cannot access it. The protection is also monitored by security guards, video cameras, sensors, or alarms.

(CMMC Assessment Guide, Level 2, Copyright 2020, 2021 Carnegie Mellon University and The Johns Hopkins University Applied Physics Laboratory LLC and/or CMMC Assessment Guide, Level 2, Version 2.11 - DRAFT, November 2023)

Assessment Focus

Also known as Assessment Objectives, these are the checklist items that an assessor will seek to verify. Each one must be addressed in your implementation and documentation:

1. the physical facility where organizational systems reside is protected
2. the support infrastructure for organizational systems is protected
3. the physical facility where organizational systems reside is monitored
4. the support infrastructure for organizational systems is monitored.

(CMMC Assessment Guide, Level 2, Copyright 2020, 2021 Carnegie Mellon University and The Johns Hopkins University Applied Physics Laboratory LLC and/or CMMC Assessment Guide, Level 2, Version 2.11 - DRAFT, November 2023)

Implementation

You will need to demonstrate that your facility is protected and monitored and your infrastructure is protected and monitored.

The steps you have already taken to prevent things like fire and burglary are assets in meeting this requirement to protect the physical facility. These protections might include alarm systems, sprinklers, and fire extinguishers.

There are many CMMC assessors that have an expectation that a facility would have camera systems with recording capabilities that cover entrances to facilities and secure areas. This is not a written requirement, but considering the low cost of these systems, the security benefits and the opinion of many assessors, it might be a good investment.

Keep in mind that the controls applied to protect the facility must be monitored. In this realm, the monitoring will often take the form of alarms for things like burglary or fire or motion on cameras when there should not be activity.

The other side of this requirement is to protect and monitor the support infrastructure. The support infrastructure includes elements such as building power and the physical network. Protections for power, including that all external disconnects are maintained with locks. Critical equipment, like servers, should all run on uninterruptable power supplies to protect against short-duration power failures. Many burglar/fire alarm systems can also provide alerts in the event of a power failure. This will provide the required monitoring.

On the physical network side, there are a couple of steps that can be taken to provide protection:

- Disable (disconnect) all network ports that are not in use
- Assure that all network switches are physically protected
- Utilize MAC address filtering to deter new devices connecting to the physical network.

The equipment already in place may provide an alert option if rogue devices attempt to connect to the wired network.

Assure that your documentation checks all four boxes:

Protect physical facility	Protect support infrastructure
Monitor physical facility	Monitor support infrastructure

Assessment Stats

- Assessment Points: 5
- Assessment POAM Eligible: No

Keys

🔧 Policy – Develop a plan of how the facility and the infrastructure will be both protected and monitored.

Physical Protection

PE.L1-3.10.3

Escort Visitors

Escort visitors and monitor visitor activity.

Impact

Diana was there to service the copier, but she was curious and not wholly ethical. So, since she had been shown the copier and left alone, she got curious about what was around her. There was an unattended computer workstation next to the copier. She picked up the keyboard and turned it over. "Oh yeah!" she whispered as she saw a username and password on a sticky note attached to the bottom of the keyboard. She quickly snapped a picture of the note on her phone. As she finished the work on the copier, she was curious about what she would be able to do with those computer credentials.

Official Interpretation*

Do not allow visitors, even those people you know well, to walk around your facility without an escort. Make sure that all non-employees wear special visitor badges and/or are escorted by an employee at all times while on the property.

(CMMC Assessment Guide, Level 2, Copyright 2020, 2021 Carnegie Mellon University and The Johns Hopkins University Applied Physics Laboratory LLC and/or CMMC Assessment Guide, Level 2, Version 2.11 - DRAFT, November 2023)

Assessment Focus

Also known as Assessment Objectives, these are the checklist items that an assessor will seek to verify. Each one must be addressed in your implementation and documentation:

1. visitors are escorted; and
2. visitor activity is monitored.

(CMMC Assessment Guide, Level 2, Copyright 2020, 2021 Carnegie Mellon University and The Johns Hopkins University Applied Physics Laboratory LLC and/or CMMC Assessment Guide, Level 2, Version 2.11 - DRAFT, November 2023)

Implementation

In a small organization where everybody knows everybody else, strangers in the building are much more obvious than in a business with thousands of employees. It is a common trick for hackers to impersonate an executive or a contractor to enter a facility and breach security. While a stranger will stand out more in a small organization, the relaxed environment lends itself toward a "They must have a reason to be here" attitude.

So, each visitor must be escorted and monitored. For many small organizations, the compliance challenge comes not from the "official visitors" like suppliers and customers that come in the front door for a visit. Often, the challenge visitors are the contractors and service people who routinely have a purpose in the building. These people may be delivery drivers, filling vending machines, changing floor mats, or performing other routine activities.

The requirement specifies not only that the visitors should be escorted but also a requirement to monitor them. This monitoring requirement says it isn't enough to be in the same general vicinity as the visitor, but their activities should be watched. The need to monitor visitors should be made clear in the policy.

While this requirement does not specify that visitor logs are required, the next requirement, PE.L1-3.10.4, does require logs, so incorporate that into your plan.

Assessment Stats

- Assessment Points: 1
- Assessment POAM Eligible: No

Keys

- Policy – Develop a policy defining how visitors will be escorted and monitored.

Physical Protection

PE.L1-3.10.4

Physical Access Logs

Maintain audit logs of physical access.

Impact

The company was in trouble. It appeared that, somehow, the competition had succeeded in establishing a means of learning exactly what they were doing. As they build a breakthrough product, their competitor would bring out an identical product just ahead of them. When they bid on a project, the competitor would bid just barely below them. Over and over, the competitor was working one step ahead of them. They felt like they had covered all the bases and eliminated everything, but one day, during a WiFi survey, Michelle, the head of the small IT department, saw something very strange. There was a rogue IP access point inside the building. Following the WiFi mapping program, they found a USB WiFi router plugged into a server. She realized that this could easily be the source of the company's loss of information to the competitor. From examining system logs, they realized that the device had been installed on July 16th around 3:12 in the afternoon. Only a few people had physical access to the server room, but there was no way to know who might have been accessing the area at that time.

Official Interpretation*

Make sure you have a record of who accesses your facility (e.g., office, plant, factory). You can do this in writing by having employees and visitors sign in and sign out or by electronic means such as badge readers. Whatever means you use, you need to retain the access records for the time period that your company has defined.

(CMMC Assessment Guide, Level 2, Copyright 2020, 2021 Carnegie Mellon University and The Johns Hopkins University Applied Physics Laboratory LLC and/or CMMC Assessment Guide, Level 2, Version 2.11 - DRAFT, November 2023)

Assessment Focus

Also known as Assessment Objectives, these are the checklist items that an assessor will seek to verify. Each one must be addressed in your implementation and documentation:

1. audit logs of physical access are maintained.

(CMMC Assessment Guide, Level 2, Copyright 2020, 2021 Carnegie Mellon University and The Johns Hopkins University Applied Physics Laboratory LLC and/or CMMC Assessment Guide, Level 2, Version 2.11 - DRAFT, November 2023)

Implementation

In the more casual environment of a small business, this requirement may get some push-back. Compliant logging is not just for visitors but for everybody entering your facility's non-public areas. For hourly employees, their time clock would suffice. In most companies, the comings-and-goings of salary employees are not generally documented. So, some challenges will likely be associated with convincing your management team that this is important.

The only exception to this logging requirement applies to portions of your facility that are considered public. Aside from that exception, everyone entering the non-public areas should have their presence logged. This includes employees, contractors, and visitors.

The log can be simple and manual or can be an electronic system. On the simple end, a log can be a paper where the individual can record their name, with time-in and time-out. Alternatively, it could also be an automated system that tracks people by their ID card swipes.

There might be multiple systems: one for visitors, another for salary employees, and a third system for hourly employees. The critical point is that all entries into and exits from the area are logged.

Auditors will want to see this logging system in action and see records of people's access to your facility.

Assessment Stats

- Assessment Points: 1
- Assessment POAM Eligible: No

Keys

- 🔧 Policy – Develop a method to record building access (aside from public areas) and how those records will be maintained.

Physical Protection

PE.L1-3.10.5

Manage Physical Access

Control and manage physical access devices.

Impact

At Stelar Psychometry, they had a problem. They realized they had completely lost track of the keys to the front door of their offices. They had the same locks on the doors for about five years, and three different people (two of whom no longer worked at the company) had been responsible for distributing the keys. Each person had their own system for handling the keys, and they each seemed to apply different levels of control to the keys. As of today, they had no idea how many keys were out there or who had them. It was clearly time to do something different.

Official Interpretation*

Identifying and controlling physical access devices (e.g., locks, badges, key cards) is just as important as monitoring and limiting who is able to physically access certain equipment. Physical access devices are only strong protection if you know who has them and what access they allow. Physical access devices can be managed using manual or automatic processes such a list of who is assigned what key, or updating the badge access system as personnel change roles.

(CMMC Assessment Guide, Level 2, Copyright 2020, 2021 Carnegie Mellon University and The Johns Hopkins University Applied Physics Laboratory LLC and/or CMMC Assessment Guide, Level 2, Version 2.11 - DRAFT, November 2023)

Assessment Focus

Also known as Assessment Objectives, these are the checklist items that an assessor will seek to verify. Each one must be addressed in your implementation and documentation:

1. physical access devices are identified;
2. physical access devices are controlled; and
3. physical access devices are managed.

(CMMC Assessment Guide, Level 2, Copyright 2020, 2021 Carnegie Mellon University and The Johns Hopkins University Applied Physics Laboratory LLC and/or CMMC Assessment Guide, Level 2, Version 2.11 - DRAFT, November 2023)

Implementation

If we have a lock protecting sensitive materials, that sounds like good security, but that assumes that only authorized personnel can open the lock. In a business environment, employees come and go and change roles within the company. These events can affect the authorization of physical access to controlled areas. There must be a plan for the management of these physical access devices.

Many types of physical access devices exist, including keys, locks, combinations, and card readers. You must have a plan in place that describes how you will manage the integrity of the use of these devices. The plan should include the assignment of responsibility for management. It should also include how events like employee onboarding, off-boarding, and role change will be handled regarding physical access devices.

The first item a CMMC assessor will look for in assessing this requirement is a listing of the physical access devices.

Then, they will look for documentation concerning how access is controlled. This would include information about the process of granting and withdrawing access. The procedures should clarify who has what responsibility and how the process is documented. The control process must be able to answer the question, who currently has access?

With physical keys, an assessor will expect that your procedure will address:

- Who gets keys?
- How are keys controlled?
- How is copying of keys controlled?
- How are keyholder terminations addressed (are locks changed)?
- How are keyholder position changes handled?

The final CMMC assessment question concerns the management of the access control system. Management would include elements such as

- audits of the system to ensure that processes are being followed,
- establishing resilient systems so the integrity of the process is maintained through the potential loss of key individuals,
- seeking continuous improvement.

Assessment Stats

- Assessment Points: 1
- Assessment POAM Eligible: No

Keys

- Document – Develop a list of the physical access devices
- Policy – Develop a written plan of how physical access devices will be controlled and managed.

Physical Protection

PE.L2-3.10.6

Alternative Work Sites

Enforce safeguarding measures for CUI at alternate work sites.

Impact

Nicole works remotely from her home. While she is careful about security, her laptop is occasionally used by her 11-year-old son. She didn't know that he had downloaded a bootleg copy of the greatest game of the day, and what he didn't know was that the "free" copy was contaminated with a remote access trojan (RAT). After that, when Nicole performed her duties as a tooling engineer, all of the CUI that she received was being sent off to unknown people in a distant country.

Official Interpretation*

Many people work from home or travel as part of their job. Define and implement safeguards to account for protection of information beyond the enterprise perimeter. Safeguards may include physical protections, such as locked file drawers, as well as electronic protections such as encryption, audit logging, and proper access controls.

(CMMC Assessment Guide, Level 2, Copyright 2020, 2021 Carnegie Mellon University and The Johns Hopkins University Applied Physics Laboratory LLC and/or CMMC Assessment Guide, Level 2, Version 2.11 - DRAFT, November 2023)

Assessment Focus

Also known as Assessment Objectives, these are the checklist items that an assessor will seek to verify. Each one must be addressed in your implementation and documentation:

1. safeguarding measures for CUI are defined for alternate work sites; and
2. safeguarding measures for CUI are enforced for alternate work sites.

(CMMC Assessment Guide, Level 2, Copyright 2020, 2021 Carnegie Mellon University and The Johns Hopkins University Applied Physics Laboratory LLC and/or CMMC Assessment Guide, Level 2, Version 2.11 - DRAFT, November 2023)

Implementation

If a manager takes CUI home to work on the weekend, their home is an alternate worksite. Similarly, if an employee is working with CUI from a hotel room, then that must be considered an alternative worksite. Anywhere an employee works with CUI outside of the office must be viewed as an alternate worksite, whether in a coffee shop, at the beach, on an airplane, or in the dentist's waiting room.

The creators of CMMC were wise in recognizing that not all CUI activities will occur within the confines of the business facility. However, it is ironic that so many explicit requirements must be applied to the "official" workplace, and so much flexibility is available at an "alternative worksite."

The key to meeting this requirement is that you will define a set of controls that will protect CUI at alternative worksites. Furthermore, you will need to describe how those controls are enforced. While this PE.L2-3.10.6 requirement does not define what those controls will consist of, an assessor might question controls that don't appear to control anything.

Controlling many elements of the alternate worksite is problematic, considering the diversity of possible worksites. When an alternative worksite has some element of permanence, like a home office of a remote worker, then there are more options available than for an ad hoc work location. Under many circumstances, the only thing that can be controlled is the device that the employee is using and a few procedural policies.

It is possible to utilize a Mobile Device Manager (MDM) to maintain a level of enforceable control for devices outside the office. Using a Mobile Device Manager allows greater control, but that is an added expense. Some providers of these products will provide a free version for a limited number of devices.

Many of the controls consist of a commitment from the employee that they will follow a list of do's and don'ts. If the organization has provided the laptop or other equipment, then the organization has more clout in making demands about how that equipment is used. In many organizations, providing equipment is contingent upon the employee signing a Laptop Security Policy. However, enforcement of the alternative worksite controls is part of this requirement, so any employee policy must have teeth and some effort to identify non-conformance.

The controls that affect the handling of CUI and those over remote access must be addressed. These include:

AC.L2-3.1.3	Control CUl Flow	Control the flow of CUI in accordance with approved authorizations.
AC.L2-3.1.12	Control Remote Access	Monitor and control remote access sessions.
AC.L2-3.1.13	Remote Access Confidentiality	Employ cryptographic mechanisms to protect the confidentiality of remote access sessions.
AC.L2-3.1.14	Remote Access Routing	Route remote access via managed access control points.
AC.L2-3.1.15	Privileged Remote Access	Authorize remote execution of privileged commands and remote access to security-relevant information.
AC.L2-3.1.19	Encrypt CUI on Mobile	Encrypt CUI on mobile devices and mobile computing platforms.
IA.L2-3.5.3	Multifactor Authentication	Use multifactor authentication for local and network access to privileged accounts and for network access to non-privileged accounts.
MP.L2-3.8.1	Media Protection	Protect (i.e., physically control and securely store) system media containing CUI, both paper and digital.

SC.L2-3.13.8	Data in Transit	Implement cryptographic mechanisms to prevent unauthorized disclosure of CUI during transmission unless otherwise protected by alternative physical safeguards.
SC.L2-3.13.11	CUI Encryption	Employ FIPS-validated cryptography when used to protect the confidentiality of CUI.
SC.L2-3.13.16	Data at Rest	Protect the confidentiality of CUI at rest.

If your remote workers are handling CUI, the company must have a policy concerning the secure use of a laptop.

Suggested Points to be Addressed by a Company Laptop Security Policy

Clear laptop identification to include brand, model, serial number, and original condition.

A clear statement that the laptop is the property of the organization. The company may request the laptop to be returned at any time. The company is the sole owner of any data and software on the laptop. As the data and software owner, the company can change or remove those digital assets at any time. The company reserves the right to monitor the location of the laptop and activities performed on the laptop.

State that the laptop is provided for business purposes and should not be used for purposes unrelated to the employee's job at the company.

The employee should not allow anybody else to use the laptop unless explicitly permitted by the company IT department or their supervisor.

No software should be installed on the laptop unless the company's IT department approves it.

Any company-installed management and monitoring software should not be disabled, uninstalled, or otherwise made inoperable.

The access controls (passwords or biometrics) should not be disabled from how they are set by the IT department.

The employee should be held responsible for taking steps to ensure the physical security of the laptop:

- When not in use, the laptop should be locked with a password, and caution should be taken when entering any company passwords on the laptop.
- Store the laptop in a locked cabinet or desk when not in use.
- Do not leave your laptop in your vehicle. If it is necessary to leave the laptop in your vehicle for a very short time, it must be locked in the vehicle's trunk.

- When using the laptop in public areas, do not leave the laptop unattended for any length of time.
- Do not pack your laptop in checked luggage when traveling on commercial airlines.
- Attach a name tag or business card to your laptop to clearly identify it during security checks or if it is lost.
- Store the laptop in a hotel room safe or locked suitcase when you are not in the room.

The policy agreement should hold the employee financially responsible for the loss or theft of the laptop resulting from the employee's negligence.

The employee and their supervisor should sign the policy.

HANDY LINK

The text of the suggested laptop policy points can be found at https://tinyurl.com/CMMC4SMB-441

All in all, you will find that workers outside the office create their own special challenges. This is probably why the requirement specifies that these controls should be enforced. There should be a documented effort to ensure that the controls are in place and that the employees are following the requirements of their policies.

Assessment Stats

- Assessment Points: 1
- Assessment POAM Eligible: Yes

Keys

- Policy – Define what controls must be applied when CUI is worked on outside the office. Furthermore, describe how the controls are enforced.

RA.L2-3.11.1

Risk Assessments

Periodically assess the risk to organizational operations (including mission, functions, image, or reputation), organizational assets, and individuals, resulting from the operation of organizational systems and the associated processing, storage, or transmission of CUI.

Impact

Jack was an optimistic kind of guy. He tended to focus on the positive. That was how he ran the IT department. He loved to please people by making visible and helpful improvements to the system. However, as a result, he didn't spend time considering the "what ifs." Had he looked at his system from a critical "what can go wrong" viewpoint, he probably would have realized that he had a large number of critical business functions dependent upon a single mechanical hard drive. He didn't ever acknowledge this risk until the day that the hard drive failed. At that point, it was too late to address the risk.

Official Interpretation*

Risk arises from anything that can reduce an organization's assurance of mission/business success; cause harm to image or reputation; or harm individuals, other organizations, or the Nation.

Organizations assess the risk to their operations and assets at regular intervals. Areas where weakness or vulnerabilities could lead to risk may include:

- poorly designed and executed business processes;
- inadvertent actions of people, such as disclosure or modification of information;
- intentional actions of people inside and outside the organization;
- failure of systems to perform as intended;
- failures of technology; and
- external events, such as natural disasters, public infrastructure and supply chain failures.

When conducting risk assessments use established criteria and procedures. The results of formal risk assessments are documented. It is important to note that risk assessments differ from vulnerability assessments (see RA.L2-3.11.2). A vulnerability assessment provides input to a risk assessment along with other information such as results from likelihood analysis and analysis of potential treat sources.

Risk assessments should be performed at defined regular intervals. Mission risks include anything that will keep an organization from meeting its mission. Function risk is anything that will prevent the performance of a function. Image and reputation risks refer to intangible risks that have value and could cause damage to potential or future trust relationships.

This requirement, RA.L2-3.11.1, which requires periodically assessing the risk to organization systems, assets, and individuals, is a baseline Risk Assessment requirement. RA.L2-3.11.1 enables other Risk Assessment requirements (e.g., RA.L2-3.11.3, Vulnerability Remediation), as well as CA.L2-3.12.2, Plan of Action.

(CMMC Assessment Guide, Level 2, Copyright 2020, 2021 Carnegie Mellon University and The Johns Hopkins University Applied Physics Laboratory LLC and/or CMMC Assessment Guide, Level 2, Version 2.11 - DRAFT, November 2023)

Assessment Focus

Also known as Assessment Objectives, these are the checklist items that an assessor will seek to verify. Each one must be addressed in your implementation and documentation:

1. the frequency to assess risk to organizational operations, organizational assets, and individuals is defined; and
2. risk to organizational operations, organizational assets, and individuals resulting from the operation of an organizational system that processes, stores, or transmits CUI is assessed with the defined frequency.

(CMMC Assessment Guide, Level 2, Copyright 2020, 2021 Carnegie Mellon University and The Johns Hopkins University Applied Physics Laboratory LLC and/or CMMC Assessment Guide, Level 2, Version 2.11 - DRAFT, November 2023)

Implementation

At some interval (defined by the organization), there needs to be a risk assessment performed. This doesn't need to be formal or comprehensive to be compliant or effective. Although some portion of the risk to be evaluated is technical, it is important to have management representation present for the risk assessment meeting to provide their perspective.

Many people in the top management of organizations of all sizes are living under the delusion that any company that experiences a cybersecurity incident must have had incompetent security management. Typically, their first response to a security incident is firing the person who let it happen. Of course, any company, even those with multi-million dollar security budgets, may experience a security incident. When management participates in risk assessment, it can open their eyes to recognize that 100% cybersecurity doesn't exist. This can be good for your own job security.

To fulfill the requirements of RA.L2-3.11.1, this risk assessment is supposed to be focused explicitly on the CUI processes. However, the protection of CUI is integrally tied to the rest of your cybersecurity. From a practical standpoint, since these are so deeply tied together, this will likely be a general assessment of data and systems risk, emphasizing CUI.

In a small business, this risk assessment might look like a meeting with players representing IT, document control, government contracting, and management responsibilities. At this meeting, they might brainstorm through a list of risk areas (like the list given above), developing a list of the risks appropriate to the organization. Then, after the list is compiled, they would go back through it, determining if the risk applies to CUI or not, identifying a probability of occurrence and a seriousness of occurrence (perhaps each of these would be on a 10-point scale). Then, this list could be sorted on probability times seriousness so the most significant risks float to the top.

A record of this risk assessment should be generated and kept. The Internet has numerous resources on how a risk assessment can be performed and forms that can be used to record your assessment. Make this process as simple as possible, and don't try to duplicate what others do if it doesn't work in your organization (most risk assessments are overly complex for the typical small organization). If your risk assessment is excessively complex, compliance will be challenging. Focus on the big picture.

Here are some questions to help bring out the risks your organization faces:

1. What are the cyber-attack methods that are currently trending?
2. How vulnerable are we to those cyber-attacks?
3. What are our most valuable data assets?
4. Are those "most valuable data assets" protected adequately from today's attack methods?
5. If we had a significant attack, would we be able to recover our systems?
6. Do our own people do things that put us at risk?
7. Do we have obsolete operating systems, software, or hardware that put us at risk?
8. Are we confident that the contractors or consultants with access to our systems are not creating risk?
9. Do we have single pieces of hardware on which large portions of our data systems depend (single-point-of-failure)?
10. What is the most likely cyber disaster for our organization?

You would want to ensure that at least one risk assessment is performed before your initial certification assessment.

Assessment Stats

- Assessment Points: 3
- Assessment POAM Eligible: No

Keys

- Policy – Determine and publish a frequency at which these risk assessments will be conducted.
- Policy – Determine a method for these risk assessments. Determine the records to be generated by the assessment process.

Risk Assessment

RA.L2-3.11.2

Vulnerability Scan

Scan for vulnerabilities in organizational systems and applications periodically and when new vulnerabilities affecting those systems and applications are identified.

Impact

The IT manager, Katie, felt she was doing a good job running the department. She was both service and security-minded. She didn't realize that she was sitting atop a proverbial powder keg. As she went about her job, she had no way of knowing that the network contained a critical security vulnerability. She signed up for a deal from an IT consulting group, where they would perform a security scan for free. When she received the report, she was astonished at the number of issues rated as "severe" and also the item listed as "critical." While she thought this might just be a scam to get business, it still concerned her. After researching and performing her own scan, she realized these vulnerabilities were real. She realized she was just plain lucky there hadn't been any significant security incidents.

Official Interpretation*

A vulnerability scanner is an application that identifies vulnerabilities in organizational assets. Most scanners can create a prioritized list of vulnerabilities ordered by their level of severity. Scan for vulnerabilities on all devices connected to the network including servers, desktops, laptops, virtual machines, containers, firewalls, switches, and printers. All assets that are within the scope of the CMMC assessment must be scanned, including assets such as laptop computers that may not routinely connect to an organization's network.

Perform reviews of your organization's custom-developed software. Vulnerability analysis of a custom-made solution may require a penetration tester to properly test and validate findings. Automated vulnerability scanners may not be as thorough when scanning custom developed applications. Source code scanners can help identify weaknesses and vulnerabilities within code prior to compilation and use.

The vulnerability scanning process is a regular activity, not a single occurrence. Organizations put in place a vulnerability scanner that updates its database each time it performs a scan so it can identify the most current known vulnerabilities. Schedule scans with consideration of the potential for impact to normal operations and use caution when scanning critical assets.

This requirement, RA.L2-3.11.2, which ensures scanning for vulnerabilities in organizational systems and application, is a baseline Risk Assessment requirement. RA.L2-3.11.2, contributes to performing risk assessments as described in RA.L2-3.11.1.

(CMMC Assessment Guide, Level 2, Copyright 2020, 2021 Carnegie Mellon University and The Johns Hopkins University Applied Physics Laboratory LLC and/or CMMC Assessment Guide, Level 2, Version 2.11 - DRAFT, November 2023)

Assessment Focus

Also known as Assessment Objectives, these are the checklist items that an assessor will seek to verify. Each one must be addressed in your implementation and documentation:

1. the frequency to scan for vulnerabilities in organizational systems and applications is defined;
2. vulnerability scans are performed on organizational systems with the defined frequency;
3. vulnerability scans are performed on applications with the defined frequency;
4. vulnerability scans are performed on organizational systems when new vulnerabilities are identified; and
5. vulnerability scans are performed on applications when new vulnerabilities are identified.

(CMMC Assessment Guide, Level 2, Copyright 2020, 2021 Carnegie Mellon University and The Johns Hopkins University Applied Physics Laboratory LLC and/or CMMC Assessment Guide, Level 2, Version 2.11 - DRAFT, November 2023)

Implementation

A vulnerability scanner is a tool that looks at your network and runs a series of tests on that machine. The things checked range from questionable configurations to critical, exploitable issues. To satisfy this requirement, you need to periodically scan your network (no information is provided about how often this needs to occur).

It should be understood that there are two different approaches to vulnerability scans. The first approach is to scan your network from the outside. Depending upon the configuration of your firewall and internet-facing services that might be available, this scan might have drastically different value to your organization. Like it or not, hostile outsiders often perform this sort of scan, just as a potential car thief might check door handles, looking for opportunities.

The next type of vulnerability scan is performed within your network. This type of scan generally yields a higher yield. You might ask why this type of scan matters if you have a good firewall. An internal scan can identify the issues that might allow ransomware to spread unchecked through your entire network or make the difference between a nuisance and a disaster. This is the type of vulnerability scan required to satisfy this requirement.

The first time you perform a vulnerability scan in your network, be prepared to be shocked. What may seem like a tightly controlled network can have an unexpectedly large number of vulnerabilities.

No guidance is provided concerning how frequently these scans need to be conducted. While you could meet the letter of the requirement with yearly scans, this might be putting your network and data at risk.

New vulnerabilities are discovered daily. This means a network considered perfectly adequate one week can have a severe vulnerability when examined the following week. This makes updating the list of vulnerabilities to be scanned especially critical. This factor also encourages more frequent scans.

If your vulnerability scans, and corresponding vulnerability list updates, are less frequent than every couple of weeks, then your documentation should address how newly added vulnerabilities should be addressed. Address how these additions will be scanned for. If you have frequent scans and updates, this issue will take care of itself.

Meeting this requirement for vulnerability scanning generally has costs associated with it. As you approach this requirement, consider that you can obtain the technology to perform the scans or hire a contractor to perform the scans on your behalf. By contracting, you might avoid the cost of obtaining and managing the software. The advantage to running it yourself is that you can perform the scans frequently without additional expense, including follow-up scans after a vulnerability has been addressed.

There are a few free options for vulnerability scanners from commercial providers, but they tend to be inflexible and slow to receive the latest updates. To graduate to a paid version is typically a giant jump in cost. Some products are suitable for very small operations (like under 25 devices, where a device is defined by having an IP address) and may even have a free option. The available options change continuously.

There are some open-source vulnerability scanners on the market. OpenVAS is free and runs on Linux. OpenVAS is pre-installed on the KALI Linux distro. Using OpenVAS, you can download a (more or less) current list of known vulnerabilities and then have it scan your network for these. These open-source options do not normally have very good or current vulnerability lists. Many users started with these options but graduated to a paid scanner after seeing how difficult the open-source options were.

In addition, some free vulnerability scanner options are available to promote cybersecurity. These include options by CISA, dibnet.dod.mil (for DoD contractors), and the NSA. These are typically limited in capability, like only performing external scans.

If you are trying to justify the cost and time associated with setting up vulnerability scans, think of how ransomware works. While a phishing email may trick a user into running malevolent code on the first computer, the malware then exploits existing system vulnerabilities to infect other systems. These vulnerabilities are generally well-known but remain unfixed within many networks. Ridding your network of these vulnerabilities can make the difference between malware that goes "fzzt" or one that goes "BOOM!"

The requirement also requires application scanning. This application scanning provision is only required if custom software is in use. Commercial software is already being evaluated in the marketplace. However, custom software may not get the scrutiny and patching that commercial products receive. The process of performing vulnerability scanning of custom software is beyond the scope of this document.

For reasons of personal liability, ensure that you have written permission from upper management before conducting vulnerability scanning on your network. Otherwise, you are breaking the law. Written permission from management to do your job may seem excessive, but this protects you from this rare possibility. I am sure everyone who got in trouble for scanning their own company believed it couldn't happen.

Assessment Stats

- Assessment Points: 5
- Assessment POAM Eligible: No

Keys

- Capability – Develop the capability to scan organizational systems and applications for vulnerabilities.
- Policy – Determine and document the frequency of scans.
- Policy – Define the specifics of the process used to perform scans. This may include information about how the vulnerability listings are to be updated. Reporting of results may also be addressed.
- Documentation – You should be able to provide evidence that the scans were being performed according to the defined schedule. This is easy for the CMMC assessor to evaluate, so expect it.
- Documentation – You should address the absence or presence of custom software in your documentation.

Risk Assessment

RA.L2-3.11.3

Vulnerability Remediation

Remediate vulnerabilities in accordance with risk assessments.

Impact

When Tori ran a vulnerability scan on the network, she was surprised by the length of the list. The list was quite intimidating for an already busy person. As a result, she did not act to address the identified vulnerabilities; instead, she waited for a time when she wasn't quite so busy. When the attack came, she immediately thought of the vulnerabilities identified in the scan and wished she had made the time to take action on the identified items.

Official Interpretation*

Not all vulnerabilities captured in a vulnerability scanner may pose the same level of risk to an organization. Prioritize mitigation efforts to close the most critical vulnerabilities first. Track all vulnerability remediation to ensure completion; also track vulnerabilities that you have determined not to remediate.

This requirement, RA.L2-3.11.3, benefits from CA.L2-3.12.2. RA.L2-3.11.3 allows remediation of vulnerabilities to take place based on the developed plans of actions for vulnerabilities from CA.L2-3.12.2.

(CMMC Assessment Guide, Level 2, Copyright 2020, 2021 Carnegie Mellon University and The Johns Hopkins University Applied Physics Laboratory LLC and/or CMMC Assessment Guide, Level 2, Version 2.11 - DRAFT, November 2023)

Assessment Focus

Also known as Assessment Objectives, these are the checklist items that an assessor will seek to verify. Each one must be addressed in your implementation and documentation:

1. vulnerabilities are identified; and
2. vulnerabilities are remediated in accordance with risk assessments.

(CMMC Assessment Guide, Level 2, Copyright 2020, 2021 Carnegie Mellon University and The Johns Hopkins University Applied Physics Laboratory LLC and/or CMMC Assessment Guide, Level 2, Version 2.11 - DRAFT, November 2023)

Implementation

After your network is scanned for vulnerabilities, action must be taken to address those found vulnerabilities. You are NOT required to fix every vulnerability identified in your scan. Still, you need to "address" all vulnerabilities through a process developed and documented that allows you to determine what vulnerabilities you will fix.

Not all vulnerabilities are equally easy to fix. Some vulnerabilities are easy to fix, and they would be considered "low-hanging fruit," regardless of the risk rating that the issue was assigned. On the other hand, fixing some problems might be unjustifiably expensive, politically unpopular, or just require more resources than are available. These are cases where the risk associated with the issue and the cost of fixing it must be considered together. Other issues may not be of consequence in your specific environment because of mitigating factors. For any decisions to ignore or postpone remediation of issues of all but low-risk items, it is a good idea to ensure management understands the issue and buys into the decision. This way, if anything goes wrong, they will not be blindsided.

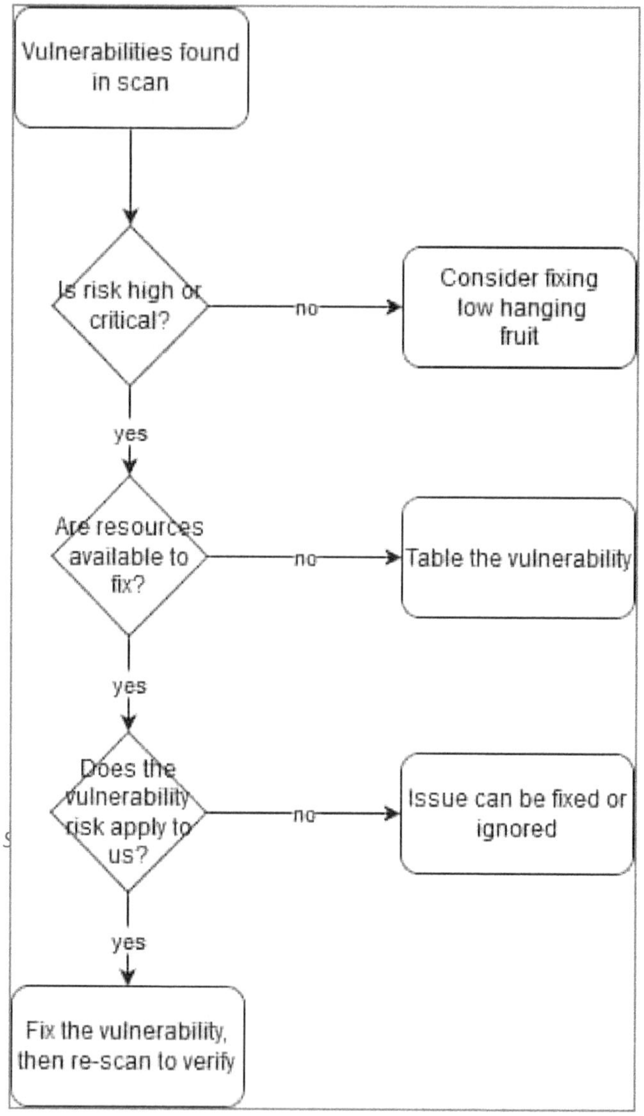

Sample Decision Tree

Your organization's policy might be to only address the vulnerabilities listed as "critical" or "high" risk, with vulnerabilities of lower risk to be taken under advisement. Compliance with RA.L2-3.11.3 does not require fixing every found vulnerability but instead addressing issues according to risk assessments. That risk assessment says you accept the risk with your eyes open. This risk assessment should be conducted according to a documented process.

There should be documentation when vulnerabilities are selected to be ignored, especially for any subjective reason. During a CMMC assessment, you want it to be clear that all vulnerabilities have been addressed, even if the selected action is to do nothing about them.

When the remediation of issues is completed, another scan should be performed to confirm the effectiveness of the remediation.

This process is a clear candidate for tracking through the POAM system. Whatever tool is used, documenttion should include:

- Justification for any decision not to address
- Action taken
- Results of efforts to confirm the effectiveness of the remediation actions.

Assessment Stats

- Assessment Points: 1
- Assessment POAM Eligible: Yes

Keys

- Process – Develop a plan for remediation of identified vulnerabilities. This must include the process for the risk assessment, record keeping, and testing of remediation actions.

Risk Management

CA.L2-3.12.1

Security Control Assessment

Periodically assess the security controls in organizational systems to determine if the controls are effective in their application.

Impact

At ABC Company, they had a control requiring their users to have a logon password of at least six characters, which was quite old. When they stop to consider the effectiveness of their controls, they recognize that, with advances in technology, 6-character passwords are no longer providing adequate security. As technology, the nature of your business, regulatory requirements, and the threat landscape change, the controls that might have provided adequate security at one time are no longer effective. However, going through our normal day-to-day, these things can easily be missed. Taking an opportunity to stop and evaluate the big-picture security effectiveness is essential.

Official Interpretation*

Avoid a "set it and forget it" mentality when implementing security controls. The security landscape is constantly changing. Reassess existing controls at periodic intervals in order to validate their effectiveness in your environment. Set the assessment schedule according to organizational needs. Consider regulatory obligations and internal policies when assessing the controls.

Outputs from security control assessments typically include:

- documented assessment results;
- proposed new controls, or updates to existing controls;
- remediation plans; and
- newly identified risks.

This requirement, CA.L2-3.12.1, which ensures determining security controls are implemented properly, promotes effective security assessments for organizational systems mandated by CA.L2-3.12.3.

(CMMC Assessment Guide, Level 2, Copyright 2020, 2021 Carnegie Mellon University and The Johns Hopkins University Applied Physics Laboratory LLC and/or CMMC Assessment Guide, Level 2, Version 2.11 - DRAFT, November 2023)

Assessment Focus

Also known as Assessment Objectives, these are the checklist items that an assessor will seek to verify. Each one must be addressed in your implementation and documentation:

1. the frequency of security control assessments is defined; and
2. security controls are assessed with the defined frequency to determine if the controls are effective in their application.

(CMMC Assessment Guide, Level 2, Copyright 2020, 2021 Carnegie Mellon University and The Johns Hopkins University Applied Physics Laboratory LLC and/or CMMC Assessment Guide, Level 2, Version 2.11 - DRAFT, November 2023)

Implementation

If this sounds the same as what you read back in RA.L2-3.11.1 (risk assessment), you would be mostly correct. The activities in these two requirements are very similar but approach risk from a different direction. This assessment of controls is supposed to focus on the effectiveness of what you are already doing.

Looking at effectiveness is different than looking at compliance. For example, a control that requires users to change their complex passwords every two weeks should be good for preventing password brute-force hacking, but standing back and looking at the effect on overall security might reveal that it isn't as good as expected. A control like that would force the users to write down their passwords, thus creating a new vulnerability. So, while this might push the risk of brute-force password attacks to a low level, it does not have good effectiveness at securing the environment.

The process needs to be conducted periodically. This periodic process can be performed simultaneously with other periodic processes. The frequency of this process should be defined.

If this assessment is performed simultaneously with the periodic evaluation of the SSP, then it is possible to run through each CMMC requirement to assess both the compliance and the effectiveness of the controls.

This assessment should focus on the big picture of how secure your system is and what can be done to make it better. Maintain a record of these discussions. This evaluation should be conducted in accordance with written policy.

The areas of improvement identified in this assessment can potentially be recorded in the POAM system to track them through the implementation process. This provides good documentation that an assessor can review. This is not a requirement. There are many other ways that the identified improvements can be documented for the benefit of an assessor.

Assessment Stats

- Assessment Points: 5
- Assessment POAM Eligible: No

Keys

- Policy – Determine the frequency that the security control assessment will be performed.
- Procedure – Create a procedure for how this security effectiveness evaluation will be conducted. This would include defining the process, who is involved, what records are created, and what will be done with the results.
- Documentation – Create records of the security control assessments.

Security Assessment

CA.L2-3.12.2

Plan of Action

Develop and implement plans of action designed to correct deficiencies and reduce or eliminate vulnerabilities in organizational systems.

Impact

Alice works in a small business doing all of their IT. She climbs under a user's desk one minute and works in Active Directory the next. As she runs from one thing to the next, she occasionally identifies a security issue that needs to be addressed. If it is something she can address quickly, she is pretty good at getting it done, but if the fix is time-consuming, it may get started but never be completed. This requirement suggests a system that tracks the various remediation efforts through effective resolution should be utilized.

Official Interpretation*

When you write a plan of action, define the clear goal or objective of the plan. You may include the following in the action plan:

- ownership of who is accountable for ensuring the plan's performance;
- specific steps or milestones that are clear and actionable;
- assigned responsibility for each step or milestone;
- milestones to measure plan progress; and
- completion dates.

This requirement, CA.L2-3.12.2, which ensures developing and implementing plans of action to correct and reduce vulnerabilities in systems, is driven by risk management requirement RA.L2-3.11.1, which promotes periodically assessing risk to organizational systems. CA.L2-3.12.2 promotes monitoring security controls on an ongoing basis as defined in requirement CA.L2-3.12.3.

(CMMC Assessment Guide, Level 2, Copyright 2020, 2021 Carnegie Mellon University and The Johns Hopkins University Applied Physics Laboratory LLC and/or CMMC Assessment Guide, Level 2, Version 2.11 - DRAFT, November 2023)

Assessment Focus

Also known as Assessment Objectives, these are the checklist items that an assessor will seek to verify. Each one must be addressed in your implementation and documentation:

1. deficiencies and vulnerabilities to be addressed by the plan of action are identified;
2. a plan of action is developed to correct identified deficiencies and reduce or eliminate identified vulnerabilities; and
3. the plan of action is implemented to correct identified deficiencies and reduce or eliminate identified vulnerabilities.

Implementation

Good security can never sit still. There are always risks to mitigate, vulnerabilities to address, or changes in the business that require addressing. Whether the action items come out of the initial implementation, responding to an incident (IR.L2-3.6.1), addressing vulnerabilities (RA.L2-3.11.3), continual improvement, or from somewhere else, these actions need to be handled following the plans of action as described in this requirement.

The essence of this requirement is that you have some sort of structure in place that assures that plans become action. In a resource-strapped organization, it is easy for plans to get lost before they are fully implemented. CMMC does not specify what this tracking structure looks like. It could be paper-based, a spreadsheet, or even a full project management system. It might utilize an existing ERP or other system already in use.

Determine what is best for your organization. Remember that this system must be <u>used</u> to be useful and maintain conformance. If this is hidden away and only pulled out in the weeks before an assessment for cramming-in updates, it is not value-added. This system can potentially serve an important role in your organization or be something thrown together to show to an assessor. Remember that your assessor will likely ask people in your organization about your POAMs. Imagine the difference between interviewed employees who are informed and where the employees have no idea about the planned changes.

In a small organization where the same person, or small team, is planning and implementing, spending a lot of time creating detailed plans is often not value-added. Unless it adds value to your specific organization for these plans to be long and formal, a plan of action might just be a couple of columns on a spreadsheet or a few sentences on a document.

The key points to a minimalist Plan of Action (POA) are:

- Assure that the POA includes "action" to be taken and isn't just a restating of the problem,
- The POA should have a specific individual that will be held accountable for the action getting done and the results being recorded,
- The POA needs to describe the action that will be taken and
- Finally, the POA needs a completion date (this might be two fields: planned and actual)
- Bonus: Since CM.L2-3.4.4 says that changes must have the security impact analyzed, it only makes sense that each POA should include a section for security analysis.

The POA documents (regardless of form) must be kept current. In a small organization, it is easy to simply jump in and start addressing an issue instead of doing paperwork about it. However, the auditors are going to expect to see completed POA records. Until a POA habit is developed, there may be a certain amount of writing the plans after the action is completed. This defeats the purpose of this requirement and won't necessarily make an auditor happy (if they find out), so the users must be encouraged to create the POA as a first step.

The Plan of Action may include multiple intermediate milestone dates and records instead of a single completion date. Multiple milestones are not required but may be appropriate for more detailed projects.

As this Plan of Action system is defined, it makes sense to determine how missed goal dates will be addressed. For example, will date adjustments be permitted? What accountability will be applied? Although a CMMC assessor will probably not be concerned if a goal date is occasionally missed, they will be concerned if this appears normal. It would be a problem if an assessor looked at POAs and found one where the POA was initiated, the goal date is missed, and there is no evidence of any action ever being taken. The CMMC assessor's guide, the CMMC Assessment Process, says, "The POAM should detail the progress of corrective actions as they are carried out and thus must be updated regularly."

There is an option for a limited set of the CMMC requirements if the CMMC assessor fails to find the organization's implementation and documentation adequate to meet the standard. An assessor may allow the organization to initiate a POAM. There are restrictions on these POAMs, and they cannot span longer than 180 days, and not all requirements are subject to this process.

This concept of an assessment POAM should never be construed as a license to be assessed before all requirements are fully implemented. The assessor's guidance of these POAMs specifically states that requirements that are not implemented would result in a NOT MET. So, all requirements must be implemented before assessment.

After you go to the effort to create a POAM system, it may be to the advantage of your organization if the system can be a value-added tool. There are circumstances where using a POAM system is required for your CMMC certification. There are other circumstances where this same system can be useful for organizing and assuring follow-through on various projects and actions. You will note that CM.L2-3.4.3 says changes should be tracked and logged. A POAM system is designed to track and log events. Placing these events into POAM provides a good repository for the documentation of the events. Possible activities to include in your POAM system:

- Conformance deployment
- Security deployment
- Incident response (IR.L2-3.6.2)
- Personnel action (PS.L2-3.9.2)
- Vulnerability remediation (RA.L2-3.11.3)
- Flaw remediation (SI.L1-3.14.1)
- Effectiveness Assessments (CA.L2-3.12.1)
- Security Alert Response (SI.L2-3.14.3)
- Contractor changes
- Scope changes
- Investigate suspicious events (AU.L2-3.3.5)
- Event Review (AU.L2-3.3.3)
- Preventive Maintenance Projects (MA.L2-3.7.1)

By adding fields to your POAM system, you can track the records for:

- Systems Change Management (CM.L2-3.4.3)
- Security Impact Analysis (CM.L2-3.4.4)

Assessment Stats

- Assessment Points: 3
- Assessment POAM Eligible: No

Keys

- Policy – In preparation for taking action to work on the security system, a Plan of Action should be written. The policy should define the procedure and responsibilities involved in the process.
- Data – Create a format for POAs that works for your organization. The POA should record a level of detail that works for your organization and the work to be done.

CA.L2-3.12.3

Security Control Monitoring

Monitor security controls on an ongoing basis to ensure the continued effectiveness of the controls.

Impact

Anthony was growing worried as he kept hearing reports of organizations with much larger budgets for cybersecurity that were getting brought down by ransomware. He decided that he was going to test some elements of his organization's controls. He set up a system to send his people some simulated phishing emails and detect if they clicked on the link. He was astonished at the number of people who mindlessly clicked on the email links. He continued testing his people as he implemented measures to fix the vulnerability and then on an ongoing basis to ensure the controls didn't slip.

Official Interpretation*

Provide a plan for monitoring the state of security controls on a recurring basis that occurs more frequently than the periodic assessments discussed in CA.L2-3.12.1. This process provides a mechanism to assess the overall security posture of your organization, which directly relates to activities discussed in CA.L2-3.12.4. As a result, the process not only maintains awareness of vulnerabilities and threats, but it also informs management of the effectiveness of the security controls in determining if security controls are current and for management to make an acceptable risk decision.

(CMMC Assessment Guide, Level 2, Copyright 2020, 2021 Carnegie Mellon University and The Johns Hopkins University Applied Physics Laboratory LLC and/or CMMC Assessment Guide, Level 2, Version 2.11 - DRAFT, November 2023)

Assessment Focus

Also known as Assessment Objectives, these are the checklist items that an assessor will seek to verify. Each one must be addressed in your implementation and documentation:

1. security controls are monitored on an ongoing basis to ensure the continued effectiveness of those controls.

(CMMC Assessment Guide, Level 2, Copyright 2020, 2021 Carnegie Mellon University and The Johns Hopkins University Applied Physics Laboratory LLC and/or CMMC Assessment Guide, Level 2, Version 2.11 - DRAFT, November 2023)

Implementation

At first glance, this looks very similar to CA.L2-3.12.1. However, the focus is different. This requirement is focused on establishing monitoring of security controls. To satisfy this requirement, it is important to consider metrics that can be utilized to monitor effective security.

These metrics do not need to cover everything to meet the requirements but should focus on effectiveness. Just as your car's dashboard provides feedback about some key data about how your vehicle is operating, you would want your security effectiveness to provide key data about your security systems. It is more important to have a few meaningful measurements than it is to have a large quantity of mixed-value metrics.

It is not necessary for the data to automatically come together into a single dashboard; it can be harvested from multiple sources or tools. However, it isn't enough that these effectiveness metrics are available if somebody goes digging for them. Since the requirement specifies "monitor," "ongoing basis," and "continued effectiveness," it isn't enough to have a tool that is capable of reporting a metric. Somebody must be looking at these identified metrics.

For the best coverage of this requirement:

- Construct a list of the metrics to be monitored, including where the data comes from and the frequency that it should be monitored,
- Then go and harvest the data at the appointed frequency and compile it into a single place (like a spreadsheet or paper form),
- Having the data charted or other graphical representation might be helpful in the identification of trends (and CMMC assessors might like it).

The selected metrics might be items already being monitored to satisfy other requirements. That is not a problem as long as they are a good indicator of security effectiveness.

It would be nice to be able to identify what you would like to see measured and monitored; however, in a small organization, that might be impractical. The pragmatic approach, subject to continual improvement, would be to look at the available data from the tools you already use in your environment. Look at your firewall, Active Directory, logging system, antivirus, facility security system, etc. for suitable data. If the data can be construed as a measurement of effectiveness, it can be utilized for this requirement.

It would be easy for this to get out of hand. Keep it simple. If you have 5-10 metrics you are monitoring, assuming they are useful metrics, that is probably better than having 1000 metrics to get lost in.

These efforts may never yield any value-added intelligence. In the small organization, this is an action that is primarily for conformance to requirements, but does not significantly contribute to real security. It should be prioritized accordingly.

Assessment Stats

- Assessment Points: 5
- Assessment POAM Eligible: No

Keys

- Policy – Determine and document several metrics that can be monitored to indicate the effectiveness of your system.
- Data – Compile the data at defined intervals and evaluate it for possible action.
- Evidence – Be prepared to demonstrate that planned monitoring occurs at the defined intervals. This is typically a record in which something was done with the data.

Security Assessment

CA.L2-3.12.4

System Security Plan

Develop, document, and periodically update system security plans that describe system boundaries, system environments of operation, how security requirements are implemented, and the relationships with or connections to other systems.

Impact

Just as a doctoral student puts everything together into a thesis, the System Security Plan is the culmination of all your efforts to implement CMMC. This pulls everything together and puts it into a form you can hand to the CMMC assessor. The assessor will use the SSP as a roadmap to understand what you have implemented, and it will guide the entire assessment.

Official Interpretation*

A system security plan (SSP) is a document that outlines how an organization implements its security requirements. At a minimum, an SSP must include:

- Description of the CMMC Assessment Scope;
- CMMC Assessment Scope Description: high-level description of the assets within the assessment scope;
- Description of the Environment of Operation: physical surroundings in which an information system processes, stores, and transmits information;
- Identified and Approved Security Requirements: requirements levied on an information system that are derived from applicable laws, Executive Orders, directives, policies, standards, instructions, regulations, procedures, or organizational mission/business case needs to ensure the confidentiality, integrity, and availability of the information being processed, stored, or transmitted;
- Implementation Method for Security Requirements: description of how the identified and approved security requirements are implemented with the system or environment;
- Connections and Relationships to Other Systems and Networks: description of related, dependent, and interconnected systems; and

- Defined Frequency of Updates: typically at least annually.

In addition to the requirements above, an SSP often includes:

- general information system description: technical and functional description;
- design philosophies: defense-in-depth strategies and allowed interfaces and network protocols; and
- roles and responsibilities: description of the roles and responsibilities for key personnel, which may include the system owner, system custodian, authorizing officials, and other stakeholders

This requirement, CA.L2-3.12.4, which requires developing, documenting, and updating system security plans, promotes effective information security within organizational systems required by SC.L2-3.13.2, as well as other system and communications protection requirements.

(CMMC Assessment Guide, Level 2, Copyright 2020, 2021 Carnegie Mellon University and The Johns Hopkins University Applied Physics Laboratory LLC and/or CMMC Assessment Guide, Level 2, Version 2.11 - DRAFT, November 2023)

Assessment Focus

Also known as Assessment Objectives, these are the checklist items that an assessor will seek to verify. Each one must be addressed in your implementation and documentation:

1. a system security plan is developed;
2. the system boundary is described and documented in the system security plan;
3. the system environment of operation is described and documented in the system security plan;
4. the security requirements identified and approved by the designated authority as non-applicable are identified;
5. the method of security requirement implementation is described and documented in the system security plan;
6. the relationship with or connection to other systems is described and documented in the system security plan;
7. the frequency to update the system security plan is defined; and
8. system security plan is updated with the defined frequency.

(CMMC Assessment Guide, Level 2, Copyright 2020, 2021 Carnegie Mellon University and The Johns Hopkins University Applied Physics Laboratory LLC and/or CMMC Assessment Guide, Level 2, Version 2.11 - DRAFT, November 2023)

Implementation

Your System Security Plan is the high-level summary of what you are doing to implement CMMC. This document serves two primary purposes:

1. It is an overview of your systems and data protection. This consists of information like
    - Roles and responsibilities,
    - A listing of security standards your organization conforms to,
    - Information about interconnected systems,
    - Data protection overview.
2. Serves as an index to all of the policies and procedures that detail how each of the CMMC Level 2 requirements is being met. These document references should include a high-level summary (without

technical details) of how your organization complies with the requirements. Then, the full details would be in the referenced documents. By starting with the SSP and following the references, it should be possible to find all the system policies and procedures.

The requirements for an SSP are very clear, but the SSP form is entirely up to the company, just so it contains all of the required elements. For example, it is not required to be a single document.

The SSP must include:

Assessment Scope

This defining of the CMMC scope is critical. Your CMMC implementation can potentially be made simpler if your scope is limited. There may be some specific headache areas in making your system conform to CMMC, but it might be possible that some of these areas could be considered out-of-scope or Contractor Risk Managed Assets and therefore get less attention during your assessment. Refer to the CMMC Level 2 Scoping Guidance document and the Scoping section of this book.

Scope Assets

This would be a description of the assets that are within the assessment scope. Although it is not identified in the requirements the Level 2 Scoping Guide makes multiple references to a network diagram, so assessors are likely to expect it. Assets would need to be divided into these categories:

- CUI Assets – These assets process, store, or transmit CUI. They will be assessed against all of the CMMC requirements.
- Security Protection Assets – These assets might process, store, or transmit CUI. The defining characteristic of these assets is that they perform some security function. These include your domain control servers, routers that divide in and out of scope assets, a vulnerability scanner, etc. These assets will be assessed against the CMMC requirements.
- Contractor Risk Managed Assets – In theory, these assets could process, store, or transmit CUI, but where "security policy, procedures, and practices" limit the devices from processing, storing, or transmitting any CUI. The controls protecting these assets are subject to evaluation. These controls must have sufficient strength and effectiveness for the assets to avoid being assessed against the CMMC requirements. An assessor has the option to evaluate them against all of the CMMC requirements if they determine that the controls are inadequate to prevent CUI from being accessed. The documentation for each CRMA asset should contain a description of the controls that keep CUI away.
- Specialized Assets – These are assets with distinct characteristics that earn their place in this category. These include:
    - Government-owned
    - Internet of Things devices (IoT) - Unmanned, Internet-connected devices on your network. They might report data or be controlled remotely.
    - Operational Technology (OT) – These devices control other physical equipment.
    - Restricted Information Systems – These are assets where the Government specifically dictates their configuration (for example, STIG)
    - Test Equipment
- Out-of-Scope Assets – These assets are incapable of any CUI access. These devices must not connect to any CUI-handling devices. They might be on a separate network or separated by a router from the CUI. These devices do not need to be addressed in the asset inventory and will not be assessed against the CMMC requirements.

Description of the Environment

This is a description of your system environment. This would include a general description of your network, the applicable facilities, the organization, and the geographic environment. If there is anything noteworthy about your company or workforce, it might also be mentioned here.

Identified Security Requirements

This would be a description of any special security requirements that your company, or specifically your information systems, might seek to comply with. These include mandatory legal requirements applicable to your industry or voluntary standards your organization chooses to comply with.

Security Requirement Implementation

This would be a listing of the 110 requirements of CMMC Level 2. It would briefly describe how your organization will ensure compliance with each requirement. This description may reference applicable procedures, policies, forms, or records.

The requirement's SSP description and the referenced documents should present a complete picture of how the organization meets the requirement and the Assessment Objectives (listed in this document as Assessment Focus).

Connection to Other Systems

This section should detail any connected system. This might be business partners, web properties, or simply the organization's Internet access.

Defined SSP Update Frequency

This is the easy part. You need to assign a frequency at which the SSP will be reviewed. Annual reviews are probably the most common frequency. This frequency should not be longer than annual. Like all periodic events, you must ensure the action gets performed according to the schedule. There should be some documentation of the review process. The SSP is expected to be a living document that is continually changed to reflect improvements and changes to the network and security processes; however, this periodic review is the opportunity to examine the whole document and identify any updates that might have been missed.

Assessment Stats

- Assessment Points: SPECIAL*
- Assessment POAM Eligible: No*

*Lack of a proper SSP will cause an assessment to immediately termininate

Keys

- Document Creation – The SSP document is a cornerstone of your auditable security system. When you are assessed, the assessor is likely to start with this document to understand your security system and then use it to find the remainder of the documentation of your fully implemented system. Assure that the SSP contains all of the required content.
- Document Maintenance - Ensure that the SSP and associated documentation are properly maintained and kept current. There should be some documentation of the periodic review being performed according to the published schedule.

Security Assessment

SC.L1-3.13.1

Boundary Protection

Monitor, control, and protect communications (i.e., information transmitted or received by organizational systems) at the external boundaries and key internal boundaries of organizational systems.

Impact

"Complexity is the enemy of security" is what Becca always said and how she managed the company network. A few years ago, when the company moved to a VOIP (voice over IP) phone system, she heard that many people moved their phone system onto its own VLAN. She considered this but decided that doing this would introduce a level of complexity that was not in the best interest of the small company. But recently, when the network was breached by way of the phone system, there were no barriers to keep the hackers from accessing all of the machines in the company. This incident caused Becca to learn the hard way why internal boundaries have value.

Official Interpretation*

Fences, locks, badges, and key cards help keep non-employees out of your physical facilities. Similarly, your company's IT network or system has boundaries that must be protected. Many companies use a web proxy and a firewall.

When an employee uses a company computer to go to a website, a web proxy makes the request on the user's behalf, looks at the web request, and decides if it should let the employee go to the website.

A firewall controls access from the inside and outside, protecting valuable information and resources stored on the company's network. A firewall stops unwanted traffic on the internet from passing through an outside "fence" to the company's networks and information systems. Internal boundaries determine where data can flow, for instance a software development environment may have its own boundary controlling, monitoring, and protecting the data that can leave that boundary.

It may be wise to monitor, control, or protect one part of the company network from another. This can also be accomplished with a firewall and limits the ability of attackers and disgruntled employees from entering sensitive parts of your internal network and causing damage.

(CMMC Assessment Guide, Level 2, Copyright 2020, 2021 Carnegie Mellon University and The Johns Hopkins University Applied Physics Laboratory LLC and/or CMMC Assessment Guide, Level 2, Version 2.11 - DRAFT, November 2023)

Assessment Focus

Also known as Assessment Objectives, these are the checklist items that an assessor will seek to verify. Each one must be addressed in your implementation and documentation:

1. the external system boundary is defined;
2. key internal system boundaries are defined;
3. communications are monitored at the external system boundary;
4. communications are monitored at key internal boundaries;
5. communications are controlled at the external system boundary;
6. communications are controlled at key internal boundaries;
7. communications are protected at the external system boundary; and
8. communications are protected at key internal boundaries.

(CMMC Assessment Guide, Level 2, Copyright 2020, 2021 Carnegie Mellon University and The Johns Hopkins University Applied Physics Laboratory LLC and/or CMMC Assessment Guide, Level 2, Version 2.11 - DRAFT, November 2023)

Implementation

The key element here is your gateway/firewall. This is the primary device that protects you from hackers breaking into your network from the Internet. It is best to block all incoming traffic (this does not mean the Internet will be inaccessible because any data conversation initiated internally will be allowed). Still, some companies find it necessary to have Internet-facing servers on their network. These are usually web or email servers that must be visible from the Internet to function. Almost any function can be placed in the cloud so that the network firewalls can be tightly closed. It should be considered that any device that is visible from the network is subject to potential hacking.

In addition, you may have routers that control communication between networks/sub-networks. In this age of ransomware that infects one machine and leap-frogs from one to another, segregating sections of your network can limit the range that an infection can spread to. These are effectively firewalls within the company to look at any communication and determine if it makes sense. For example, is there any reason why an engineering computer would want to send data packets directly to an accounting computer (email is indirect communication, with at least one server in the pathway)?

Many big, security-conscious companies seek to have every computer behind its own firewall that only allows the necessary communication and blocks everything else. With this structure, any ransomware infection would be limited to a single computer. (Security tip: Group policy can set the Windows firewalls to block communication between computers that have no business sending each other packets. Beware that this blocks shared printers or shared files.)

For compliance, you will want to list all the internal and external system boundaries. Assure that each of the internal segmenting devices or external firewalls is:

- controlled (password protection, for example),
- monitored (there needs to be some looking to see how they are doing, collecting audit data is good), and
- protected (physical protection).

The lists and their control, monitoring, and protection methods must be documented.

Assessment Stats

- Assessment Points: 5
- Assessment POAM Eligible: No

Keys

- Structure – There must be a firewall device protecting every Internet connection. These need to be defined and have some form of documented protection, monitoring, and protection.
- Structure – Any devices that set internal boundaries need the same level of definition and documented protection, monitoring, and protection as the external boundary devices.

System & Communications Protection

SC.L2-3.13.2

Security Engineering

Employ architectural designs, software development techniques, and systems engineering principles that promote effective information security within organizational systems.

Impact

This had been the worst few weeks in Andrew's professional career. He had been running IT at a small company for many years. While there had been a few bumps in the road, nothing compared to this disaster.

It all started when he learned that a bunch of the company's private data was posted on the Internet. This was information that should have never left the building, including pay rates, customer lists, and embarrassing emails. Andrew had no idea how the documents had ever gotten out of the building. The company brought in a consultant who performed a post-mortem to determine what happened. It turns out that one of the entry-level employees had connected their phone to the company WiFi network. This phone was beyond its support period, and it was also infected. Since the employee WiFi network was on the same network as the company servers, a hacker was able to easily hack into the servers from the compromised cell phone.

Andrew kicked himself because he had always known that having the employee WiFi join into the same sub-net as the business-critical equipment was a bad idea. Still, he had never gotten around to doing anything different.

Official Interpretation*

Familiarity with security engineering principles and their successful application to your infrastructure will increase the security of your environment. NIST SP 800-160 System Security Engineering: Considerations for a Multidisciplinary Approach in the Engineering of Trustworthy Secure Systems can serve as a source of security engineering and design principles.

Decide which designs and principles to apply. Some will not be possible or appropriate for a given company or for specific systems or components.

Designs and principles should be applied to policies and security standards. Starting with the baseline configuration, they should be extended through all layers of the technology stack (e.g., hardware, software, firmware) and throughout all the components of the infrastructure. The application of these chosen designs and principles should drive you towards a secure architecture with the required security capabilities and intrinsic behaviors present throughout the lifecycle of your technology.

As legacy components age, it may become increasingly difficult for those components to meet security principles and requirements. This should factor into life-cycle decisions for those components (e.g., replacing legacy hardware, upgrading or re-writing software, upgrading run-time environments).

(CMMC Assessment Guide, Level 2, Copyright 2020, 2021 Carnegie Mellon University and The Johns Hopkins University Applied Physics Laboratory LLC and/or CMMC Assessment Guide, Level 2, Version 2.11 - DRAFT, November 2023)

Assessment Focus

Also known as Assessment Objectives, these are the checklist items that an assessor will seek to verify. Each one must be addressed in your implementation and documentation:

1. architectural designs that promote effective information security are identified;
2. software development techniques that promote effective information security are identified;
3. systems engineering principles that promote effective information security are identified;
4. identified architectural designs that promote effective information security are employed;
5. identified software development techniques that promote effective information security are employed; and
6. identified systems engineering principles that promote effective information security are employed.

(CMMC Assessment Guide, Level 2, Copyright 2020, 2021 Carnegie Mellon University and The Johns Hopkins University Applied Physics Laboratory LLC and/or CMMC Assessment Guide, Level 2, Version 2.11 - DRAFT, November 2023)

Implementation

Small organizations are typically blessed with a relatively simple network architecture. If you have 20 computers on a basic network controlled by a single switch, this is not the architecture challenge of a worldwide company with 50,000 computers. Although network architecture does not have a significant role with most small businesses, you must be able to demonstrate to an assessor that you have considered the security architectural structure of your network.

Three elements need to be addressed:

- architectural designs
- software development techniques (This does not apply to many organizations)
- systems engineering

Below is a sample network architectural analysis document that might represent a small business:

Secure Computing Architecture

XYZ Manufacturing, Inc.

Facility at 123 Smith Street, Anytown, MD

Summary – This is a simple flat network with a single connection to the Internet and one switch interconnecting Windows-based computers and servers. This design has been determined to be the most appropriate for an organization of our size, complexity, and security challenges. All software is commercially purchased, and no software development occurs at this facility.

Network Physical Elements

- Switches: Netgear 78-052w
- Routers: Netgear CD842
- Modems: Arris 46052 cable modem
- Gateways: none
- Repeaters: none
- WiFi Network: Isolated from the business network, sharing only the Internet connection.

Security Elements

- Firewalls: Meraki MX46
- Intrusion Detection: Meraki MX46
- Intrusion Prevention: none
- Anti-malware: Microsoft Defender for Office 365 and ESET Endpoint
- Anti-spyware: ESET Endpoint
- Anti-phishing: Microsoft Defender for Office 365 and ESET Endpoint

Security Framework

- CMMC Level 2

A document like this will illustrate to an assessor that you have evaluated your network architecture and engineering. You would not want to present an outdated architecture analysis document, so it makes sense to schedule a periodic, like annual, review to bring it up to date.

Assessment Stats

- Assessment Points: 5
- Assessment POAM Eligible: No

Keys

🔧 Compile – Document a simple analysis of your system security architecture.

SC.L2-3.13.3

Role Separation

Separate user functionality from system management functionality.

Impact

Bart is the whole IT department at his company. Since he is always doing something or another in the network, he has figured out several shortcuts to improve his efficiency in performing his various jobs. One of those shortcuts is that he made sure he could access the SQL Management Console from any computer in the building. He didn't recognize that as a problem until one of his users got on and thought DROP might be the tool to delete a single record. Through this event, Bart learned that his database backups worked and that he should guard against users having access to certain powerful tools.

Official Interpretation*

Prevent users and user services from accessing system management functionality on IT components (e.g., databases, network components, workstations, servers). This reduces the attack surface to those critical interfaces by limiting who can access and how they can be accessed. By separating the user functionality from system management functionality, the administrator or privileged functions are not available to the general user.

The intent of this requirement is to ensure:

- general users are not permitted to perform system administration functions; and
- system administrators only perform system administration functions from their privileged account.

This can be accomplished using separation like VLANs or logical separation using strong access control methods.

(CMMC Assessment Guide, Level 2, Copyright 2020, 2021 Carnegie Mellon University and The Johns Hopkins University Applied Physics Laboratory LLC and/or CMMC Assessment Guide, Level 2, Version 2.11 - DRAFT, November 2023)

Assessment Focus

Also known as Assessment Objectives, these are the checklist items that an assessor will seek to verify. Each one must be addressed in your implementation and documentation:

1. user functionality is identified;

2. system management functionality is identified; and
3. user functionality is separated from system management functionality.

(CMMC Assessment Guide, Level 2, Copyright 2020, 2021 Carnegie Mellon University and The Johns Hopkins University Applied Physics Laboratory LLC and/or CMMC Assessment Guide, Level 2, Version 2.11 - DRAFT, November 2023)

Implementation

The response to this requirement will be very similar to that of AC.L2-3.1.7 (Privileged Functions).

The tools used by system administrators wield enough power that they are capable of significant disruption if used carelessly or with malicious intent. The goal of this requirement is to implement protections to prevent that.

To address this, it is important to define the functions that regular users should be permitted and what should be exclusive to the system administrators. Your system administrators will need the tools required to administer workstations, servers, databases, and network components, but those same tools could be a massive problem in the wrong hands.

At the same time, system administrators should not use privileged accounts to perform routine tasks. Your administrators should typically have two separate accounts: one for mundane tasks (with low privilege) and another for administrator tasks (with high privilege). This will prevent their email and internet activities from granting some malware their high-privilege access to the network.

The first step of seeking conformance with this requirement is to make lists of the functions that users are permitted to access and then a list of the functions that only the administrators should be permitted to use. This can be painted with broad strokes to avoid attempting to make a list of every single function. For example:

System management functionality shall incorporate all other Windows functions, plus management of non-Windows network components.

User functionality shall include all the functionality granted by default to domain users.

The next step is to ensure that there are protections that make it impossible for users to access the administrator-only functions. These protections can be physical (like tools on a particular computer that only the administrator can get physical access to) or logical (making good use of Windows access controls). The way the requirement and documentation is written, it is clear that there is a preference for physical protections. However, logical controls do meet the requirements. Your listing of the administrator-only functions might be expanded to describe the protections that apply to each function.

Keep in mind that these tools might prove to be a pain if the wrong user accessed them, they could be disastrous if a hacker accessed them.

Assessment Stats

- Assessment Points: 1
- Assessment POAM Eligible: Yes

Keys

- Document – Identify the functions that are applicable to basic users. Then, document the functions granted for system management.

- Implement – Implement and document controls that make it impossible for basic users to access each of the administrator-only functions.

System & Communications Protection

SC.L2-3.13.4

Shared Resource Control

Prevent unauthorized and unintended information transfer via shared system resources.

Impact

Troy shared the computer used by another employee who worked during the day shift. Troy noticed that he could go to the users section of the C: drive and see the documents that the other guy had accessed recently. Since that guy had higher-level responsibilities than Troy, Troy could use this method to see some materials he wasn't normally allowed to view. Troy didn't know of any regular PC that allowed viewing another user's documents and assumed that this computer had been configured strangely.

Official Interpretation*

No shared system resource, such as cache memory, hard disks, registers, or main memory may pass information from one user to another user. In other words, when objects are reused no residual information should exist on that object. This protects the confidentiality of the information. This is typically a feature provided by operating system and software vendors.

(CMMC Assessment Guide, Level 2, Copyright 2020, 2021 Carnegie Mellon University and The Johns Hopkins University Applied Physics Laboratory LLC and/or CMMC Assessment Guide, Level 2, Version 2.11 - DRAFT, November 2023)

Assessment Focus

Also known as Assessment Objectives, these are the checklist items that an assessor will seek to verify. Each one must be addressed in your implementation and documentation:

1. unauthorized and unintended information transfer via shared system resources is prevented.

(CMMC Assessment Guide, Level 2, Copyright 2020, 2021 Carnegie Mellon University and The Johns Hopkins University Applied Physics Laboratory LLC and/or CMMC Assessment Guide, Level 2, Version 2.11 - DRAFT, November 2023)

Implementation

Having a Windows-based network makes this requirement easy to check off as complete. Windows does this out of the box. In fact, it would be a lot more work to make your Windows system violate this requirement.

The shared resources that this requirement refers to are shared SYSTEM resources. Specifically, this is residual data of prior users or processes being accessible to current users or processes. This can be from data residing in registers, memory, or on disks. Systems with multiple users/roles must be evaluated for possible information leakage. Virtualized machines residing on a single host should also be evaluated for proper object reuse procedures.

Any non-Windows devices with multiple roles or users should be evaluated for proper shared resource controls.

Assessment Stats

- Assessment Points: 1
- Assessment POAM Eligible: Yes

Keys

- Evaluate any VM Hosts for possible leakage
- Evaluate and non-Windows systems with multiple roles or Windows for potential data leakage.
- For Windows systems, no action is required.

System & Communications Protection

SC.L1-3.13.5

Public-Access System Separation

Implement subnetworks for publicly accessible system components that are physically or logically separated from internal networks.

Impact

The sales department wanted access to a particular service from out on the road. The software provided simple instructions on how to make the service available from the Internet. For a few months, this didn't seem to be a problem. One day, however, there was a complete panic when the company bank accounts were emptied. Looking into the situation, it was determined that the order to transfer funds was generated from inside their building. Further investigation revealed that an unknown person had hacked the application exposed to the Internet and then used that hole to install a RAT (remote access trojan) in the accounting computer. This incident revealed the value of a DMZ for all Internet-facing applications.

Official Interpretation*

Separate the publicly accessible systems from the internal systems that need to be protected. Do not place internal systems on the same network as the publicly accessible systems and block access by default from DMZ networks to internal networks.

One method of accomplishing this is to create a DMZ network, which enhances security by providing public access to a specific set of resources while preventing connections from those resources to the rest of the IT environment. Some OSAs achieve a similar result through the use of a cloud computing environment that is separated from the rest of the company's infrastructure.

(CMMC Assessment Guide, Level 2, Copyright 2020, 2021 Carnegie Mellon University and The Johns Hopkins University Applied Physics Laboratory LLC and/or CMMC Assessment Guide, Level 2, Version 2.11 - DRAFT, November 2023)

Assessment Focus

Also known as Assessment Objectives, these are the checklist items that an assessor will seek to verify. Each one must be addressed in your implementation and documentation:

1. publicly accessible system components are identified; and
2. subnetworks for publicly accessible system components are physically or logically separated from internal networks.

(CMMC Assessment Guide, Level 2, Copyright 2020, 2021 Carnegie Mellon University and The Johns Hopkins University Applied Physics Laboratory LLC and/or CMMC Assessment Guide, Level 2, Version 2.11 - DRAFT, November 2023)

Implementation

There is no getting away from the concept that every system that is accessible from the Internet is especially vulnerable. What may seem like an absolutely un-hackable system might be tomorrow's open door to hacking access. Hosting any Internet services on your network carries risks. If somebody thinks they are saving money by hosting their own website, they could risk the company's existence to save a few bucks. However, there are situations where it is necessary to have a web service with access to data on local servers. This needs to be carefully planned to minimize the risk so that if the web service gets hacked, it doesn't lead to disaster.

If it is necessary to have Internet-facing applications, then the use of a DMZ is essential. Essentially, this requires that you have your web applications with firewalls on each side of them. There is a firewall on the Internet side that only allows only the essential types of packets. Then, the second firewall, between the web application and the rest of your network, would block all connections initiated from the web application side, except those generated by your web application for the essential data it needs. Because of the inherent risks, these firewalls should be configured with immense care and minimal permissions. (see SC.L2-3.13.6)

Plan your DMZ with the expectation that the web application will be compromised. Consider what access a hacker might gain if they were able to take control of the web application computer. Specifically, consider whether their control of that computer might be a portal into the rest of your network. As DMZ firewalls are set, the goal is to allow the absolute minimum of access necessary for the required functionality. Risk is associated with all web application access to the network, so the more restrictive, the better.

Any Internet-visible applications on your network must be identified. Then, you should document the firewall protections that separate those applications from the rest of your network.

Assessment Stats

- Assessment Points: 5
- Assessment POAM Eligible: No

Keys

🔧 Policy - Assure that any internet-facing applications are in a DMZ and separated from the rest of the network.

System & Communications Protection

SC.L2-3.13.6

Network Communication by Exception

Deny network communications traffic by default and allow network communications traffic by exception (i.e., deny all, permit by exception).

Impact

Melanie thought she had done well when she established a sub-net to place all her users who were allowed CUI access. She had a router between their sub-net and the rest of the company's network. One day, she noticed some odd traffic passing between the sub-nets. She suddenly realized that somebody was establishing an RDP session to one of the restricted computers. Apparently, when she set up the router, she had not thought of blocking RDP traffic. She referred the incident to the company security officer and proceeded to remedy the problem. She realized the easiest and most effective answer was to block everything and then set rules that would allow only the intended traffic. This way, she couldn't again omit a specific method that should be banned.

Official Interpretation*

Block all traffic entering and leaving the network, but permit specific traffic based on organizational policies, exceptions, or criteria. This process of permitting only authorized traffic to the network is called whitelisting and limits the number of unintentional connections to the network.

This requirement, SC.L2-3.13.6, requires a deny-all permit by exception approach for all network communications. In doing so, it adds specifics for SC.L2-3.13.1, which only requires monitoring, control, and protection of communication channels.

(CMMC Assessment Guide, Level 2, Copyright 2020, 2021 Carnegie Mellon University and The Johns Hopkins University Applied Physics Laboratory LLC and/or CMMC Assessment Guide, Level 2, Version 2.11 - DRAFT, November 2023)

Assessment Focus

Also known as Assessment Objectives, these are the checklist items that an assessor will seek to verify. Each one must be addressed in your implementation and documentation:

1. network communications traffic is denied by default; and
2. network communications traffic is allowed by exception.

(CMMC Assessment Guide, Level 2, Copyright 2020, 2021 Carnegie Mellon University and The Johns Hopkins University Applied Physics Laboratory LLC and/or CMMC Assessment Guide, Level 2, Version 2.11 - DRAFT, November 2023)

Implementation

The challenge of defensive cybersecurity is that we must defend ourselves from all possible attacks, whereas the attacker only needs to find a single unprotected point of vulnerability. The attackers have the easier job by far. While we might be able to identify all of the attacks that are known today, we cannot anticipate what attacks may be in use tomorrow. Because of this, the ability to use a "deny all" structure is an excellent method to make a sweeping blow to the attacks of today and the unknown attacks of the future.

Most modern firewalls and routers have rules that follow this pattern. Their rule set will show a series of "allow," followed by the final rule, a "deny all" rule. The "allow" rules define the limited set of communications that are allowed to pass, and then everything else will hit the "deny all" rule. A decade ago, the common practice was to allow everything except for a few things that would be blocked. This method was inefficient because the lists were always just behind the latest attack. Because this paradigm shift has been recent, older devices should be suspect.

Make a list of your firewalling devices and be prepared to present an assessor a copy of the rulesets so they can confirm that rules conform to this allow-by-exception/deny-all structure.

Assessment Stats

- Assessment Points: 5
- Assessment POAM Eligible: No

Keys

- Documentation – Have the ruleset of all firewalling devices available to demonstrate a "deny all" rule structure.

SC.L2-3.13.7

Split Tunneling

Prevent remote devices from simultaneously establishing non-remote connections with organizational systems and communicating via some other connection to resources in external networks (i.e., split tunneling).

Impact

It never seemed like an issue. When Alfred used the VPN to access company resources remotely, he also wanted to keep an eye on Internet sales. So, he would simultaneously maintain a connection into the heart of the company network and the Internet. While the VPN connection was secure enough to have acceptable security, even when accessed on the hotel Wi-Fi connection, his other Internet activities were not. Alfred did not know that his teenage son had modified a few settings on the laptop to make a gaming application work better. A hacker who was monitoring the traffic on the hotel network saw an opportunity. He managed to leverage Alfred's Internet activity to slide through his laptop and Alfred's VPN connection, going right into the heart of the company network.

Official Interpretation*

Split tunneling for a remote user utilizes two connections: accessing resources on the internal network via a VPN and simultaneously accessing an external network such as a public network or the internet.

Split tunneling presents a potential opportunity where an open unencrypted connection from a public network could allow an adversary to access resources on internal network. As a mitigation strategy, the split tunneling setting should be disabled on all devices so that all traffic, including traffic for external networks or the internet, goes through the VPN.

(CMMC Assessment Guide, Level 2, Copyright 2020, 2021 Carnegie Mellon University and The Johns Hopkins University Applied Physics Laboratory LLC and/or CMMC Assessment Guide, Level 2, Version 2.11 - DRAFT, November 2023)

Assessment Focus

Also known as Assessment Objectives, these are the checklist items that an assessor will seek to verify. Each one must be addressed in your implementation and documentation:

1. remote devices are prevented from simultaneously establishing non-remote connections with the system and communicating via some other connection to resources in external networks (i.e., split tunneling).

(CMMC Assessment Guide, Level 2, Copyright 2020, 2021 Carnegie Mellon University and The Johns Hopkins University Applied Physics Laboratory LLC and/or CMMC Assessment Guide, Level 2, Version 2.11 - DRAFT, November 2023)

Implementation

This control requires that any devices authorized to connect remotely to your network, laptops, for instance, are configured to prohibit "split tunneling." Split tunneling is where a user could remotely connect to your network while simultaneously connecting to an uncontrolled external network. This configuration could allow a hacker to bypass all network boundary controls by going through the user's laptop.

Microsoft calls this capability "Network Bridging." It is disabled by default. Windows provides a method to use Group Policy to ensure it stays disabled. When a group policy, as described below, is applied, it will prevent split tunneling, but only when the computer is connected to the domain DNS. Network Bridging can be disabled at:

Computer Configuration -> Administrative Templates -> Network -> Network Connections -> Prohibit installation and configuration of network bridge on your DNS domain network.

If any third-party VPN tools are in use, they should be examined for conformance to this requirement. Some split-tunneling issues, in the products, are a matter of configuration, but a few products are reportedly innately deficient in this area.

Assessment Stats

- Assessment Points: 1
- Assessment POAM Eligible: Yes

Keys

- Group Policy - Create a group policy object to prohibit Network Bridging.

System & Communications Protection

SC.L2-3.13.8

Data in Transit

Implement cryptographic mechanisms to prevent unauthorized disclosure of CUI during transmission unless otherwise protected by alternative physical safeguards.

Impact

Erin had always sent drawings and specifications to her suppliers by email as simple attachments. To Erin, email seemed like a secure way to send digital materials to somebody. What she didn't realize was that the email messages she sent didn't really have any security. All her outbound emails were being monitored by an unauthorized person, who was convinced there was a market for some of the DoD materials Erin sent out. Erin had no idea that her messages were being viewed by somebody other than the intended recipient.

Official Interpretation*

The intent of this requirement is to ensure CUI is cryptographically protected during transit, particularly on the internet. The most common way to accomplish this is to establish a TLS tunnel between the source and destination using the most current version of TLS. This requirement does not specify a mutually authenticated handshake, but mutual authentication is the most secure approach to creating a tunnel.

Because the use of cryptography in this requirement is to protect the confidentiality of CUI, the cryptography used must meet the criteria specified in requirement SC.L2-3.13.11.

This requirement, SC.L2-3.13.8, requires cryptographic mechanisms be used to prevent the disclosure of CUI in-transit and leverages SC.L2-3.13.11, which specifies that the algorithms used must be FIPS-validated cryptography.

(CMMC Assessment Guide, Level 2, Copyright 2020, 2021 Carnegie Mellon University and The Johns Hopkins University Applied Physics Laboratory LLC and/or CMMC Assessment Guide, Level 2, Version 2.11 - DRAFT, November 2023)

Assessment Focus

Also known as Assessment Objectives, these are the checklist items that an assessor will seek to verify. Each one must be addressed in your implementation and documentation:

1. cryptographic mechanisms intended to prevent unauthorized disclosure of CUI are identified;

2. alternative physical safeguards intended to prevent unauthorized disclosure of CUI are identified; and
3. either cryptographic mechanisms or alternative physical safeguards are implemented to prevent unauthorized disclosure of CUI during transmission.

(CMMC Assessment Guide, Level 2, Copyright 2020, 2021 Carnegie Mellon University and The Johns Hopkins University Applied Physics Laboratory LLC and/or CMMC Assessment Guide, Level 2, Version 2.11 - DRAFT, November 2023)

Implementation

In the course of doing business, it is often essential to send CUI to business partners. We might be accustomed to sending various files via email. Although email leaves most non-technical users with an impression of good security, there are many points, as a message travels from sender to recipient, where third parties can easily read a message. Even a message sent to a co-worker down the hall may travel outside the country before it reaches the intended recipient.

This requirement identifies sending CUI in email as an unacceptable practice due to the inherent insecurity of standard email.

The challenge to the smaller organization associated with this requirement is that emailing files may have been standard practice for as long as there has been email. Emailing documents is extremely easy for our users. Because of this, imposing a new procedure will be challenging. To smooth user acceptance, ease of use should be a serious consideration in evaluating solutions.

Although the requirement says that "alternative physical safeguards" may be used to protect the CUI during transmission, this is not really a viable option in most modern organizations. This leaves encryption as the method of choice. The encryption implementation must be validated under FIPS 140-2 whenever encryption is used to protect CUI (So, the specific application must be listed in the CMVP list).

Many different services are available to provide file transfer. A smaller number of the choices provide FIPS 140-2 encrypted communication. Often, the providers of FIPS-validated file transfer services will cost more to cover the cost of maintaining the validation.

Often, the expense is a per-user cost. So, limiting the number of people authorized to send CUI outside the organization is advantageous. Then, inside the organization, you can share files using the organization's in-house CUI repository file server.

When shopping for a file-transfer service, there are various considerations. First, the service MUST utilize FIPS 140-2 validation of their encryption (required under SC.L2-3.13.11). Any cloud service that handles CUI should be FedRAMP. Then, for good user acceptance, sending files securely should be as easy as possible.

A free alternative is to use the DoD Secure Access File Exchange (SAFE). This website is not easy, quick, or accessible in all situations. Either the sender, receiver, or both must have a Government-issued Common Access Card (CAC). The sender submits a file, checking the box so it will be encrypted. After a wait (up to 4 hours), the receiver can retrieve the file from the service. The inconvenience of this process might result in poor user compliance, however, the service is free. SAFE can be accessed at https://safe.apps.mil

While you and your management may be able to convince the users of the importance of using secure file transfer, it will still be easy for them to slip back into the easier and more comfortable mode of emailing the documents. A CMMC assessor will be looking for CUI being sent by non-secure modes. Because of this genuine possibility, monitoring what people are actually doing with redirection as necessary will be important. Your file-sharing service probably has an audit function that allows you to see who is using the service. If you have a user that sends files regularly and their use of the service drops off, that should be noted as suspicious.

HANDY LINK

The author's preferred tool for secure and compliant transmission of CUI for the small organization can be found here https://tinyurl.com/CMMC4SMB-938

Assessment Stats

- Assessment Points: 3
- Assessment POAM Eligible: No

Keys

- Policy – Clearly identify who is authorized to transmit CUI outside the organization.
- Policy – Define the procedure employees should use to send CUI within the organization.
- Policy - Create a policy defining how CUI will be transmitted to outside entities.

System & Communications Protection

SC.L2-3.13.9

Connections Termination

Terminate network connections associated with communications sessions at the end of the sessions or after a defined period of inactivity.

Impact

On Tuesday, Antonio makes his secure connection to remote servers, but he leaves his computer and heads to a meeting when he finishes with the task at hand. While the computer is still logged into the secure site, but he is no longer at the computer, Liz slides over to his workstation and begins exploring the secure site. She is looking for a specific document, which she finds with little difficulty. She is quickly able to download the file onto a USB drive. She loves the idea that when it becomes clear that the file has been stolen, the logs will show that Antonio accessed it, and he will be blamed. Nobody will ever suspect Liz.

Official Interpretation*

Prevent malicious actors from taking advantage of an open network session or an unattended computer at the end of the connection. Balance user work patterns and needs against security to determine the length of inactivity that will force a termination.

This requirement, SC.L2-3.13.9, specifies network connections be terminated under certain conditions, which complements AC.L2-3.1.18 that specifies control of mobile device connections.

(CMMC Assessment Guide, Level 2, Copyright 2020, 2021 Carnegie Mellon University and The Johns Hopkins University Applied Physics Laboratory LLC and/or CMMC Assessment Guide, Level 2, Version 2.11 - DRAFT, November 2023)

Assessment Focus

Also known as Assessment Objectives, these are the checklist items that an assessor will seek to verify. Each one must be addressed in your implementation and documentation:

1. a period of inactivity to terminate network connections associated with communications sessions is defined;

2. network connections associated with communications sessions are terminated at the end of the sessions; and
3. network connections associated with communications sessions are terminated after the defined period of inactivity.

(CMMC Assessment Guide, Level 2, Copyright 2020, 2021 Carnegie Mellon University and The Johns Hopkins University Applied Physics Laboratory LLC and/or CMMC Assessment Guide, Level 2, Version 2.11 - DRAFT, November 2023)

Implementation

If you have servers (or similar resources) where clients are establishing communication sessions, you need to ensure that there is a method of automatically terminating those sessions. A communication session that continues for days (or weeks) presents an unacceptable security risk. The most common applicable communication session is VPN. So, if somebody connects to your network via VPN, there must be a process by which the connection is terminated automatically if the user doesn't terminate the session. This termination should be controlled on the server-side, rather than the client-side.

To automatically terminate VPN communication sessions based on session duration on a Windows server that uses NPS, you can follow these steps:

1. Open the NPS console on the Windows server.
2. In the left-hand pane, select "Policies" and "Network Policies."
3. Locate the policy used to grant VPN access and double-click on it to open its properties.
4. In the "Constraints" tab, scroll down to the "Conditions" section.
5. Click on "Add" to add a new condition.
6. Select "Session Timeout" as the condition type, and click "Add."
7. In the "Edit Session Timeout" window, set the maximum duration of the VPN session in minutes. For example, if you want to limit VPN sessions to 2 hours, enter "120" in the "Maximum session duration (minutes)" field.
8. Click "OK" to save the session timeout condition, then click "OK" again to close the policy properties window.

You will also find session termination options based on "idle" time. However, it is reported that this is ineffective for a VPN connection because there is ongoing traffic across that connection, even if the user is inactive.

If your organization has other circumstances where a user remotely logs onto your data systems different than VPN, then those will each need to be addressed.

Assessment Stats

- Assessment Points: 1
- Assessment POAM Eligible: Yes

Keys

- Policy – Identify the process where users will create connections to your data systems, then define a policy for terminating each network connection.
- Configuration – Establish a mechanism that terminates network connections in accordance with your policy.

System & Communications Protection

SC.L2-3.13.10

Key Management

Establish and manage cryptographic keys for cryptography employed in organizational systems.

Impact

Jonathan was instructed to set up the server data backups for his company. He assured the backups were encrypted. However, he placed the work documentation, including the backup encryption keys, in the IT folder on the shared drive. A few months later, a student intern who got interested in what the company did used those credentials to gain access to every bit of information the company valued.

Official Interpretation*

Develop processes and technical mechanisms to protect the cryptographic keys' confidentiality, authenticity, and authorized use in accordance with industry standards and regulations. Key management systems provide oversight, assurance, and the capability to demonstrate the cryptographic keys are created in a secure manner and protected from loss or misuse throughout their lifecycle (e.g., active, expired, revoked). For a small number of keys, this can be accomplished with manual procedures and mechanisms. As the number of keys and cryptographic units increase, automation and tool support will be required.

The first intent of this requirement is to ensure cryptographic keys are properly created in a secure manner that prevents them from being reproduced by an adversary. The second intent of this requirement is to ensure cryptographic keys are managed in a secure manner that prevents them from being stolen by an adversary.

Key establishment involves the creation of keys and coordination among parties that will use the keys of the methodology for generating the final keying material. This is discussed in detail in SP 800-56A, B, and C.

Key management involves protecting keys when they are distributed, when they are stored, when they are being used, and when they are being recovered.

Key establishment best practices are identified in NIST SP 800-56A, B, and C. Key management best practices are identified in NIST SP 800-57 Parts 1, 2, and 3.

This requirement, SC.L2-3.13.10, complements AC.L2-3.1.19 by specifying that any cryptographic keys in use must be protected.

Assessment Focus

Also known as Assessment Objectives, these are the checklist items that an assessor will seek to verify. Each one must be addressed in your implementation and documentation:

1. cryptographic keys are established whenever cryptography is employed; and
2. cryptographic keys are managed whenever cryptography is employed.

Implementation

Certificate cryptography is complex. Microsoft has done its best to streamline the processes and provide a system to do the bulk of the heavy lifting, but that does not make it simple. Cryptography has its own language, and many aspects are incomprehensible to individuals who have not been trained in it. To satisfy this requirement, establishing a PKI (Public Key Infrastructure) structure within your networks will be necessary; doing that correctly is challenging.

This requirement says cryptographic keys should be established and managed whenever cryptography is used. Although Windows can perform many cryptographic functions without a Certificate Authority and the other elements of PKI, that does not allow for satisfaction of this requirement's need to establish and manage the cryptographic keys.

Before installing a Certificate Authority (CA), it is crucial to plan the architecture of your PKI. Because the Certificate has great power (for example, signing code that computers will run without question), it is essential to protect it.

PKI is a system of "trusts." For example, my computer trusts a specific certificate because it is trusted by this issuing server, which is itself trusted by a root CA, which my computer has been told is trustworthy. Each of these "trusts" is set up so they cannot be faked. If a hacker compromised the issuing server, they could issue some certificates, but those certificates could be canceled and the harm corrected as long as the root CA remains safe. So, the optimal way to set up PKI is to have the root certificate authority issue the certificate to the issuing CA, then the root CA is pulled offline and kept safe.

Another optional security consideration is whether you can justify an HSM (hardware security module). This device costs around $1000 for a FIPS model. It takes the high-risk elements of the certificate management process and moves it to where it is effectively inaccessible to hacking. Having an HSM on your CA would be an excellent tool to demonstrate your ability to conform to this requirement. While it is NOT required, it is good from a security and conformance standpoint. The HSM must be installed on the Windows server BEFORE the CA is created.

Here are the basic instructions for setting up a certificate authority:

1. Log on as a member of both the Enterprise Admins group and the root domain's Domain Admins group.
2. In Server Manager, click **Manage** and **Add Roles and Features**. The Add Roles and Features Wizard opens.
3. In **Select Installation Type**, ensure that **Role-Based or feature-based installation** is selected, and then click **Next**.
4. In **Select destination server**, ensure that **Select a server from the server pool** is selected. In the **Server Pool**, ensure that the local computer is selected. Click **Next**.
5. In **Select Server Roles**, in **Roles**, select **Active Directory Certificate Services**. When prompted to add required features, click **Add Features** and **Next**.
6. In **Select features**, click **Next**.
7. In **Active Directory Certificate Services**, read the provided information and click **Next**.
8. In **Confirm installation selections**, click **Install**. Do not close the wizard during the installation process. When installation is complete, click **Configure Active Directory Certificate Services on the destination server**. The AD CS Configuration wizard opens. Read the credentials information and, if needed, provide the credentials for an account that is a member of the Enterprise Admins group. Click **Next**.
9. In **Role Services**, click **Certification Authority** and **Next**.
10. On the **Setup Type** page, verify that **Enterprise CA** is selected, and then click **Next**.
11. On the **Specify the type of the CA** page, verify that **Root CA** is selected, and then click **Next**.
12. On the **Specify the type of the private key** page, verify that **Create a new private key** is selected, and then click **Next**.
13. On the **Cryptography for CA** page, keep the default settings for CSP (**RSA#Microsoft Software Key Storage Provider**) and the hash algorithm (**SHA2**), and determine the best key character length for your deployment. Large key character lengths provide optimal security; however, they can impact server performance and might not be compatible with legacy applications. It is recommended that you keep the default setting of 2048. Click **Next**.
14. On the **CA Name** page, keep the suggested common name for the CA or change the name according to your requirements. Ensure that the CA name is compatible with your naming conventions and purposes because you cannot change the CA name after you have installed AD CS. Click **Next**.
15. On the **Validity Period** page, in **Specify the validity period**, type the number and select a time value (Years, Months, Weeks, or Days). The default setting of five years is recommended. Click **Next**.
16. On the **CA Database** page, in **Specify the database locations**, specify the folder location for the certificate database and the certificate database log. If you specify locations other than the default locations, ensure that the folders are secured with access control lists (ACLs) that prevent unauthorized users or computers from accessing the CA database and log files. Click **Next**.
17. In **Confirmation**, click **Configure** to apply your selections, then click **Close**.

After setting up your Certificate Authorities, you can use Group Policy to tell the domain members to trust that root authority. From there, it is possible to start issuing certificates to computers and users.

The protections you apply to your root Certificate authority are how you will "establish and maintain" the keys for cryptography. Your response to this requirement would be to detail how your PKI is set up and secured.

If you have any other cryptographic keys within your system (application's encryption keys, for example), you will want to address how those will be protected.

Assessment Stats

- Assessment Points: 1
- Assessment POAM Eligible: Yes

Keys

- System - Set up one or more Certificate Authorities
- Documentation – Document the controls that protect the cryptographic keys.

System & Communications Protection

SC.L2-3.13.11

CUI Encryption

Employ FIPS-validated cryptography when used to protect the confidentiality of CUI.

Impact

In an effort to save cost, the CUI data was stored in a digital vault that used encryption to protect the data, but somebody in the company developed the encryption. They thought that it should be more secure because nobody knew the algorithm that was used to encrypt and decrypt the documents. They had hired a new guy in accounting who was a bit of a computer geek. Although his role in the company did not earn him permission to access the CUI vault, he took getting access to it as a challenge. It didn't take him long to gain access. As he got access, it didn't take him long to decide that the materials in the vault were pretty boring. Still, he wondered if the materials might have some monetary value to anybody else. Soon, he had a copy of the data for sale on the dark web.

Official Interpretation*

FIPS-validated cryptography means the cryptographic module has to have been tested and validated to meet FIPS 140-2 requirements. Simply using an approved algorithm is not sufficient – the module (software and/or hardware) used to implement the algorithm must be separately validated under FIPS 140. Accordingly, FIPS-validated cryptography is required to protect CUI when transmitted or stored outside the protected environment of the covered OSA information system (including wireless/remote access). Encryption used for other purposes, such as within applications or devices within the protected environment of the covered OSA information system, would not need to use FIPS-validated cryptography.

This requirement, SC.L2-3.13.11, complements AC.L2-3.1.19, MP.L2-3.8.6, SC.L2-3.13.8, and SC.L2-3.13.16 by specifying that FIPS-validated cryptography must be used.

(CMMC Assessment Guide, Level 2, Copyright 2020, 2021 Carnegie Mellon University and The Johns Hopkins University Applied Physics Laboratory LLC and/or CMMC Assessment Guide, Level 2, Version 2.11 - DRAFT, November 2023)

Assessment Focus

Also known as Assessment Objectives, these are the checklist items that an assessor will seek to verify. Each one must be addressed in your implementation and documentation:

1. FIPS-validated cryptography is employed to protect the confidentiality of CUI.

(CMMC Assessment Guide, Level 2, Copyright 2020, 2021 Carnegie Mellon University and The Johns Hopkins University Applied Physics Laboratory LLC and/or CMMC Assessment Guide, Level 2, Version 2.11 - DRAFT, November 2023)

Implementation

The industry-accepted cryptography methods are the product of a huge amount of effort from people who have dedicated their lives to the field. It is easy to screw it up if a person doesn't really know what they are doing. In fact, a programmer can try to implement a standardized and respected algorithm, like AES, but can have a flawed implementation that leaves it insecure. Many applications brag about their "military-grade encryption," which could never get a FIPS certification because of their flawed implementation of the cryptography.

There are some sellers of application that will advertise products as being FIPS validated, when they are merely using encryption algorithms that are validated, but their application's implementation has never been validated. Your assessor will want to be able to check the actual FIPS status of any tool used to protect CUI. Demonstrating that the application's website says "FIPS 140-2" isn't adequate.

As each provider of encryption-enabled software or services gets their cryptography validated by NIST CVMP, the approval of each specific product gets publically listed.

HANDY LINK

The lists can be found at https://tinyurl.com/CMMC4SMB-780

The process that companies have to go through to get their product validated is long and expensive. At the time of this writing, Windows 11 was released for almost a year and a half but is still not FIPS validated. The process is so slow that some have questioned whether running outdated, FIPS-validated software is the best security option. However, when FIPS validation is a requirement, then it is a requirement.

FIPS encryption can be enabled in Windows computers through Group Policy:

Computer Configuration -> Policies -> Windows Settings -> Security Settings -> Local Policies -> Security Options, and enable the "System cryptography: Use FIPS compliant algorithms for encryption, hashing, and signing"

FIPS mode has a reputation for breaking some software, so you must test your various configurations. These issues are rare, but do happen. Some software will have hard-coded instructions to use specific encryption methods that aren't allowed within a FIPS-enabled computer, thus occasionally causing the software to break. If you encounter something that breaks in a FIPS environment, you should contact the software vendor since they have likely dealt with this before and may have fixes available.

If software on workstations or servers uses encryption to protect CUI, then all of those encryption processes must be FIPS validated. Any software that does not perform this function is expressly excluded.

If software is used with CUI but does not perform encryption, it does not need to be FIPS validated. For example, you may use a PDF viewer to open certain CUI documents. If that PDF viewer does not use encryption to protect the CUI, then FIPS validation is not required.

Your operating system, on the other hand, does use encryption to protect how CUI travels across the network, through authentication and authorization processes. When CUI is downloaded from the Internet, the Windows SSL secures the transaction with encryption. So, any computer's operating system that handles CUI must be FIPS validated.

Some have taken the phrase "when used to protect the confidentiality of CUI" down a slippery slope. It is possible to logically justify all kinds of processes that are indirectly involved in protecting CUI. This can lead to an expectation for FIPS-validated door locks and all sorts of other ancillary processes. In general, just plan on FIPS-validated encryption for the systems that directly protect CUI. You should note the language used in the Assessment Guide, "Encryption used for other purposes, such as within applications or devices within the protected environment of the covered OSA information system, would not need to use FIPS-validated cryptography."

At the time of writing, this interpretation is still evolving. Hopefully, common sense will prevail.

Many people are looking at the most current software and OS versions that are not yet FIPS validated and are concluding that the correct answer is to implement those (in FIPS mode) and initiate a POAM. This POAM stands to say that the official FIPS designation is pending, so we use this software or operating system awaiting that determination.

Assessment Stats

- Assessment Points: 3 or 5*
- Assessment POAM Eligible: No

*If encryption is employed, but is not FIPS-validated, 3 points are subtracted from the maximum score; if encryption is not employed; 5 points are subtracted from the maximum score.

Keys

- Discover– Identify how encryption is used to protect CUI within your data processes.
- Implement – You should be able to demonstrate how each applicable process has the encryption implementation FIPS approved.

System & Communications Protection

SC.L2-3.13.12

Collaborative Device Control

Prohibit remote activation of collaborative computing devices and provide indication of devices in use to users present at the device.

Impact

Top management and the top minds from the R&D department were crammed into the conference room. The goal of this meeting was to chart the course of their future products. However, there was one more silent participant in the meeting. There was a supplier that thought they were supposed to join up for a video conference. Yet when they tried to sign into the meeting, they found themselves listening and watching a fascinating meeting. The official meeting participants were unaware of the supplier's eavesdropping. Since this supplier sold to many companies in this same field, getting insights into this company's plans was very valuable information that could be leveraged into more sales. The participants had no idea that their meeting wasn't private.

Official Interpretation*

Notification that a device is in use can include an indicator light that turns on or a specific text window that appears on screen. If a device does not have the means to alert a user when in use, the organization should provide manual means. Manual means can include, as necessary:

- paper notification on entryways; and
- locking entryways when a collaborative computing device is in use.

This requirement is not intended to include technologies that enable users to share the contents of their computer screens via the internet.

(CMMC Assessment Guide, Level 2, Copyright 2020, 2021 Carnegie Mellon University and The Johns Hopkins University Applied Physics Laboratory LLC and/or CMMC Assessment Guide, Level 2, Version 2.11 - DRAFT, November 2023)

Assessment Focus

Also known as Assessment Objectives, these are the checklist items that an assessor will seek to verify. Each one must be addressed in your implementation and documentation:

1. collaborative computing devices are identified;

2. collaborative computing devices provide indication to users of devices in use; and
3. remote activation of collaborative computing devices is prohibited.

(CMMC Assessment Guide, Level 2, Copyright 2020, 2021 Carnegie Mellon University and The Johns Hopkins University Applied Physics Laboratory LLC and/or CMMC Assessment Guide, Level 2, Version 2.11 - DRAFT, November 2023)

Implementation

Although many different types of "collaborative computing devices" are available, by far, the most common device in small organizations is the webcam. We find ourselves with many webcams throughout our organizations as video conferencing becomes the usual way of doing business. Some of these webcams are permanent fixtures on laptops, while others may be USB add-ons. Typically, the webcam has a built-in microphone. The cameras on these devices may or may not have indicator lights to show when the device is in use. If there is a camera indicator light, that does not mean the light will actuate if only the microphone is in use.

If a webcam does not have an indicator light that indicates the use of either the camera or the microphone, then action needs to be taken to address this requirement. If a webcam fails to indicate camera or microphone usage, then options include:

- Replace the device with one that has the required indications,
- Remove the device,
- Permanently disable the device (if it is not removable, like on a laptop) or
- Install a utility that provides an on-screen indication of active use.

Less common are the other "collaborative computing devices," like electronic whiteboards that allow remote users to observe/participate in visual collaboration. Similarly, these devices need to have clear indicators of remote participants.

The other requirement is that none of these devices be permitted to be remotely activated. This prohibition is typically a function of the settings of the device. Examine the documentation associated with each device to determine the best way to accomplish this goal.

It should be noted that in NIST SP 800-171 R1, where this requirement came from, there was a footnote (27) that said, "Dedicated video conferencing systems, which rely on one of the participants calling or connecting to the other party to activate the video conference, are excluded."

Compile a list of all collaborative computing devices within your scope. For each device, identify how the user can know when the device is active and how it is known that the device cannot be remotely activated. Assuring remote activation is disabled on certain inexpensive, no-name devices might be impossible. Any devices that cannot be configured to meet these requirements may have to be replaced.

Assessment Stats

- Assessment Points: 1
- Assessment POAM Eligible: Yes

Keys

- Identification – Compile a list of all collaborative computing devices within your scope.
- Configuration – Remediate any webcams, collaborative devices, or other audio/video recording devices that lack a clear indication that they are active.
- Configuration – Assure that none of the audio/video recording devices or collaborative computing devices can be remotely activated.

SC.L2-3.13.13

Mobile Code

Control and monitor the use of mobile code.

Impact

When Mike went to a website, it told him that he needed to install Flash so he could fully access their materials. Without question, he downloaded the Flash plugin and proceeded to explore the website. About a week later, Mike was viewing materials on a reputable advertising-supported website when one of the ads utilized a Flash vulnerability to install a piece of malware on his computer. That incident started a catastrophic chain of events that led to the compromise of the entire network.

Official Interpretation*

Ensure mobile code is authorized to execute in company systems only in accordance with policy and technical configuration, and that unauthorized mobile code is not. Monitor the use of mobile code through boundary devices (e.g., firewalls), audit logs, or security utilities (e.g., mobile device management, advanced endpoint protection) and implement remediation activities as needed.

The first intent of this requirement is to ensure the limits of mobile code usage and usage restrictions are documented and enforced. This includes documenting all authorizations for the use of mobile code and ensuring it is not used in other ways. Usage restrictions and implementation guidance apply to the selection and use of mobile code installed on servers and mobile code downloaded and executed on individual workstations and devices to include all mobile devices and smart phones.

The second intent is to monitor the use of mobile code and implement remediation steps if its use does not align with policy.

(CMMC Assessment Guide, Level 2, Copyright 2020, 2021 Carnegie Mellon University and The Johns Hopkins University Applied Physics Laboratory LLC and/or CMMC Assessment Guide, Level 2, Version 2.11 - DRAFT, November 2023)

Assessment Focus

Also known as Assessment Objectives, these are the checklist items that an assessor will seek to verify. Each one must be addressed in your implementation and documentation:

1. use of mobile code is controlled; and
2. use of mobile code is monitored.

(CMMC Assessment Guide, Level 2, Copyright 2020, 2021 Carnegie Mellon University and The Johns Hopkins University Applied Physics Laboratory LLC and/or CMMC Assessment Guide, Level 2, Version 2.11 - DRAFT, November 2023)

Implementation

This requirement refers to controlling technologies like Java, JavaScript, ActiveX, Postscript, PDF, Shockwave movies, Flash animations, and VBScript. With the vast number of vulnerabilities attributed to Flash alone, this is a significant problem. Malicious code in this family is most famously delivered through Internet browsing but can also be in macros in documents.

Although these code technologies carry risks, they have become ubiquitous on the Internet. To turn off all of these technologies, which would be the safest option, will cause many web interfaces to fail. That might lead to employees being unable to do their jobs and lead to you being unpopular. So, your approach to these technologies must include research and balancing risk against benefit.

You will need to determine a policy for the company of which technologies will be allowed and which will be prohibited. Although the policy can have exceptions, a specific user or maybe a department has access that is prohibited to others. However, those exceptions add management complexity and should only be made when there is a strong necessity.

An additional mobile code policy consideration is that situations change, and various mobile code technologies come and go out of popularity. Flash was very popular a few years ago, and now it is rarely used. Whatever decisions you make about mobile code should be reevaluated as the world changes.

The first line of defense against malicious mobile code is in the browser security settings. All of the major browsers can be controlled through group policy. The browsers that are not Microsoft products require the addition of administrative templates (ADMX files) to Group Policy. After these templates are installed, the browser settings can be controlled in the same way that Edge can be controlled. The ADMX templates can be downloaded from the browser support sites.

Through Group Policy, the use of mobile code should be controlled for all browsers in use in your organization. Remember that "control" of these technologies does not necessarily mean prohibiting their use.

Some of these mobile code technologies are also used through the operating system or software. Your standard builds should be consistent with your mobile code policy. Some technologies that are in the operating system can be controlled through Group Policy.

Some mobile code technologies that can be addressed in your control policy:

- Javascript
- VBScript
- HTML
- XHTML
- CSS
- AJAX

Assessment Stats

- Assessment Points: 1
- Assessment POAM Eligible: Yes

Keys

- Policy – Determine and document what mobile code will be prohibited and what will be permitted (and under what circumstances it will be permitted).
- Configuration – Set controls in browsers and Windows to enforce the mobile code policy.

System & Communications Protection

SC.L2-3.13.14

Voice over Internet Protocol

Control and monitor the use of Voice over Internet Protocol (VoIP) technologies.

Impact

The sales pitch for the new Voice Over IP (VOIP) phone system never mentioned any security concerns. Instead, the purveyors emphasized how simple it was to set up the system. Luke found the phone system to be extremely simple. When the phones were attached to the network, they linked in and were functional. There was never any hint to Luke that he had just installed the method that would be used for hackers to attack the company and drain the bank accounts. As it turned out, this particular phone system had an unpatched vulnerability that could be remotely leveraged.

Official Interpretation*

Controlling VoIP technologies starts with establishing guidelines and enforcing the appropriate usage that is described in organizational policies. Monitoring should include the users' activity for anything other than what is permitted and authorized and detection of insecure or unauthorized use of the VoIP technology. Security concerns for VoIP include eavesdropping on calls and using ID spoofing to impersonate trusted individuals.

Selecting a solution that can encrypt VoIP traffic is helpful in maintaining the confidentiality and integrity of the voice data.

(CMMC Assessment Guide, Level 2, Copyright 2020, 2021 Carnegie Mellon University and The Johns Hopkins University Applied Physics Laboratory LLC and/or CMMC Assessment Guide, Level 2, Version 2.11 - DRAFT, November 2023)

Assessment Focus

Also known as Assessment Objectives, these are the checklist items that an assessor will seek to verify. Each one must be addressed in your implementation and documentation:

1. use of Voice over Internet Protocol (VoIP) technologies is controlled; and
2. use of Voice over Internet Protocol (VoIP) technologies is monitored.

(CMMC Assessment Guide, Level 2, Copyright 2020, 2021 Carnegie Mellon University and The Johns Hopkins University Applied Physics Laboratory LLC and/or CMMC Assessment Guide, Level 2, Version 2.11 - DRAFT, November 2023)

Implementation

If you utilize VoIP, you should approach it with the knowledge that it has been leveraged for attacks. Your VoIP must be configured and maintained in accordance with best practices. Contact your VoIP provider for recommendations for preventing your VoIP system from becoming an attack vector.

The top security recommendation is that VOIP devices should be on a VLAN by themselves, isolated from the data network. While these devices need access to the Internet, there is no need for direct communication between these devices and the rest of your network. Although you may have applications on the desktops that interact with the VOIP system, these interactions typically occur through the internet and not device-to-device over the network. If the devices can be segregated and isolated from company resources, the risk of the VOIP being an effective attack vector is significantly reduced.

The requirement says that VoIP technologies should be "controlled"; it does not explicitly say they should be segregated from other systems. However, this represents a security-conscious form of control. Control plans might also involve assuring that all software and firmware remain patched. The manufacturer of your VoIP products may have other product-specific security recommendations.

The second aspect of this requirement is that your VoIP systems are monitored. If you Google "VoIP monitoring," you will see dozens of products you could purchase to monitor various aspects of VoIP. Many of these products would be overkill for the typical small organization. Check with your VoIP vendor and see if they have any monitoring or analytics products available. Remember, the requirement does NOT say what must be monitored, so if you are monitoring <u>any</u> aspect of your VoIP technologies, you can comply with this requirement.

Assessment Stats

- Assessment Points: 1
- Assessment POAM Eligible: Yes

Keys

- System Configuration – Set some controls on your VoIP technologies.
- System Monitoring – Establish some sort of monitoring of your VoIP systems.

System & Communications Protection

SC.L2-3.13.15

Communications Authenticity

Protect the authenticity of communications sessions.

Impact

The company had its most important secrets on a special server set up by an IT guy who had long since left the company. On this particular day, when the CEO needed to log onto the server and do some work, he didn't know that his communication with the server had been hijacked. He was actually connected to a virtual machine set up by a disgruntled employee, which in turn was passing his keystrokes and server output through and serving as an intermediary between the CEO and the server. However, the "man in the middle" machine recorded everything that passed through, capturing the CEO's credentials and the files he accessed.

Official Interpretation*

The intent of this requirement is to ensure a trust relationship is established between both ends of a communication session. Each end can be assured that the other end is who it is supposed to be. This is often implemented using a mutual authentication handshake when the session is established, especially between devices. Session authenticity is usually provided by a security protocol enforced for a communication session. Choosing and enforcing a protocol will provide authenticity throughout a communications session.

(CMMC Assessment Guide, Level 2, Copyright 2020, 2021 Carnegie Mellon University and The Johns Hopkins University Applied Physics Laboratory LLC and/or CMMC Assessment Guide, Level 2, Version 2.11 - DRAFT, November 2023)

Assessment Focus

Also known as Assessment Objectives, these are the checklist items that an assessor will seek to verify. Each one must be addressed in your implementation and documentation:

1. the authenticity of communications sessions is protected.

(CMMC Assessment Guide, Level 2, Copyright 2020, 2021 Carnegie Mellon University and The Johns Hopkins University Applied Physics Laboratory LLC and/or CMMC Assessment Guide, Level 2, Version 2.11 - DRAFT, November 2023)

Implementation

This requirement ensures that attackers cannot capture and use the session IDs of validly authenticated sessions.

The good news is that when performing communication within a domain information system, Microsoft handles all of the details of proper authentication. Then, during the remainder of the communication session, Windows will ensure that the properly authenticated user is the one performing activities on the network. For example, when accessing a Windows domain share from a domain account, Windows assures that the user is authenticated and authorized to access the share.

Communication with entities outside the network should utilize SSL/TLS security that (in addition to encryption) assures the entity's identity. Modern browsers make it difficult or impossible to connect to sites that do not utilize current certificates and encryption.

For a higher level of security in communication authentications inside the network, it is possible to implement IPSec. IPSec utilizes the PKI-issued certificates of each party to ensure that communication is with exactly who it is supposed to be with. You have all the tools to implement IPSec in your Windows domain environment. While IPsec provides a higher level of communication security, it will also elevate setup and management complexity.

Assessment Stats

- Assessment Points: 5
- Assessment POAM Eligible: No

Keys

- Configuration – Assure that communication is between domain members so Windows can conduct proper authentication processes.
- Configuration – Assure that Internet communication uses SSL/TLS to ensure good authentication.

System & Communications Protection

SC.L2-3.13.16

Data at Rest

Protect the confidentiality of CUI at rest.

Impact

Leo was a contractor brought in to implement a new ERP system. While at the company, he became very interested in the Defense items he saw being manufactured there. His interest grew over time, and he wanted to understand better how the product did what it did, but nobody was eager to talk to him about the details of the product. So, as he sat at a company computer, he decided to see for himself. Leo scanned the network and discovered they had all their DoD drawings and specifications in a shared folder. He found no particular security surrounding the folder, and copying the contents onto a portable drive was easy. He could now examine the contents of the folder at his convenience.

Official Interpretation*

CUI at rest means information that is not moving through the network; typically this means data currently stored on hard drives, media, and mobile devices. Implement the necessary security controls to protect the confidentiality of CUI at rest. Although an approved encryption method protects data stored at rest, there are other technical and physical solutions. The methods chosen should depend on the environment and business needs.

Implementing encryption for CUI is one approach to this requirement, but it is not mandatory. Physical security is often employed to restrict access to CUI, particularly when it resides on servers within a company's offices. Other approaches for protecting CUI include system-related protections such as configurations and rule sets for firewalls, gateways, intrusion detection/prevention systems, filtering routers, and authenticator content that eliminate attempts at exfiltration. You may also employ other security requirements including secure off-line storage.

Because the use of cryptography in this requirement is to protect the confidentiality of CUI, the cryptography used must meet the criteria specified in requirement SC.L2-3.13.11.

This requirement, SC.L2-3.13.16, specifies confidentially be provided for CUI at rest and complements MP.L2-3.8.9, which specifies confidentially of CUI at backup storage locations. This requirement, SC.L2-3.13.16, also leverages SC.L2-3.13.11, which specifies that the algorithms used must be FIPS-validated cryptography.

(CMMC Assessment Guide, Level 2, Copyright 2020, 2021 Carnegie Mellon University and The Johns Hopkins University Applied Physics Laboratory LLC and/or CMMC Assessment Guide, Level 2, Version 2.11 - DRAFT, November 2023)

Assessment Focus

Also known as Assessment Objectives, these are the checklist items that an assessor will seek to verify. Each one must be addressed in your implementation and documentation:

1. the confidentiality of CUI at rest is protected.

(CMMC Assessment Guide, Level 2, Copyright 2020, 2021 Carnegie Mellon University and The Johns Hopkins University Applied Physics Laboratory LLC and/or CMMC Assessment Guide, Level 2, Version 2.11 - DRAFT, November 2023)

Implementation

This control applies to all stored CUI, whether on network storage, hard drives, portable devices, or file cabinets. The requirement says that you must "protect the confidentiality," but it does not specify how the protection should be achieved. The way this requirement is written allows for protection by encryption, physical controls, logical controls, or combinations of those controls. The generally accepted best solution is to maintain this data encrypted*.

Some assessors will be skeptical of any system that has "at rest" CUI that is unencrypted. There is a strong bias toward this solution.

As an alternative (or in addition) to encryption, the CUI can be stored in an area with restrictive permissions and auditing. In the Windows domain, the CUI-containing folders can have security settings that only allow access by specific users (or groups of users) that the domain has authenticated.

The most basic protection in a Windows environment for digital CUI is to require all CUI to be kept in a specific folder on the server. Encryption can be enabled on the shared folder by using this PowerShell command:

> New-SmbShare –Name <sharename> -Path <pathname> –EncryptData $true
>
> [Testing should be performed to ensure that access to the encrypted data can be made from the devices in your environment since this technology was new in 2023]

Then, a security group can be created for CUI access, and the CUI-authorized users are placed into that group. Then, the CUI folder's security is set so only the CUI user's security group members can access the CUI assets. This would need to be supplemented by training and audits to support users only using this folder as a location for CUI. If your environment requires that CUI be processed in some way on users' computers, then careful consideration and planning will need to evaluate whether local copies of the CUI are created during processing. Bitlocker Full Disk Encryption (FDE) can be applied to the workstation to provide encryption for any local copies of CUI.

You can set your share up so access can be restricted to both a CUI-users security group AND a CUI-computers group. You can set the share permissions to the user group, then set the folder's NTFS permissions to make it accessible to the security group of computers. In this way, access can only be achieved by an authorized user, using an authorized computer.

Whatever controls are implemented, the most challenging part will often be ensuring that the protections apply to every location and circumstance of CUI storage. For example, if a user copies a file from the controlled folder to their desktop, it is no longer controlled. Similarly, if a CUI document is printed, appropriate controls must be applied to the paper version.

HANDY LINK

The author's preferred tool for secure and compliant cloud storage of CUI for the small organization can be found here https://tinyurl.com/CMMC4SMB-938

*When encryption protects CUI, then SC.L2-3.13.11 applies, so the encryption implementation must be FIPS-validated.

Assessment Stats

- Assessment Points: 1
- Assessment POAM Eligible: Yes

Keys

- Policy – Determine what controls will protect CUI in storage within your organization. These controls may be encryption, physical protections, or logical protections.
- Training - Employees must clearly understand the acceptable locations and suitable handling for CUI so it always complies with the CUI at rest policy.
- Configuration – Set up controlled storage areas that can only be accessed by authorized users.

System & Communications Protection

SI.L1-3.14.1

Flaw Remediation

Identify, report, and correct system flaws in a timely manner.

Impact

Since the Dynamic Defense Systems Group had evolved the use a specific software package has decreased, it was decided that they no longer needed to keep paying the annual software maintenance fees. This might have been a good decision, except that a nasty security vulnerability was discovered soon after they stopped getting the updates. The security flaw was being exploited before the software manufacturer knew there was an issue. They got a patch out to their customers on maintenance agreements but assumed that those no longer on maintenance were no longer using the product. For DDSG, this software flaw was an entry point for a hacking group out of Asia. When the DDSG management had to explain to the Defense Investigative Service agents why their software was never patched against this known vulnerability, the amount of money saved by not paying the software maintenance looked awfully petty.

Official Interpretation*

All software and firmware have potential flaws. Many vendors work to remedy those flaws by releasing vulnerability information and updates to their software and firmware. OSAs must have a process to review relevant vendor notifications and updates about problems or weaknesses. After reviewing the information, the OSA must implement a patch management process that allows for software and firmware flaws to be fixed without adversely affecting the system functionality. OSAs must define the time frames within which flaws are identified, reported, and corrected for all systems. OSAs should consider purchasing support from their vendors to ensure timely access to updates.

(CMMC Assessment Guide, Level 2, Copyright 2020, 2021 Carnegie Mellon University and The Johns Hopkins University Applied Physics Laboratory LLC and/or CMMC Assessment Guide, Level 2, Version 2.11 - DRAFT, November 2023)

Assessment Focus

Also known as Assessment Objectives, these are the checklist items that an assessor will seek to verify. Each one must be addressed in your implementation and documentation:

1. the time within which to identify system flaws is specified;

2. system flaws are identified within the specified time frame;
3. the time within which to report system flaws is specified;
4. system flaws are reported within the specified time frame;
5. the time within which to correct system flaws is specified; and
6. system flaws are corrected within the specified time frame.

(CMMC Assessment Guide, Level 2, Copyright 2020, 2021 Carnegie Mellon University and The Johns Hopkins University Applied Physics Laboratory LLC and/or CMMC Assessment Guide, Level 2, Version 2.11 - DRAFT, November 2023)

Implementation

New security vulnerabilities are continuously being identified and patched. For some software products, like Microsoft Windows, those patches are automatically distributed, downloaded, and installed. A manual process must be followed for other products, especially hardware, to check for updates and install them. Unless the organization is willing to invest in a Patch Management System (these are not typically designed for small organizations), then this can be a burden. Different providers require different methods to check for updates and apply them.

This requirement mandates that flaws be addressed. It also specifies that these remediations will be made "in a timely manner." As you look at the Assessment Focus section, you will see that your organization needs to establish (documented) timetables for the following:

- Identification of system flaws
- Reporting of system flaws
- Correction of system flaws

Then, there is an expectation that these steps will be achieved within the established timeframe. Since you are the creator of those timetables and are being held to them, you would want to set them very conservatively.

Consider this situation: researchers identify a flaw, but the vendor is very slow to address the issue. You do not want to be in a situation where you have committed to correction within 30 days, but the vendor takes 4 months to get a patch. While completely out of your control, this situation could result in your organization being non-compliant with this requirement.

So, while it is important, for security reasons, to implement flaw remediation as quickly as possible, your CMMC documented timetables should be set to be longer than you can possibly imagine the process ever taking. Your published timetables are maximum lengths of time. Nothing prevents fully addressing the flaws in hours, even if the published goal might be several months.

Most hardware and software vendors have the means to auto-update to fix identified flaws automatically, and there are some that do not. In those cases, you must create a documented system to address flaws.

Identification – There are a couple of circumstances where auto-update of flaws will not be applicable. The first of these situations is where products are not capable of automatically finding and installing fixes. Things without this capability are often older or more specialized devices or software that do not provide support. The second circumstance is where the provider does not have a fix for the issue, but the problem has been published or is being actively exploited. When issues are not being automatically fixed, you need an active means to seek out the issue. This might involve visiting the manufacturer's website, reading security newsletters, or paying attention to the Common Weakness Enumeration (CWE) database or Common Vulnerabilities and Exposures (CVE) databases. You need to document what efforts will be made to identify flaws applicable to your systems and a maximum length of time between the public disclosure and your identification of the flaw.

Potentially, you should create a list of the various manufacturer websites where you need to make manual checks for updates. Then, you can periodically review each web page to check for updates. There are also webpage monitoring services that can inform you when changes are made to these pages. Other items may require a different process to check for updates, like logging onto a device and clicking a "check for updates" option in the user interface. Whatever is needed to determine if pending updates exist, can become part of a periodic process.

You can also use a webpage monitoring service like changetower.com to monitor the specific web pages for changes. These services (many are free) can periodically (like daily) check a specific webpage, and then send you an email if any changes are detected.

Reporting – This reporting is supposed to be made to "designated personnel with information security responsibilities." In a small organization, this is potentially instantaneous since the same person might be responsible for identifying and fixing the flaw. Even though the same person might typically conduct these steps, you should publish a maximum reporting time that allows for future responsibility changes and people on leave time.

Correction – This step is the application of the patch, update, hotfix, or other corrections. Sometimes, a patch may not be available, but there is a workaround (perhaps a special firewall rule that protects a device from a specific type of packet). While these workarounds can protect your security temporarily, they are still a temporary fix. You need to document the maximum time this process could take in a worst-case situation.

You will want to provide documentation of how this process has been followed. The best place to document it is within your POAM system, which can track the process from start to end and provide documentation for your assessor.

The application of patches should be prioritized based on the risk associated with the hardware or software. Some of the highest priorities should be:

- Firewalls
- Internet-facing services
- Operating systems
- Browsers
- Email Clients
- Other software that accesses the Internet in normal operation.

Rarely do the patches themselves cause problems. In larger organizations, patches undergo a careful testing process to ensure they won't cause any problems. This testing phase is typically outside what is justified in a smaller organization. It comes down to recognizing that these software and firmware providers are experts who will produce patches that fix more problems than they cause. Additionally, by utilizing the automatic patching features, patches get applied much faster than in the big companies, thus reducing vulnerability exposure time.

To protect your network, it is vital to address applicable vulnerabilities promptly. You should promptly apply new patches, service packs, hotfixes, firmware updates, and anti-virus signatures.

Assessment Stats

- Assessment Points: 5
- Assessment POAM Eligible: No

Keys

- Configuration – Turn on automatic updates wherever possible
- Process – Determine the method and maximum timetable for identification of flaws
- Process - Determine the method and maximum timetable for internal communication of flaws
- Process - Determine the method and maximum timetable for remediation of flaws
- Configuration – Use the POAM system or similar to alert and track the identification and application of specific patches to systems that do not perform automatic updates.

System & Information Integrity

SI.L1-3.14.2

Malicious Code Protection

Provide protection from malicious code at designated locations within organizational systems.

Impact

Desi was responsible for configuring new workstation computers. Although he was usually systematic about following his checklist, on this one day, he was off his game due to a bad fight he had with his girlfriend. As he set up this one computer for an accounts payable clerk, he neglected to install the anti-malware program. This might have never been a problem, except the clerk received a phishing email that said, "Please see your attached invoice." The clerk failed to identify the signs of a phishing email, and there was nothing on his computer to stop the email's malware from infecting his new computer.

Official Interpretation*

A designated location may be a network device such as a firewall or an end user's computer.

Malicious code, which can be delivered by a range of means (e.g., email, removable media, or websites), includes the following:

- virus – program designed to damage, steal information, change data, send email, show messages, or any combination of these things;
- spyware – program designed to gather information about a person's activity in secret when they click on a link, usually installed without the person knowing ;
- trojan horse – type of malware made to look like legitimate software and used by cyber criminals to get access to a company's systems; and
- ransomware – type of malware that threatens to publish the victim's data or perpetually block access to it unless a ransom is paid.

Use anti-malware tools to stop or lessen the impact of malicious code.

(CMMC Assessment Guide, Level 2, Copyright 2020, 2021 Carnegie Mellon University and The Johns Hopkins University Applied Physics Laboratory LLC and/or CMMC Assessment Guide, Level 2, Version 2.11 - DRAFT, November 2023)

Assessment Focus

Also known as Assessment Objectives, these are the checklist items that an assessor will seek to verify. Each one must be addressed in your implementation and documentation:

1. designated locations for malicious code protection are identified
2. protection from malicious code at designated locations is provided.

Implementation

This is where your anti-virus software can be the hero in your organization. As it monitors what comes into your computer and also evaluates code before executables are run, it can identify many different kinds of malicious code and stop them before becoming a problem. This software is a key element of your defense. While no anti-virus is 100% effective, there is a wide range of effectivenesses from one antivirus product to another, so careful selection is justified.

Antivirus is a form of blacklisting; it compares code against a list of known malicious software. Malicious code can also be prevented by using a whitelist. Whitelist software has a list of all of the software pieces that ARE allowed to run. This can be more effective than a blacklist but typically has a higher maintenance burden. The challenges of maintaining a whitelist typically place these products outside of the scope of smaller organizations.

Applocker, the Microsoft whitelist application, is included in enterprise-level editions of Windows. Both the server and client machines need to be running the enterprise version of their operating systems. Applocker has some tools that help address the maintenance challenges, like the ability to whitelist all code that specific publishers digitally sign.

Whether using endpoint anti-virus or application whitelisting software, there must be a tool to protect systems from running malicious code. Sometimes, CMMC implementation in a small organization is about doing the least necessary to gain certification. However, this element is essential enough to your organization's security that it should be given close and careful consideration. There do exist some "free" anti-virus systems, however this is sometimes a case of getting what you pay for. The most effective anti-malware systems have some cost to use, which pays for ongoing research to ensure the product stays ahead of evolving threats.

Assessment Stats

- Assessment Points: 5
- Assessment POAM Eligible: No

Keys

🔧 Analysis – Determine and document the locations in your organization where malicious software mitigation is required. This could be in broad rules, like "all workstations."

🔧 Configuration – Establish endpoint anti-virus or whitelisting on all the required systems.

System & Information Integrity

SI.L2-3.14.3

Security Alerts & Advisories

Monitor system security alerts and advisories and take action in response.

Impact

Last Tuesday, it hit the security news. The router used at Jonah's company had been found to have a backdoor that was remotely accessible. Furthermore, the vulnerability was being actively exploited in the wild. However, Jonah was very busy and didn't have time to bother with security news. He was focused on his specific network. While a simple firmware update could have fixed the problem, Jonah didn't know that. His ignorance about the issue ended up costing him his job and almost caused the business to close.

Official Interpretation*

Solicit and receive security alerts, advisories, and directives from reputable external organizations. Identify sources relevant to the industry and technology used by your company. Methods to receive alerts and advisories may include:

- signing up for email distributions;
- subscribing to RSS feeds; and
- attending meetings.

Review alerts and advisories for applicability as they are received. The frequency of the reviews should be based on the frequency of the alerts and advisories to ensure you have the most up-to-date information.

External alerts and advisories may prompt you to generate internal security alerts, advisories, or directives, and share these with all personnel with a need-to-know. The individuals should assess the risk related to a given alert and act to respond as appropriate. Sometimes it may require a configuration update. Other times, the information may also require adjusting system architecture in order to thwart a threat described in an advisory.

(CMMC Assessment Guide, Level 2, Copyright 2020, 2021 Carnegie Mellon University and The Johns Hopkins University Applied Physics Laboratory LLC and/or CMMC Assessment Guide, Level 2, Version 2.11 - DRAFT, November 2023)

Assessment Focus

Also known as Assessment Objectives, these are the checklist items that an assessor will seek to verify. Each one must be addressed in your implementation and documentation:

1. response actions to system security alerts and advisories are identified;
2. system security alerts and advisories are monitored; and
3. actions in response to system security alerts and advisories are taken.

(CMMC Assessment Guide, Level 2, Copyright 2020, 2021 Carnegie Mellon University and The Johns Hopkins University Applied Physics Laboratory LLC and/or CMMC Assessment Guide, Level 2, Version 2.11 - DRAFT, November 2023)

Implementation

Subscribe to one or more security bulletins like the SANS Newsbites or US-CERT alerts to keep informed about vulnerabilities, news, and trends being seen outside your doors. Take actions to address issues that apply to your network. Your POAM system can provide simple documentation for the identification of applicable issues and the resulting actions for presentation in your assessment. The conduct of this activity should be defined in your policy.

HANDY LINK
SANS Newsletter - https://tinyurl.com/CMMC4SMB-750
US-CERT Newsletter - https://tinyurl.com/CMMC4SMB-214
DIB CS Program - https://tinyurl.com/CMMC4SMB-697

Assessment Stats

- Assessment Points: 5
- Assessment POAM Eligible: No

Keys

- Subscribe – Ensure you receive one or more security alert newsletters.
- Document – When items in the alerts are actionable within your systems, ensure they are documented. This allows demonstration of your actions as a result of the news.

System & Information Integrity

SI.L1-3.14.4

Update Malicious Code Protection

Update malicious code protection mechanisms when new releases are available.

Impact

Juan was very confident in the anti-virus product they used to protect from malware. It had done an excellent job for a long time. However, a couple of weeks ago, their subscription to updates had lapsed, and the reminder emails were unread in the mailbox of a woman on maternity leave. So, their computers were relying upon malware recognition algorithms that were rapidly becoming outdated. Because hackers and phishers are continuously seeking new opportunities to cause problems, it wasn't long before the company had a malware infection. They didn't even know they were at risk.

Official Interpretation*

Malware changes on an hourly or daily basis, and it is important to update detection and protection mechanisms frequently to maintain the effectiveness of the protection.

(CMMC Assessment Guide, Level 2, Copyright 2020, 2021 Carnegie Mellon University and The Johns Hopkins University Applied Physics Laboratory LLC and/or CMMC Assessment Guide, Level 2, Version 2.11 - DRAFT, November 2023)

Assessment Focus

Also known as Assessment Objectives, these are the checklist items that an assessor will seek to verify. Each one must be addressed in your implementation and documentation:

1. malicious code protection mechanisms are updated when new releases are available.

(CMMC Assessment Guide, Level 2, Copyright 2020, 2021 Carnegie Mellon University and The Johns Hopkins University Applied Physics Laboratory LLC and/or CMMC Assessment Guide, Level 2, Version 2.11 - DRAFT, November 2023)

Implementation

Because money is on the line, hackers always seek new ways to infect systems. Because of their ongoing innovations, your defenses must be kept as current as possible to protect you from new threats. Antivirus software depends upon their teams of computer scientists that identify malware and develop signatures from each new threat. Those signatures are sent out regularly to users, so each computer is on guard for the latest threat.

Antivirus software in use in your organization should be receiving continuous updates and virus signatures. This necessitates that a subscription for updates is paid. This subscription pays for the software provider to do the necessary research and development to keep their product effective in an ever-changing threat landscape. Your anti-virus software should continuously update the malware signatures.

This continuous update for every new bit of malware is where whitelisting of executables has a significant advantage. Instead of trying to have the protection software watching to stop every known piece of malware, it only allows what it knows is good. This eliminates the cat-and-mouse game that is played by antivirus. However, any utilized whitelisting software should be kept current, and all updates applied.

Assessment Stats

- Assessment Points: 5
- Assessment POAM Eligible: No

Keys

🔧 System – Ensure your malware protection has (paid) support and automatically receives updates.

SI.L1-3.14.5

System & File Scanning

Perform periodic scans of organizational systems and real-time scans of files from external sources as files are downloaded, opened, or executed.

Impact

Two of the 46 computers at the company did not have the anti-malware software installed. Today, Leigh was using one of those computers. She was attempting to find a graphics tool to address a specific need. Without realizing it, she downloaded a tool that was infected with malware. The site looked legitimate, and the tool appeared to be what she needed, but when she installed it, she was simultaneously installing a remote access trojan (RAT) onto that computer. Without the anti-malware, nothing could stop her from downloading and installing it. After it was installed, there were no scans to detect the malicious code on her hard drive.

Official Interpretation*

Use anti-malware software to scan for and identify viruses in your computer systems and determine how often scans are conducted. Real-time scans look at the system whenever new files are downloaded, opened, and saved. Periodic scans check previously saved files against updated malware information.

(CMMC Assessment Guide, Level 2, Copyright 2020, 2021 Carnegie Mellon University and The Johns Hopkins University Applied Physics Laboratory LLC and/or CMMC Assessment Guide, Level 2, Version 2.11 - DRAFT, November 2023)

Assessment Focus

Also known as Assessment Objectives, these are the checklist items that an assessor will seek to verify. Each one must be addressed in your implementation and documentation:

1. the frequency for malicious code scans is defined;
2. malicious code scans are performed with the defined frequency; and

3. real-time malicious code scans of files from external sources as files are downloaded, opened, or executed are performed.

(CMMC Assessment Guide, Level 2, Copyright 2020, 2021 Carnegie Mellon University and The Johns Hopkins University Applied Physics Laboratory LLC and/or CMMC Assessment Guide, Level 2, Version 2.11 - DRAFT, November 2023)

Implementation

This requirement can be satisfied by most anti-virus software installed on the end-point computers. There are two different types of scans performed by anti-malware programs:

- The real-time scans are preventive in nature because their goal is to detect the malware before it is installed. This function examines downloads and other files entering the system and evaluates all programs attempting to run. The goal of this is to find malicious code before it is run.
- Periodic scans look at drives and memory to find evidence of malware saved, installed, or running on the system. These scans are corrective in nature.

Both types of scans are essential to providing an additional layer of defense.

Malware scanning in your border devices or email servers may also be utilized. There is value in having files scanned twice by different algorithms at different points because this increases the probability of finding malware. However, border scans are ineffective at identifying malware within SSL/TLS encrypted communications. Email is generally not encrypted.

To achieve conformance to this requirement, you must document the frequency at which systems will be scanned for malicious code. You will need to be able to provide documentation that the scans are actually occurring at the designated frequency. Finally, you will need to provide documentation concerning the performance of real-time scans as files are downloaded, opened, or executed.

Assessment Stats

- Assessment Points: 3
- Assessment POAM Eligible: No

Keys

🔧 Documentation – Determine and document the frequency of periodic scans of your systems.

🔧 Verify – Assure that your anti-virus products are designed and configured to perform both periodic and real-time scans of the computer systems. Assure that the periodic scans are being performed at a frequency consistent with your documentation.

System & Information Integrity

SI.L2-3.14.6

Monitor Communications for Attacks

Monitor organizational systems, including inbound and outbound communications traffic, to detect attacks and indicators of potential attacks.

Impact

During the last week, there was a massive upsurge in outbound traffic. The IT manager might have been suspicious, but the traffic level was not being monitored. During this time, the entire contents of the engineering file storage was sent to a server in Albania. With no recognition that anything was wrong, the IT staff performed their normal activities while CUI and proprietary information was exfiltrated from the facility.

Official Interpretation*

Think of indicators of attack as a set of footprints an adversary leaves during an attack. Indicators of attack provide information on the steps the adversary followed and its intent. Indicators of attacks on organizational systems may include:

- internal traffic that indicates the presence of malicious code;
- anomalous activity detected during non-business hours;
- unauthorized data leaving the organization; and
- communicating to external information systems.

To detect attacks and indicators of attacks, deploy monitoring devices or agents. Place these sensors at strategic points within the systems and networks to collect essential information. Strategic points include internal and external system boundaries. Monitor both inbound traffic and outbound traffic as well as actions on hosts.

This requirement, SI.L2-3.14.6, provides details for the communications of organizational systems. SI.L2-3.14.6 supports the requirement AU.L2-3.3.1, which involves creating and retaining records for monitoring, analysis, and investigations.

Assessment Focus

Also known as Assessment Objectives, these are the checklist items that an assessor will seek to verify. Each one must be addressed in your implementation and documentation:

1. the system is monitored to detect attacks and indicators of potential attacks;
2. inbound communications traffic is monitored to detect attacks and indicators of potential attacks; and
3. outbound communications traffic is monitored to detect attacks and indicators of potential attacks.

Implementation

Within a security-conscious network, there are likely to be several tools that contribute to meeting this requirement. It is entirely possible that you will not need to do anything new to meet this, but just take credit for what you are already doing.

The first place to look is your border device (i.e. firewall) because it may be configured to fulfill some of this requirement. To comply with the detection portion, the device should be running IDS or set with some alerts when certain unusual events occur that might indicate an attack. These alerts might be in the form of logging events being communicated to your logging system. Notice that the requirement includes the evaluation of outbound traffic. For example, if packets are attempting to leave your network that list their "from" address as something other than your network's address space, it would be an indication of malware activity (Google "Egress Traffic Filtering" for similar ideas). Typically, firewall rules can be attached to a notification or audit event.

If the end-point antivirus systems report detections to a central location, this can be another element of attack detection. Certainly, your system log reporting can also play a role in the detection of attacks.

You may have other devices or systems monitoring some communication elements for suspicious activity. These systems should also be acknowledged as contributing toward satisfying this requirement.

Because of the requirement that the signs of potentially malicious activity are monitored, it is not adequate to have the data available if somebody chooses to go look at it. Either you need to have a system that notifies or there needs to be a process to periodically check the results.

You will need to create a listing of the systems that are monitoring communications. Your list should define whether the system monitors inbound, outbound, or both types of communication. There must be monitors of both inbound and outbound traffic.

Assessment Stats

- Assessment Points: 5
- Assessment POAM Eligible: No

Keys

- Identify – Determine which tools within your systems can be useful in identifying attacks or potential attacks.
- Document – Describe how the identified tools will be used to detect suspicious activity and how that will be monitored. Assure that these tools consider inbound and outbound traffic.

SI.L2-3.14.7

Identify Unauthorized Use

Identify unauthorized use of organizational systems.

Impact

Chuck has a side business. While at work, he sends thousands of "spam" messages daily to promote sales in this side business. He is sending those out through the company network. After a period of time, the company has its IP address flagged as a source of spam, and real company emails are blocked and never make it to their intended recipients. This is affecting purchasing, contact with customers, and accounts payable. Suddenly, the company is in a crisis because most of its outbound messages are being rejected. While Chuck's activity did not seem much worse than wasting time when he should be working, it has brought much of the company's essential business activities to a sudden halt.

Official Interpretation*

Define authorized use of your systems. Create an acceptable use policy to establish the baseline for how users access devices, internal network services, and the internet. Define authorized use by specific roles such as: user, administrator, and technician. After authorized use is defined, identify unauthorized use of systems.

Monitor systems by observing audit activities from the system logs. This can be accomplished in real time using automated solutions or by manual means. To identify unauthorized use, leverage existing tools and techniques, such as:

- intrusion detection systems;
- intrusion prevention systems;
- malicious code protection software;
- scanning tools;
- audit record monitoring software; and
- network monitoring software.

This requirement, SI.L2-3.14.7, which deals with identifying unauthorized use of organizational systems, is related to requirements: AC.L2-3.1.1, AU.L2-3.3.1, IA.L2-3.5.1, and IA.L2-3.5.2. All of these requirements help create the building blocks that support SI.L2-3.14.7.

(CMMC Assessment Guide, Level 2, Copyright 2020, 2021 Carnegie Mellon University and The Johns Hopkins University Applied Physics Laboratory LLC and/or CMMC Assessment Guide, Level 2, Version 2.11 - DRAFT, November 2023)

Assessment Focus

Also known as Assessment Objectives, these are the checklist items that an assessor will seek to verify. Each one must be addressed in your implementation and documentation:

1. authorized use of the system is defined; and
2. unauthorized use of the system is identified.

(CMMC Assessment Guide, Level 2, Copyright 2020, 2021 Carnegie Mellon University and The Johns Hopkins University Applied Physics Laboratory LLC and/or CMMC Assessment Guide, Level 2, Version 2.11 - DRAFT, November 2023)

Implementation

Every company needs to have their users comply with a written Acceptable Use Policy (AUP). This document provides the company with many legal protections. For the purpose of this requirement, it is impossible to identify "unauthorized use" if it hasn't been determined and communicated what is acceptable and what is not. There should be some form of documentation by the employees showing that they understand and accept the AUP.

This requirement entails monitoring activity at the border of your network and what occurs within the network. The internal monitoring may include audit activities and access patterns. Tools such as intrusion detection systems, intrusion prevention systems, scanning tools, or audit record monitoring software may be used.

Sample Acceptable Use Policy (adapted from https://www.getsafeonline.org)

This document should be tailored to your organization's specific requirements. Every organization is different. Remove, add, or substitute text where appropriate. Legal review of your Acceptable Use Policy is advised.

This Acceptable Usage Policy covers the security and use of all (Acme Corporation's) information and IT equipment. It also includes the use of email, internet, voice, and mobile IT equipment. This policy applies to all (Acme Corporation's) employees, contractors, and agents (hereafter referred to as 'individuals').

This policy applies to all information, in whatever form, relating to (Acme Corporation's) business activities worldwide and to all information handled by (Acme Corporation) relating to other organizations with whom it deals. It also covers all IT and information communications facilities operated by (Acme Corporation) or on its behalf.

<u>Computer Access Control – Individual's Responsibility</u>

Access to the (Acme Corporation) IT systems is controlled by the use of User IDs, passwords, biometrics, or tokens. All User IDs and passwords are to be uniquely assigned to named individuals, and consequently, individuals are accountable for all actions on the (Acme Corporation's) IT systems.

Individuals must not:

- Allow anyone else to use their user ID/token and password on any (Acme Corporation) IT system.
- Leave their user accounts logged in at an unattended and unlocked computer.
- Use someone else's user ID and password to access (Acme Corporation's) IT systems.
- Leave their password unprotected (for example, writing it down).
- Perform any unauthorized changes to (Acme Corporation's) IT systems or information.

• Attempt to access data they are not authorized to use or access.
• Exceed the limits of their authorization or specific business need to interrogate the system or data.
• Connect any non-(Acme Corporation) authorized device to the (Acme Corporation) network or IT systems.
• Store (Acme Corporation) data on any non-authorized (Acme Corporation) equipment.
• Give or transfer (Acme Corporation) data or software to any person or organization outside (Acme Corporation) without the authority of (Acme Corporation).

Line managers must ensure that individuals are given clear direction on the extent and limits of their authority with regard to IT systems and data.

Internet and Email Conditions of Use

Use of (Acme Corporation) internet and email is intended for business use. Personal use is permitted where such use does not affect the individual's business performance, is not detrimental to (Acme Corporation) in any way, is not in breach of any term and condition of employment, and does not place the individual or (Acme Corporation) in breach of statutory or other legal obligations.

All individuals are accountable for their actions on the Internet and email systems.

Individuals must not:

• Use the internet or email for the purposes of harassment or abuse.
• Use profanity, obscenities, or derogatory remarks in communications.
• Access, download, send, or receive any data (including images) that (Acme Corporation) considers offensive in any way, including sexually explicit, discriminatory, defamatory, or libelous material.
• Use the internet or email to make personal gains or conduct a personal business.
• Use the internet or email to gamble.
• Use the email systems in a way that could affect its reliability or effectiveness, for example, distributing chain letters or spam.
• Place any information on the Internet that relates to (Acme Corporation), alter any information about it, or express any opinion about (Acme Corporation) unless they are expressly authorized to do this.
• Send unprotected sensitive or confidential information externally.
• Forward (Acme Corporation) mail to personal (non-Acme Corporation) email accounts (for example, a personal Hotmail account).
• Make official commitments through the Internet or email on behalf of (Acme Corporation) unless authorized to do so.
• Download copyrighted material such as music media (MP3) files, film, and video files (not an exhaustive list) without appropriate approval.
• In any way infringe any copyright, database rights, trademarks, or other intellectual property.
• Download any software from the internet without prior approval of the IT Department.
• Connect (Acme Corporation) devices to the internet using non-standard connections.

Clear Desk and Clear Screen Policy

In order to reduce the risk of unauthorized access or loss of information, (Acme Corporation) enforces a clear desk and screen policy as follows:
• Personal or confidential business information must be protected using security features provided, for example, secure print on printers.
• Computers must be logged off/locked or protected with a screen-locking mechanism controlled by a password when unattended.
• Care must be taken not to leave confidential material on printers or photocopiers.
• All business-related printed matter must be disposed of using confidential waste bins or shredders.

Working Off-site

It is accepted that laptops and mobile devices will be taken off-site. The following controls must be applied:
• Working away from the office must align with (Acme Corporation) remote working policy.

• Equipment and media taken off-site must not be left unattended in public places and not left in sight in a car.
• Laptops must be carried as hand luggage when traveling.
• Information should be protected against loss or compromise when working remotely (for example, at home or in public places). Laptop encryption must be used.
• Particular care should be taken with the use of mobile devices such as laptops, mobile phones, smartphones and tablets. They must be protected at least by a password or a PIN and, where available, encryption.

Mobile Storage Devices

Mobile devices such as memory sticks, CDs, DVDs, and removable hard drives must be used only in situations when network connectivity is unavailable or there is no other secure method of transferring data. Only (Acme Corporation) authorized mobile storage devices with encryption enabled must be used when transferring sensitive or confidential data. Software

Employees must use only software that is authorized by (Acme Corporation) on (Acme Corporation's) computers. Authorized software must be used in accordance with the software supplier's licensing agreements. All software on (Acme Corporation) computers must be approved and installed by the (Acme Corporation) IT department.

Individuals must not:

• Store personal files such as music, video, photographs, or games on (Acme Corporation) IT equipment.

Viruses
The IT department has implemented centralized, automated virus detection and virus software updates within the (Acme Corporation). All PCs have antivirus software installed to detect and remove any virus automatically.

Individuals must not:
• Remove or disable anti-virus software.
• Attempt to remove virus-infected files or clean up an infection, other than by using approved (Acme Corporation) anti-virus software and procedures.

Telephony (Voice) Equipment Conditions of Use
Use of (Acme Corporation) voice equipment is intended for business use. Individuals must not use (Acme Corporation's) voice facilities for sending or receiving private communications on personal matters except in exceptional circumstances. All non-urgent personal communications should be made at an individual's expense using alternative communication means.

Individuals must not:
• Use (Acme Corporation's) voice for conducting private business.
• Make hoax or threatening calls to internal or external destinations.
• Accept reverse charge calls from domestic or International operators, unless it is for business use.

Actions upon Termination of Employment

All (Acme Corporation) equipment and data, for example, laptops and mobile devices, including telephones, smartphones, USB memory devices, and CDs/DVDs, must be returned to (Acme Corporation) at the termination of the contract. All (Acme Corporation) data or intellectual property developed or gained during the period of employment remains the property of (Acme Corporation) and must not be retained beyond termination or reused for any other purpose.

Monitoring and Filtering

All data that is created and stored on (Acme Corporation) computers is the property of (Acme Corporation), and there is no official provision for individual data privacy; however, wherever possible, (Acme Corporation) will avoid opening personal emails.

IT system logging will occur where appropriate, and investigations will be commenced where reasonable suspicion exists of a breach of this or any other policy. (Acme Corporation) has the right (under certain conditions) to monitor activity on its systems, including internet and email use, to ensure systems security and effective operation and protect against misuse.

Any monitoring will be carried out in accordance with audited, controlled internal processes, the UK Data Protection Act 1998, the Regulation of Investigatory Powers Act 2000, and the Telecommunications (Lawful Business Practice Interception of Communications) Regulations 2000.

This policy must be read in conjunction with:

- Computer Misuse Act 1990
- Data Protection Act 1998

It is your responsibility to report suspected breaches of security policy without delay to your line management, the IT department, the information security department, or the IT helpdesk.

All breaches of information security policies will be investigated. Where investigations reveal misconduct, disciplinary action may follow in line with (Acme Corporation) disciplinary procedures.

HANDY LINK

The text of this sample Acceptable Use Policy can be found at https://tinyurl.com/CMMC4SMB-533

The next element is to document some monitoring tools for occasions when users might violate of their Acceptable Use Policy. For example, the system you put in place to meet the requirements of CM.L2-3.4.9, User-Installed Software, would be useful in your list of monitoring to meet this requirement. So, when creating this list, evaluate the things you are already monitoring and see if you can take credit for them to help meet this requirement.

There is no expectation that every item in your AUP would be monitored. You just need to develop a list of several AUP items that are being monitored.

Assessment Stats

- Assessment Points: 3
- Assessment POAM Eligible: No

Keys

- Policy – Provide all system users with a clear policy that defines acceptable uses of the computer systems.
- Identify – Identify those tools within your environment that can be useful in identifying unauthorized activities.
- Document – Describe how the specified tools will be used to identify unauthorized activities.

INDEX

www.ingramcontent.com/pod-product-compliance
Lightning Source LLC
LaVergne TN
LVHW062143200926
848484LV00007B/1850
* 9 7 8 1 7 3 3 1 9 5 1 4 0 *